Public Infrastructure, Private Finance

Traditionally, the public sector has been responsible for the provision of all public goods necessary to support sustainable urban development, including public infrastructure such as roads, parks, social facilities, climate mitigation and adaptation, and affordable housing. With the shift in recent years towards public infrastructure being financed by private stakeholders, the demand for transparent guidance to ensure accountability for the responsibilities held by developers has risen.

Within planning practice and urban development, the shift towards private financing of public infrastructure has translated into new tools being implemented to provide joint responsibility for upholding requirements. Developer obligations are contributions made by property developers and landowners towards public infrastructure in exchange for decisions on land-use regulations which increase the economic value of their land. This book presents insight into the design and practical results of these obligations in different countries and their effects on municipal financial health, demonstrating the increasing importance of efficient bargaining processes and the institutional design of developer obligations in modern urban planning.

Primarily written for academics in land-use planning, real estate, urban development, law, and economics, it will additionally be useful to policy makers and practitioners pursuing the improvement of public infrastructure financing.

Demetrio Muñoz Gielen (ORCID: http://orcid.org/0000-0001-6863-2336) is Lecturer of Land Policies at two universities: the Institute of Housing and Urban Development Studies (IHS) at the Erasmus University of Rotterdam, and also at the Radboud University, both in the Netherlands. He combines his lectureship and research position with a position as public officer at the Dutch Municipality of Purmerend. He does research on, and is involved in the design, implementation and evaluation of land policies and land-based finance in urban development.

Erwin van der Krabben is Professor of Urban Planning at Radboud University (the Netherlands), and Honorary Professor of Planning and Real Estate at Hong Kong University, Faculty of Architecture. His research focuses on the interrelationships between urban planning and land and real estate markets, and includes work on land policy and value capture, financial aspects of urban management and decision-making processes.

Routledge Research in Planning and Urban Design

Routledge Research in Planning and Urban Design is a series of academic monographs for scholars working in these disciplines and the overlaps between them. Building on Routledge's history of academic rigour and cutting-edge research, the series contributes to the rapidly expanding literature in all areas of planning and urban design.

For a full list of titles in this series, please visit www.routledge.com/Routledge-Research-in-Planning-and-Urban-Design/book-series/RRPUD

Public Infrastructure, Private Finance

Developer Obligations and
Responsibilities

Edited by Demetrio Muñoz Gielen and
Erwin van der Krabben

LONDON AND NEW YORK

First published 2019
by Routledge
4 Park Square, Milton Park, Abingdon, Oxon OX14 4RN

605 Third Avenue, New York, NY 10017

First issued in paperback 2022

Routledge is an imprint of the Taylor & Francis Group, an informa business

British Library Cataloguing-in-Publication Data
A catalogue record for this book is available from the British Library

Library of Congress Cataloging-in-Publication Data
Names: Muñoz Gielen, Demetrio, 1970– editor. | Krabben, Erwin van
    der, editor.
Title: Public infrastructure, private finance : developer obligations
    and responsibilities / edited by Demetrio Muñoz Gielen and Erwin
    van der Krabben.
Description: Abingdon, Oxon ; New York, NY : Routledge, 2019. |
    Series: Routledge research in planning and urban design | Includes
    bibliographical references and index.
Identifiers: LCCN 2018056318 | ISBN 9780815355854 (hardback)
Subjects: LCSH: City planning. | Real estate development. |
    Municipal services. | Public works. | Public-private sector
    cooperation.
Classification: LCC HT166 .P795 2019 | DDC 307.1/216—dc23
LC record available at https://lccn.loc.gov/2018056318

ISBN 13: 978-1-03-247562-2 (pbk)
ISBN 13: 978-0-8153-5585-4 (hbk)
ISBN 13: 978-1-351-12916-9 (ebk)

DOI: 10.4324/9781351129169

Typeset in Sabon
by Apex CoVantage, LLC

Contents

Contributors

David Amborski is a professor at the School of Urban and Regional Planning, Ryerson University.

Fatma Belgin Gumru is currently pursuing her PhD degree at Istanbul Technical University (ITU). In her research, she strives to investigate the sustainability of the planning profession through the lens of planners themselves by focusing on the concept of planning agreements/developer obligations and its use in Turkey.

Vicente Burgos Salas is an urban planning lawyer from Universidad de Chile, with an MSc in Development Administration and Planning from the University College of London, where he is undertaking PhD research.

Nico Calavita is Professor Emeritus at San Diego State University. His areas of interest include affordable housing and community development, smart growth, and comparative planning. He has coauthored *Inclusionary Housing in International Perspective: Affordable Housing, Social Inclusion, and Land Value Recapture*, published in 2010 by the Lincoln Institute. In 2016, he was presented with the Marilyn Gittel Activist Scholar Award by the Urban Affairs Association.

K. W. Chau is Chair Professor of Real Estate and Construction and Head, Department of Real Estate and Construction and Ronald Coase Centre for Property Rights Research, The University of Hong Kong.

Lennon Choy is Associate Professor of Real Estate Economics and Finance and Associate Head, Department of Real Estate and Construction and Ronald Coase Centre for Property Rights Research, The University of Hong Kong.

Paulo Vasconcelos Dias Correia (ORCID: https://orcid.org//Q-2815–2017) is an associate professor and Past President of the Department of Management Sciences of IST – Instituto Superior Tecnico, Lisbon University. He is Past Director General of Territorial Development, Researcher and Past President of the Center of Management Studies of IST, and Past President of ECTP.

Hsiu-yin Ding is an assistant professor in the Department of Land Economics, National Chengchi University, Taipei, Taiwan. Her research interests include land-use controls and land consolidation in both urban and rural contexts.

Catherine Gilbert (ORCID: https://orcid.org//0000-0002-8944-8009) is a research associate at the University of Sydney. She is an urban planner with a research interest in housing. Her research focuses on examining the impacts of planning regulation and, in particular, regulatory reform on rates, patterns, and diversity of housing supply.

Nicole Gurran (ORCID: https://orcid.org//0000-0003-2646-384X) is Professor of Urban and Regional Planning at the University of Sydney and directs the University's AHURI (Australian Housing and Urban Research Institute) research centre. Her research focuses on intersections between urban planning and the housing system, and she has led and collaborated on a series of studies on aspects of urban policy, housing, sustainability, and planning, funded by AHURI, the Australian Research Council (ARC), as well as state and local governments.

Myounggu Kang is Professor of Urban and Regional Planning at the University of Seoul, where he is also the editor of the *International Journal of Urban Sciences* (IJUS). His former appointments include the position of Senior Urban Specialist at the World Bank in Washington and Director-General of International Urban Development Collaboration at Seoul Metropolitan Government, among others.

Eran S. Kaplinsky is an associate professor at the Faculty of Law, University of Alberta.

Sang-Il Kim is a senior research fellow at the City of Seoul's urban think tank 'The Seoul Institute' where he holds the position of Director of the Department of Urban Planning, Design and Housing. His major research projects include Estimation of Planning Gain from Zoning Regulation Change and the Introduction of the Negotiation for Rezoning and Developer Obligations.

Klaas Kresse is a professor at Ewha Womans University in Seoul. His research and practical work revolves around spatial design, the supporting rules and regulations, and the belonging financing structures. Previously, he worked as a visiting professor at the University of Seoul and practiced in Rem Koolhaas' Office for Metropolitan Architecture.

Lawrence W. C. Lai is Professor of Planning and Real Estate, Department of Real Estate and Construction and Ronald Coase Centre for Property Rights Research, The University of Hong Kong, and a registered professional planner.

Sébastien Lambelet (ORCID: https://orcid.org/0000-0002-7803-3836) is a research assistant and PhD student in the Department of Political Science and in the Institute for Environmental Governance & Territorial Development at the University of Geneva, Switzerland. His research concentrates around urban power and governance, land management, and the implementation of urban policies in Switzerland. See https://unige. academia.edu/SébastienLambelet.

Tzu-Chin Lin is a professor in the Department of Land Economics, National Chengchi University, Taipei, Taiwan. His research focuses on the areas of land market and land policies. He has published widely in journals such as *Land Economics*, *American Journal of Agricultural Economics*, and *Land Use Policy*.

Zhi Liu is Director of Peking University – Lincoln Institute Center for Urban Development and Land Policy, and Senior Research Fellow and China Program Director with the Lincoln Institute of Land Policy. He specializes in infrastructure finance, municipal finance, land policy, and urban planning.

Marcio Alex Marcelino is an architect and an urban planner, Master of Science in Urban Management and Development, and MBA in project management. He is a public officer at the Municipality of Curitiba, Brazil, where he develops projects and studies in the areas of social housing, transportation, and urban development.

Pia Mora is a sociologist from Pontificia Universidad Católica de Chile who has worked around 10 years in investigating and coordinating projects at the Public Policy Center of the Chilean Catholic University.

Ana Morais de Sá (ORCID: 0000-0003-0591-9369) is an assistant professor at Instituto Superior Técnico, Lisbon University, where she teaches spatial planning and urban management. Her research interests focus on the relationships between land policies, land economics, land and property taxation, and the planning practice.

Demetrio Muñoz Gielen (ORCID: https://orcid.org/0000-0001-6863-2336) is Lecturer of Land Policies at two universities: the Institute of Housing and Urban Development Studies (IHS) at the Erasmus University of Rotterdam, and also at the Radboud University, both in the Netherlands. He combines his lectureship and research position with a position as public officer at the Dutch Municipality of Purmerend. His research work involves the design, implementation, and evaluation of land policies and land-based finance in urban development. He can be contacted at d.munozgielen@icloud.com.

Tomasz Ossowicz is a professor in the Faculty of Architecture at Wrocław University of Science and Technology, Poland. His field of expertise is urban planning and land policies. He is also a public officer in Municipality of Wrocław, and from 1998 to 2015, he was Director of the Office of Development and Principal Urban Designer of Wrocław City.

Adjie Pamungkas is the head of the Urban and Regional Planning Department, Institut Teknologi Sepuluh Nopember (ITS), Indonesia. He is a member of several professional associations in Indonesia including, among others, the Indonesian Planning Expert Association and the Surabaya Planning Expert Team.

Juan Felipe Pinilla is a lawyer from the University of Los Andes (Bogotá) with a master's degree in Territorial and Urban Policy from the Carlos III University of Madrid, Spain. He coordinates consultancy and research projects through his firm JFP & Asociados-Derecho Urbano (www. jfpyasociados.com). He has published diverse articles regarding, among other topics, property and land management tools, and has given lectures of urban law in various Colombian universities.

Laura Pogliani (ORCID ID https://orcid.org/0000-0003-0048-102X) is Associate Professor, MSc Architecture, Dipartimento di Architettura e Studi Urbani, Politecnico di Milano, piazza Leonardo da Vinci 26,. Her research focuses on land-use planning and regulation tools. She is a member of the Editorial Board of *Urbanistica* Journal and Coordinator of the INU Community 'Policies for Inclusive Housing'.**Ary A. Samsura** is a lecturer and researcher at the Department of Geography, Planning and Environment, Radboud University, the Netherlands. His research mainly focuses on the collective decision-making in urban development processes in Europe, and also some Asian countries including Indonesia.

Glen Searle (ORCID: https://orcid.org//0000-0002-9661-7931) is Honorary Associate Professor of Planning at the Universities of Sydney and Queensland. He was formerly Director of the Planning Programs at the University of Technology Sydney and the University of Queensland. He has held urban policy and planning positions at the UK Department of the Environment and the New South Wales Departments of Decentralisation and Development, Treasury, and Planning, where he was Manager of Policy.

Sevkiye Sence Turk is a professor at the Department of Urban and Regional Planning, Faculty of Architecture, Istanbul Technical University (ITU). Her main interests are land development processes, use of land readjustment (LR) in urban areas, serviced land supply for housing, and location theory.

Erwin van der Krabben is Professor of Urban Planning at Radboud University (the Netherlands), and Honorary Professor of Planning and Real Estate at Hong Kong University, Faculty of Architecture. His research focuses on the interrelationships between urban planning and land and real estate markets, and includes work on land policy and value capture, financial aspects of urban management, and decision-making processes.

François-Xavier Viallon (ORCID: https://orcid.org/0000-0001-8718-2756) is a postdoctoral researcher in the Swiss Graduate School of Public Administration at the University of Lausanne and an associated researcher in the Institute for Environmental Governance & Territorial Development at the University of Geneva. His research interests are policy instruments and value redistribution, natural resource management, property rights, and property governance.

Tomasz Zaborowski (ORCID: https://orcid.org/0000-0001-9656-5169) is an assistant professor at the Faculty of Geography and Regional Studies, University of Warsaw, and public officer in the Municipality of Radom. His fields of scientific and professional interests are the legal and economic issues in urban and city-regional planning. He has carried out comparative cross-country studies in Poland, Germany, England, and Spain.

Xinman Zeng is Research Fellow at Peking University – Lincoln Institute Center for Urban Development and Land Policy. Her main research areas are urban planning, area development, and policy.

Figures

Tables

Acknowledgements

The editors thank the Lincoln Institute of Land Policy for its support to the participation of many of the authors in the 11th Annual Conference International Academic Association Planning, Law and Property Rights, held in Hong Kong, China, in February 2017. The discussions that took place there greatly inspired us and many of the chapters in this book are based on the papers presented there.

Introduction

Demetrio Muñoz Gielen and
Erwin van der Krabben

Traditionally, in most countries, the public sector is responsible for the provision of all public goods that are necessary to support sustainable urban development, including among many other things public urban infrastructure (road infrastructure, parks, social, health and educational facilities, affordable and social housing, climate adaption and mitigation, etc). Public bodies increasingly rely on private financing of this infrastructure. As a consequence, value capture instruments, and among them developer obligations, are gaining prominence in public-private relationships in urban development. In line with that, debates take place in many countries with regard to the effectiveness and efficiency of value capture practices. Such debates are relevant to urban planning, since they address the financial feasibility of its implementation.

This book gathers contributions of authors from around the world addressing the institutional design and results, in different countries, of one specific type of value capture tool: developer obligations (DO). DOs are contributions of property developers and landowners made in exchange for public bodies making decisions on land-use regulations that increase the economic value of their land and buildings. They can be the result of previously prescribed requirements that do not leave room for negotiation (non-negotiable developer obligations, N-NDOs). In contrast, in many jurisdictions, developer obligations are negotiated between public bodies and developers (negotiable developer obligations, NDOs).

1. Definition of the problem: lack of systematic international comparative knowledge

DOs most of the time derive from an indirect economic rationale, i.e. that developers should pay for the costs of the negative externalities caused by their development projects, and less from a direct rationale, i.e. the more ideological rationale that land value increase belongs to the community (see Section 4.1 for more explanation about indirect and direct rationales). Because of their less evident ideological background, variety and local character, DOs – especially negotiable ones and those based on indirect rationales – have been less discussed in international scholarly literature than tools based on direct rationales. Historically, particular attention has been paid to the Uthwatt report in 1942, the subsequently announced (and largely not implemented) nationalization of development rights in the British 1947 Town and Country Planning Act and the vicissitudes of the betterment tax since then. This makes sense: direct tools as this one have a strong ideological nature and challenge principles of property rights, and correspondingly do strongly impact on planning debates, policies and legislation. Any proposal to introduce direct tools does inevitably attract much attention of scholars.

Among DOs, N-NDO practices are better documented than NDO practices. N-NDOs are regulated, often in detail, in regional and/or national legislation, and have thus also attracted some scholarly attention (generally not so much, however, as taxes and charges based on direct rationales). Their institutional design is usually well documented, though not so much their results in practice: we often know how they should work, but not always whether they are effective. The use of NDOs usually is poorly documented for most countries in academic publications, both their institutional design (which often has a local character only) and their results in practice.

There have been previous and very valuable contributions in English scholarly literature dealing with DOs.[1] However, we are not aware of any systematic international comparative study about the institutional design and practical results of the negotiable ones. Also, there is, with some exceptions (UK, North America and in some cases Latin America), not much recent evidence of the results in practice of N-NDOs. And finally, there is in academic literature also not much trace of knowledge about the interaction between N-NDOs and NDOs. In many countries, this interaction plays a relevant role in the introduction and evolution of both sorts of obligations. This book has the ambition of filling these knowledge gaps. We believe that more knowledge can help to improve the effectiveness of developer obligations in achieving better urban infrastructure and, ultimately, sustainable and inclusive cities.

This book has primarily been written for scholars and academics of urban planning, real estate and urban development, planning law and urban and land economics. It offers both a systematic and international overview and a critical evaluation of the design, working and results of developer obligations globally, detailed enough to feed their research and teaching programs. Also, it has been written for policy makers who devise

---

1   For example, Hagman & Misczynski (1978), Alterman (1988), Healey et al. (1995), Smolka (2013) and Crook et al. (2016).

improvements of value capture instruments. Practitioners in the field of urban planning and land and property development will find in this book a valuable source to contextualize their practices (and to feed their proposals if they are involved in policy-making processes), but not a 'manual' to feed their daily practices.

2. Structure of this book

This introductory chapter briefly introduces some basic concepts and discussions about public value capture (Section 3) and elucidates the different sorts of value capture instruments and the place of DOs among them (Section 4). We paid special attention to their categorization in order to allow an accurate international comparison and positioning of DOs. Section 5 presents the theoretical framework that is used to reflect on the practices around DOs, introducing four theoretical lenses: 'Georgism', public finance theory, collaborative planning and the communicative rationality in planning, and property rights theory.

Next chapters of this book focus each on one of the 18 countries. The authors of these chapters address several of a common list of relevant questions and follow the categorization presented in Section 4. The countries are presented in geographical order: Canada, US, Colombia, Brazil, Chile, Poland, the Netherlands, Switzerland, Italy, Spain, Portugal, Turkey, China and Hong Kong, Korea, Taiwan, Indonesia and Australia.

Finally, we infer in Chapter Conclusions some reflections based on these 18 country chapters and other literature (including the experience in five other countries: UK, India, Israel, Vietnam and Qatar). These reflections focus on those variables that seem to be relevant for the effectiveness of DOs.

3. Introduction to public value capture

This section briefly introduces the principles of, and main discussions about, public value capture.

3.1 To whom belongs the increase in value of land and property?

When the value of a plot of land and/or the property (the building) on it increases, this is usually due to one or more of the following 'events':

1   The owner of the land and/or property makes efforts himself and invests in the qualities or accessibility of his plot of land and/or property (by fertilizing agricultural land, by renovating or rebuilding the property, by constructing access roads, etc.).
2   Others, public and/or private parties, make efforts and investments that positively affect the qualities of the location (accessibility, status,

proximity to economic activities, views, etc.) in which the plot of land and property are located; this may include the provision of new infrastructure (like an airport, motorway or a park), general population growth and economic growth, which is the result of efforts and investments by others than the owner.

3   Public bodies allow more profitable use and building possibilities through land-use regulation decisions of any kind: rezoning, additional development rights, relaxation of existing land-use regulations, issuing of building permit, property subdivision and readjustment decisions leading to new use and/or building possibilities, etc.

When land is public or communal property, there should be not much discussion: the land value increase goes to the community.[2] When land is private property (freehold) and the value increase is the result of the owner's own efforts, there usually is not much discussion too about who is the legitimate 'owner' of this increase: the owner himself.

However, when land is private property and the value increase is the result of investments or decisions by others (e.g. the result of public investment in infrastructure, general economic growth or public decisions on land-use regulations), it is often questioned to whom the increment value belongs. It is this very dependency on the efforts, investments and regulations of parties other than the owner himself that has long stimulated fundamental discussions about whether (part of) the value increase of the land caused by previously listed 'events' 2 and 3 legitimately belongs to the landowner or not. The terms used to name this value increase often betray the normative nature of these discussions: *unearned increment* or *betterment, windfalls, givings*, etc. On one side, there is the thesis of full or conservative liberal ownership, where any value increase of land, no matter who or what caused it, belongs to the landowner. An alternative thesis, to be found also amongst liberal scholars, advocates that the use value can be indeed considered as fundamental to individual and social well-being, but that the exchange value (should the property be exchanged) does not. Any value increase resulting from exchange belongs to the community, because it is the community after all that is responsible for it (MacIntyre, 1984: 251; Christman, 1994; Krueckeberg, 1995). Consequently, taxes or other types of charges or DOs should cream off (part of) the land value increase. A popular topic in the neo-classical theory of economic rent is the idea of taxing land value increase, which, when removed, will not affect the output or the price of the product produced on that plot of land. Variants

2   However, sometimes in situations of long-term lease contracts on public land (as in countries like China and Vietnam, many African countries but also in some Dutch cities), the question of who deserves the value increases can still lead to a lot of public and political debate.

of this argument have been advanced by Adam Smith, David Ricardo, J.S. Mill, Alfred Marshall, A. Pigou and, specially, Henry George (George, 1879: 89–94, 219–241; Prest, 1981: 7–21; Oxley, 2006: 103; Alterman, 2009: 4–5).

3.2 Proposals for land value capture (LVC)

The debate on whether and how public bodies should capture land value increase has crystallized in different regulations, in various jurisdictions. The capture of land value increase is documented as early as in the Roman Empire (Smolka, 2013: 13), but more recent examples regard the UK just after WWII, Spain in 1978, Brazil in the 1980s, Colombia in 1989, Switzerland in the 1970s, and many others. Land value capture is sometimes 'disguised' under similar, related concepts such as *land-based finance* (e.g. UN-Habitat, 2015).

Proposals for a full or partial LVC based on the direct rationale that it is the community to whom all or part of the land value increase belongs have often led to (political) controversies and have not always been fully or sufficiently implemented (e.g. the proposals of betterment taxation in the Netherlands in the 2000s). The perhaps most documented dispute over taxing land value increase took place in the UK after publication of the Uthwatt report in 1942. The Uthwatt Committee discussed among other things the introduction of a betterment levy to capture the planning gain. A 100% betterment levy was introduced in the 1947 Town and Country Planning Act, and no development could take place without payment to the Central Land Board. The levy would apply where land in private ownership was sold to developers. However, the political controversy about the new regulation became clear soon after, when the subsequent Conservative government immediately decided to abolish it by the 1954 Planning Act. Similarly, a 40% levy introduced by Labour in 1967 was abandoned by a Conservative government in 1971. The last major attempt in UK to tax development gains was the Development Land Tax Act 1976, introduced by a Labour government. This betterment tax was severely modified by a Conservative administration that came into power in 1979 and eventually scrapped in 1985 (García-Bellido, 1975; Spaans et al., 1996: 302–304; Oxley, 2006: 104; Clusa & Mur, 2007: 124–127; Alterman, 2009: 8, 15–17). The British example shows the strong ideological nature of LVC debates.[3]

---

3 Internationally less known is the political crisis that developed in the Netherlands in 1977, after incompatible views had arisen with respect to land policy between the Labour Party and the Christian Democrats that formed a coalition at that time. The debate was not about introducing a land value tax, but about a related theme: the compensation to be paid in case

A study of 14 advanced-economy countries (Australia, Austria, Canada, Finland, France, Germany, Greece, Israel, the Netherlands, Poland, Sweden, the UK and the US) found that only three included LVC instruments based on direct rationales (Israel, Poland and UK), and that only one of them did actually successfully apply such an instrument (the betterment levy in Israel, Alterman, 2012).

We are, however, not so pessimistic about the potential use of tools based on direct rationales because, as following chapters show, there are also examples of countries that have successfully, or partially successfully, introduced taxes based on direct rationales. And moreover, because many countries have had success in introducing direct instruments shaped as DOs (so not taxes, but contributions made in exchange for land-use regulations decisions; see Section 4 for more details about these categories). A good example of a country in which direct rationales have successfully being introduced shaped as DOs is Brazil.

Besides proposals of LVC based on a direct rationale (the community is the rightful owner of all or part of the increased value and should therefore capture it), other proposals have come forward that are based on different, 'indirect' rationales, of which the internalization of negative impacts of urban development is the most common one. These proposals do not challenge fundamental ideological principles and do not always require a detailed regulation, which make them easier to introduce. The findings presented in this book suggest that indirect LVC tools are nowadays successfully applied in many countries around the world.

3.3 Increasing private financing of public infrastructure

In many countries, the discussions about the legitimacy and practicality of LVC comes along with a general trend of decreasing direct public responsibility in the financing of public goods. The public sector is not anymore expected or – as is the case in many developing countries – able to be the only one responsible for financing them. In recent decades, public bodies therefore increasingly pursued the private financing of urban infrastructure. A well-known example is the inclusionary housing regulation used in many places around the US and in other countries. This increasing

---

of expropriation. While the Labour Party advocated a compensation based on the value of the land in its original use (the planning gain as the result of the government decision to change the use of the land would go to the state), the Christian Democrats did not want to change the existing regulation which prescribes compensation based on the market value of the land (the planning gain would remain with the owner that would be expropriated). The coalition partners couldn't agree on the method to define compensation (which added up to some other disagreements within the coalition) and decided to step down. Compensation for expropriation would continue since then to include planning gain.

need of private financing can be related to public sector expenditure constraints, and to a shift towards privatization and managerial strategies and economic liberalization.[4] Also, the rise of environmentalism, which has concentrated public attention on the impacts of urban development, its limitation and mitigation, fiscal decentralization towards local public bodies, the influence of multilateral agencies promoting LVC and other variables like prosperous real estate markets (or the opposite: real estate markets in crisis, as the Netherlands shows) have contributed to this fundamental shift (Loughlin, 1981: 95; Kirwan, 1989; Bailey, 1990: 428, 431; Callies & Grant, 1991; Peddle & Lewis, 1996: 131–132; Healey et al., 1996: 144; O'Neill, 2010: 5–6; Burge, 2010: 183; Monk & Crook, 2016: 233–234, 237, 252–253, 256; Smolka, 2013: 10–12; Fox-Rogers & Murphy, 2015: 41–43; Crook, 2016: 73; Muñoz & Lenferink, 2018). This topic has kept the attention of the professional and scholarly communities in recent decades, and special attention has been given to the financing of transit systems (e.g. Smith & Gihring, 2006; Suzuki et al., 2015; Nguyen et al., 2018).

3.4 Definition of land value capture (LVC) and public value capture (PVC)

Before categorizing all different sorts of value capture tools, there is need first to clarify the meaning of and discussions about some related concepts. There is agreement that land value capture (LVC) refers not to the capture of value created by the efforts of the landowner himself because there is no discussion that this value belongs to him. LVC refers thus first to the capture of the land value created by efforts of public bodies. It could be discussed whether LVC should also include the capture of the land value created not by public bodies but by other private parties than the owner or the general economic growth. Besides, there is agreement that LVC refers to the capture of land value increase, excluding thus the capture of the increase in value of buidings. Another discussion regards whether LVC can be considered a tax or not (e.g. Smolka, 2013: 8–9, 21–22; Ingram & Hong, 2012: 4–5; UN-Habitat, 1976: recommendation D.3).

Because it is often difficult to assess from the available information whether tools in practice capture value increase belonging to land or to buildings, and because this book has not the ambition of elaborating on the mentioned discussions, it uses the generic term public value capture (PVC, excluding thus the term 'land') to include all instruments that capture all possible increases

---

4 Some use the term 'neoliberalism' to characterize this trend, e.g. Fox-Rogers & Murphy (2015).

of the value of land and buildings, whether they are considered taxes or not. Public value capture includes thus land value capture, and more.

4. Categorization of public value capture instruments

This section introduces some categories of PVC tools that seem to be relevant for their feasibility (is there enough support in the specific context to introduce them?) and their effectiveness (do they provide good results?).

4.1 Categorization based on the supporting rationale: direct and indirect

When trying to capture the value increase of land and property, public bodies either use direct or indirect PVC instruments that, as said before, build on two motivating rationales (Alterman, 2012: 763–766, 775–779; Muñoz Gielen et al., 2017: 126–127). This categorization is relevant because it may influence the feasibility of PVC instruments.

Direct instruments seek to capture all or some of the value increase under the explicit or implicit rationale that this value increase belongs to the community and not to the landowner because it has not been caused by him ('events' 2 and 3 mentioned in Section 3.1). Direct instruments are considered wealth redistribution instruments, and are thus often seen as a tax (which, formally speaking, often they are not) that needs explicit and detailed legislative base at the regional and/or national level.

Indirect instruments are more pragmatic and seek to capture value increase under different motivating rationales other than the rationale that the value increase belongs to the community. As mentioned before, the most common one is that landowners and developers should internalize the costs of mitigating the impacts of their building plans, i.e. to pay for the maintenance and improvement of existing public infrastructure, or to pay the new public infrastructure directly or indirectly needed to support the new developed (or redeveloped) areas. The value of these impacts represents the social costs or compensation that the community that bears such costs can exact on the developer (Bowers, 1992; Webster, 1998).

Often instruments are based on a mixture of rationales. For example, for property tax, the indirect rationale (landowners must internalize negative externalities) and the direct rationale (they should pay back to the community the value created by investments of the community) are blurred and/or not well defined in legislation or policies. Also, 'betterment contributions' (contributions paid in exchange for public investment in infrastructure) might support on different rationales: they support on a direct rationale when landowners must pay the value increase (the full value increase or a share of it) caused by the public investment in infrastructure, regardless whether they cover or not the costs of the public infrastructure. Examples are the *contribución por valorización* in Colombia, the *opłaty adiacenckie* in Poland and the *Encargo de Mais-Valia* in Portugal.[5] Here, the implicit or explicit argument is that this value increase is created by this investment and should therefore be paid back. However, betterment contributions seem to follow also an indirect rationale when they charge only the costs of the public infrastructure, i.e. when they do not charge the value increase or a standardized share of it, but only the costs of the specific infrastructure (which can be higher or lower than the value increase). Examples are the Dutch *baatbelasting* and the German *Erschließungsbeitrag*. Here, the implicit or explicit argument, besides the idea that landowners somehow do not deserve the (full) value increase, is mainly that landowners must internalize the impacts of development.

We will see in Chapter Conclusions of this book that the supportive rationale might be relevant for their feasibility as it influences the socio-political support for deploying them.

4.2 Categorization based on whether charged in exchange for land-use regulation decisions or not (definition of developer obligations)

PVC tools can be charged independently from the moment in which land-use regulation decisions are made:[6] sometimes recurrently, e.g. *capital gains tax on land or property* and the *property tax*; sometimes only once, e.g. a *tax upon transfer of title* (also known as *stamp duty*); and those taxes meant to capture land value increase that are paid when land is transferred (the most common one is the *land value tax*,[7] e.g. the *impuesto de plusvalías* in Spain, the *opłata planistyczna* in Poland and the *tu di zeng zhi shui* in Taiwan).

Besides these taxes and fees, another sort of PVC tool charged independently from the moment of land-use regulation decisions consists of contributions to be paid by property owners who benefit from a public investment in the improvement of public infrastructure, regardless of whether the owners are developing or not their land and regardless land-use regulation decisions. They are often referred to as 'betterment contributions' or 'charges'. Some examples, besides those just mentioned in the previous section, are

---

5 All of them when used in exchange for a public investment in infrastructure.
6 Land-use regulation decisions are rezoning, additional development rights, relaxation of existing land-use regulations, issuing of building permit, property subdivision or readjustment decisions leading to new use and/or building possibilities, etc.
7 Land value taxes charge only the value increase of the land, not of the land and the building on it together, like the property tax does. Land value taxes build on a direct rationale, while the property tax often has a vague supporting rationale that includes also indirect arguments: that landowners must pay for the costs of local services.

Community Development Fees (*gong cheng shou yi fei zheng shou tiao li*) in Taiwan, *special assessments* in the US, *Contribuição de melhoria* in Brazil and *Contribución especial de mejoras* in Ecuador.

Alternatively, PVC tools can also be charged linked to land-use regulations decisions (as a compensation in exchange for such a decision, levied usually on the one who asks for it).

This categorization of instruments (charged independently from or directly related to the land-use regulation decision) is relevant for their feasibility, e.g. property taxes are charged on all landowners independently from land-use regulation decisions, and often proportional to the market value of their property, but not always proportional to their liquidity (an old lady living on a small pension in an inherited apartment in the city centre might be required to pay the same as the rich investor who just bought the apartment right next door).

Contributions charged in exchange for land-use decisions, however, can be charged on those who benefit from these decisions, right at the moment at which they dispose of liquidity. We believe that, in general, this peculiarity favours the political and social feasibility of these contributions, which are thus paid by property owners or developers in exchange for land-use regulations decisions of any kind.[8] Public bodies require these contributions as a condition for owners and developers if they want to enjoy the new use and/or building possibilities of their property, i.e. when they want to enjoy the development possibilities created by a public decision on land-use regulations that increases the value of their property. Note that here the public delivery consists of a public decision, not any other form of compensation like public investments in infrastructure or the selling of public land. The actual moment of payment is not necessarily the same moment of approval of the land-use regulations; actually, the payment is often deferred in time to the moment when the developer actually wants to build and asks for the necessary permits. In the US, these contributions are known as *exactions*, but we follow here Alterman (2012) and name them generically *developer obligations* (DOs).

Most developer obligations belong to the category of indirect instruments, but some, if based on the rationale that the economic value increase belongs to the community and should therefore be paid back to the public, belong to the direct value capture instruments, e.g. the Spanish N-NDO *cesiones* is based on the Spanish constitutional principle that 'the community shall have a share in the benefits from the town-planning policies of public bodies',[9] or the Italian *Contributo straordinario per la plusvalenza*, which charges 50%

---

8 Rezoning, additional development rights, relaxation of existing land-use regulations, issuing of development or building permits, property subdivision and readjustment decisions leading to new use and/or building possibilities, etc.

9 Section 47, 1978 Spanish Constitution.

of the development profit, or the Portuguese *Encargo de Mais-Valia*, when used to charge a share of the increased economic value due to a land-use regulation decision, or the Taiwaneese contributions in urban land (land or value-equivalent payment) and the feedback fee (*hui kui ji*, payment), used in farmland conversion, both charging a share of the increased economic value due to a land-use regulation decision.

There are several reasons why DOs gain in practice increasing popularity: first because as mentioned before, they are charged on those who actually benefit from value increase and spare the wider public (the old lady doesn't have to pay); second, because DOs are often based on indirect rationales and thus often do not require a detailed prescription in regional or national legislation. As a consequence, local public bodies are often relatively free to prescribe and frame them. This relative ease of introducing DOs, together with the need for innovative funding sources for public services mentioned in Section 3.3, has stimulated since at least the 1970s a plethora of locally inspired forms of DOs. Some of them can operate without almost any legislative authority. This being said, DOs still require a minimum of regulation and policy framing because there is need of some sort of legal and policy legitimacy to prescribe requirements on landowners and other private parties when they develop their land. At least national or regional legislation and/or jurisprudence must explicitly recognize the legality of negotiating such obligations. In addition to this, legislation and/or policy framing can (but not always does) prescribe (with fewer or more details) the scope of the contributions and the degree of transparency. We will see later, however, that there are also countries where, even if there is no such minimum legal base, municipalities do sometimes in practice introduce some sorts of DOs that in theory are not allowed (for example, but not exclusively, Poland).

4.3 Categorization of developer obligations based on the discretional room of public bodies: non-negotiable and negotiable

There are two sorts of developer obligations: non-negotiable (N-NDO) and negotiable (NDO).

Non-negotiable obligations have a statutory status, which means that they are regulated, most of the time in supra-municipal legislation that prescribe precisely their scope with legal standards and categorizations,[10] but sometimes also in legally binding local (municipal) regulations and policies. Thanks to this legal prescription, they can be prescribed without

---

10 Supra-municipal legislation can be produced at the national, regional, state or provincial level, depending on the institutional structure of the public administration in the respective country.

negotiation, at least in theory. N-NDOs are also sometimes referred to as taxes (although, formally speaking, often they are not). Generally speaking, they have a less local character than the negotiable ones. Examples of N-NDOs are building permit fees, which charge whomever solicits such fees the administrative costs of issuing them. Other N-NDOs charge larger contributions that go further than administrative costs; for example, *development impact fees* and *commercial linkage fees* in the US; *diretrizes básicas* in Brazil; *Participación en plusvalías* in Colombia; *opłaty adiacenckie* in Poland;[11] *Encargo de Mais-Valia*,[12] *Taxa Municipal de Urbanização* (TMU), *Taxa pela Realização, Manutenção e Reforço das Infraestruturas Urbanísticas* (TRIU) and *Cedências* in Portugal; the *Community Infrastructure Levy* in England; the *Tax d'aménagement* in France; *Cargas de Urbanización, cesiones* and *reservas de suelo* in Spain; *oneri di urbanizzazione, standard urbanistici* and *contributo sul costo di construzione* in Italy; *exploitatiebijdrage* in a *Exploitatieplan* in the Netherlands; *Section 94/7.11 Contribution Plans* in Australia; *development charges* in Canada; *public facility land contributions* and *public rental housing land contributions* in land readjustment (LR) and *joint (hapdong) redevelopments* in Korea; *development impact fees (kai fa ying xiang fei)* and *feedback fees (hui kui jin)* in Taiwan; and *compulsory dedication, inclusionary zoning* (of land for public uses or affordable housing) and *transfer of development rights by private bodies* (TDR) or *sale of development rights by public bodies* (SDR) in many other countries.

Transfer and sale of development rights include different instruments that have one characteristic in common, which makes them DOs: they always involve public bodies allowing property owners to build on their land (sometimes to build more than initially allowed in the land-use regulations) in exchange for any form of obligation. For example, in the case of transferable development rights (TDR), a landowner who wants to build must buy first development rights from another landowner that is not allowed to build (e.g. because his land has an ecologic or environmental value, or because he delivered his land to be used for a public goal) or must fulfill certain conditions (e.g. to preserve existing buildings with a cultural-historic value or to build social/affordable housing). TDRs are used to a certain extend in the US (Pruetz, 2016: 148–149), Brazil (Smolka, 2013: 42–44), Mumbai, India (Walters et al., 2016: 163–164), Northern and Central Italy (TDR are called there *perequazione*) and some other countries. Another type is the sale of development rights (SDR), whereby landowners who want to build must

---

11 When used to charge landowners that benefit from administrative decisions that allow plot subdivision.
12 When used in exchange for land-use regulation decisions.

buy development rights from public bodies. SDRs can be found in many countries, for example in Rajkot, Bangalore and Mumbai in India (Mathur, 2015; Walters et al., 2016: 88–89, 163–164). Brazil uses this instruments since the 1990s, first with the *Outorga Onerosa do Direito de Construir*, OODC (Smolka, 2013: 37–42). The city of São Paulo has developed SDRs to its most sophisticated form: development rights there are auctioned (sold) in the stock market to finance public infrastructure provision (the CEPAC, Sandroni, 2010; Smolka, 2013: 53–57).

Often, N-NDOs offer in practice room for negotiations, for example because prescriptions do in practice allow much room for interpretation, because practice doesn't strictly follow the prescriptions or because they are prescribed after negotiations take place. Therefore, they could also be considered NDOs, i.e. they are a hybrid between non-negotiable and negotiable. 'Pure' NDOs are usually only vaguely regulated in legislation, e.g. Dutch and Spanish NDOs (*exploitatiebijdrage* and *bijdrage ruimtelijke ontwikkeling* in a *anterieure overeenkomst*, and *costes adicionales* and *compromisos complementarios*, respectively) are based on some basic regulation (from central respectively central and regional governments), but it is the municipality which should (but in practice does often not) regulate them in detail. Or the Indonesian contributions as part of corporate social responsibility legislation, which are poorly regulated. Hybrid cases are regulated in legislation, e.g. the Italian *Contributo straordinario per la plusvalenza* charges 50% of the development profit, but there is room for interpreting how to appraise this profit. Or the Chilean *ZUDCs*, *PDUCs* and *ZUCs*, that are prescribed in the Regional Zoning Plan of Santiago de Chile but do in practice offer room for negotiation. Or the Swiss tax on added land value (*taxe sur la plus-value foncière, Mehrwertabgabe, compensazione del plusvalore*) and extended land service tax, which both are prescribed in legislation but in practice are negotiable (see cases in chapter Switzerland). Or the Indonesian agreements for surrounding infrastructure, which are framed within local regulation specifying the percentage of land to be contributed for public infrastructure but offer in practice much room to negotiate the form of infrastructure. Or the Taiwanese development impact fees (free cession of land for public infrastructure), of which legislation prescribes only minimum percentages and whose equivalent cash payments are calculated based on discretionary premises. Other examples of NDOs (pure and hybrid negotiable and non-negotiable) are negotiated exactions in the US, Section 37 Agreements in Canada (Amborski, 2017), planning gains and planning obligations in the UK, agreements with developers *(Heskemim Im Yazamim)* in Israel, *Medidas mitigadoras e compensatórias* in Brazil, *participation* in France and *FAR adjustments* in China.

Some NDOs are more negotiable than others. When NDOs are prescribed in indicative, non-legally binding local policy,[13] this policy reduces somehow the room for the negotiating parties to decide which obligations can be asked and agreed upon. But still, these NDOs can to a certain extend be negotiated because this local policy has no direct legal consequences for the rights of landowners, and municipalities (staff and local politicians or councils) can deviate from them without the need for extensive procedure, or they can just ignore them. As a consequence, parties can decide to agree lower obligations than prescribed in the local policy, or just to omit or add one specific obligation. Sometimes NDOs are not or almost not prescribed in local policy, so the outcome of negotiations will depend mainly on specific circumstances and the negotiating skills of involved persons. Here there are by definition no deviations, as the policy framework from which negotiations deviate, if existing, is vague. In this circumstance, the room for negotiation is the largest.

4.4 Sui generis *categorization: public and public-private land assembly*

Finally, there is a *sui generis* sort of PVC instrument: when a public or public-private body deploys an active governance approach to land development (see Chapter Conclusions for more explanation of governance approaches), i.e. when this body owns or acquires the land previously to its development (through nationalization, expropriation, or regular acquisition) and captures land value increase by selling and/or developing it. Some authors categorize active governance approaches as a value capture tool,[14] and they often unmistakably serve as such. Actually, one of the main motivations of active governance approaches is that they allow, under certain circumstances, for a public capture of land value increase. By providing the infrastructure and selling the serviced building plots, public bodies (sometimes disguised in a public-private body) can recover the costs made and, maybe make some profit. For example, in the Netherlands until recently, municipalities financed new public infrastructure in this way. A similar effect is achieved when public bodies, as the owners of the land, just sell the 'raw' land (freehold or leasehold), without providing the infrastructure, to developers or to a public-private partnership bodies (PPP). Public bodies can capture the land value increase through the land price (or through a share of development profits in case of PPP), or they can prescribe in the selling contract that developers will construct the infrastructure, and maybe

---

13 For example, indicative, non-legally binding master plans, or internal guidelines.
14 For example, Alterman mentions active governance approaches as a 'macro' category of value capture (2012), and Alexander mentions the selling of public land to developers (freehold or freehold) as a specific form of value capture, which he names 'land endowment' (2012).

pay public bodies for other expenses. This looks similar to DOs, but is not always the case: when the contributions are made in exchange for transfer of property rights on public land (freehold or leasehold), they are not DOs because it is not the land-use regulation decision that is used as leverage. When, in addition to negotiating the transfer of land, public bodies and developers also agree on specific contributions in exchange for land-use regulation decisions, they could be considered as DOs. Often, developers first negotiate with the public body selling the land (freehold or leasehold), and then they discuss the modification of the land-use regulations, maybe with a different public body or department. Contributions agreed in the first negotiations are not DOs, but rather a form of profit accruing from property selling. Contributions made in the second step are DOs because they are made in exchange for a public decision on land-use regulations. Sometimes both the transfer of land and the land-use regulation decisions are simultaneously used as leverage, which makes it harder to distinguish which are DOs and which not, e.g. in China, where land-use regulation decisions (the detailed land-use plan, which includes also contributions) prescribe the conditions that must be fulfilled by the buyer of land-use rights of public land. Despite being prescribed in the detailed land-use plan, which makes them look like DOs, actually these contributions are in fact the result of using as leverage the selling of land-use rights, not the land-use regulation decision itself.

Particularly in countries that have been in transition from a communist regime towards a socialist market system and where all land (e.g. China and Vietnam) or part of it (e.g. Poland) is still state owned, income from selling the land (freehold or long-term land leases) serves as a major source of income for local authorities.

See Table 0.1 for an overview of all mentioned PVC tools within all mentioned categorizations.

5. Reflections on developer obligations practices: theoretical lenses

The main objective of this book is to analyse and discuss the effectiveness and impact of developer obligations practices. To conceptualize and reflect on these practices we use four theoretical 'lenses'.

5.1 'Georgism'

In Section 3.1, we mentioned as a popular topic in the neo-classical theory of economic rent (also known as land rent theory) the idea of taxing land value increase, which, when removed, will not affect the output or the price of the product. Variants of this argument have been advanced by Adam Smith, David Ricardo, J.S. Mill, Alfred Marshall, A. Pigou and, especially, Henry George. The Georgist paradigm, relating to the famous

Table 0.1 Overview categorizations of public value capture instruments

		Other value capture tools (taxes, charges and fees) Require detailed regulation in legislation	Developer obligations (DO)		Public and public-private land assembly
			Non-negotiable (N-NDO) Require detailed regulation in legislation and often also in local policy	Negotiable (NDO) Require only basic regulation in legislation	
Based on direct rationale: landowner does not deserve value increase	Charged independently from modification land-use regulation	-Capital gains tax -Tax upon transfer title -Property tax -Land value tax -Impuesto de Plusvalías (SP) -Opłata planistyczna and Opłaty adiacenckie (PL) -Betterment tax (UK until 1970s) -Some of the betterment contributions mentioned under can also fit here, if they charge value increase independently from the costs of public infrastructure.			Nationalization, expropriation or voluntary acquisition of land + selling 'raw' land or public or public-private land development
	Charged linked to modification land-use regulation		-Participación en plusvalías (COL) -Cesiones (SP) -Sale of development rights (e.g. OODC and CEPACs, BRA) -Contributo straordinario per la plusvalenza (IT) -Encargo de Mais-Valia (in exchange for land-use plan, PT) -'Tax on added land value' [taxe sur la plus-value / Mehrwertabgabe / compensazione del plusvalore], CHE)	-Compromisos complementarios? (SP) -Contributo straordinario per la plusvalenza (IT) -Feedback fee (hui kui jin) (TW)	

		Other value capture tools (taxes, charges and fees) Require detailed regulation in legislation	Developer obligations (DO)		Public and public-private land assembly
			Non-negotiable (N-NDO) Require detailed regulation in legislation and often also in local policy	Negotiable (NDO) Require only basic regulation in legislation	
Based on indirect rationale: commonly that landowner should internalize negative externalities development	Charged independently from modification land-use regulation	-Betterment contribution -Special assessment (US) -Contribuição de melhoria (BRA) -Contribución especial de mejoras (ECU) -Baatbelasting (NL) -Erschließungsbeitrag (GER) -Contribución por valorización (COL) -Some taxes charged independently from land-use regulation decisions mentioned above can also fit here.			
	Charged linked to modification land-use regulation		-Building permit fee -Development impact fee (sort of exaction) (US) -Diretrizes Básicas (BRA) -Opłaty adiacenckie (PL) -TMU, TRIU and Cedências (PT) -Community infrastructure levy (ENG) -Tax d'aménagement (FR) -Cargas de urbanización and reservas de suelo (SP) -Section 94/7.11 CPs (AUS) -oneri di urbanizzazione, standard urbanistici and contributo sul costo di construzione (IT) -Exploitatiebijdrage (NL) prescribed in development contributions plan -Compulsory dedication or inclusionary zoning -Transfer of development rights -Development charges (CAN)	-Exactions (US) -Medidas mitigadoras e compensatórias (BRA) -Negotiated Exploitatiebijdrage and Bijdrage ruimtelijke ontwikkeling (NL) -Compromisos complementarios? (SP) -Costes adicionales (SP) -Exactions (US) -Section 37 Agreement (CAN) -Planning gains and obligations (UK) -Heskemim Im Yazamim (ISL) -Tax on added land value and Extended land service tax (CHE) -Participation (FR) -FAR adjustments (CHN) -Development impact fee (kai fa ying xiang fei) (TW)	Nationalization, expropriation or voluntary acquisition of land + selling 'raw' land or public or public-private land development

economic-philosophical work by Henry George, states that while people should own the value they produce themselves, economic value derived from land, natural resources and natural opportunities should belong equally to all members of society. In the second half of the 19th Century, Henry George advocated, in his famous work *Progress and Property* (1879), the introduction of a land value tax – also referred to as a 'Single Tax' on land. Before him, Adam Smith had already called it 'the perfect tax' (Smith, 1776; Webb, 2013) because of its economic effects. George argued that because the supply of land is fixed and its location value is created by communities and public works, the economic rent of land is the most logical source of public revenue. While many taxes distort economic decisions and suppress beneficial economic activity, land value tax is payable regardless of how well or poorly land is actually used. Noble Prize winner William Vickrey believed that "removing almost all business taxes, including property taxes on improvements, excepting only taxes reflecting the marginal social cost of public services rendered to specific activities and replacing them with taxes on site values, would substantially improve the economic efficiency of the jurisdiction" (Vickrey, 1996: 603). Despite the strong economic arguments in favor of land value tax as the main – or single – revenue source for public finance and despite (ongoing) debates in many countries around the world to introduce land value tax, only a few countries actually implemented land value tax (but never as a single tax), including some states in Australia, Hong Kong, Taiwan, Colombia, Denmark, Spain and Mexico (Andelson, 1971; chapter Spain). Some have criticized George's ideas because of the alegued injustice and immorality of the principle to existing landowners (Andelson, 2004).

5.2 Public finance theory

Public finance is the study of the role of the government in the economy. It is the branch of economics that assesses the revenue and expenditure of public authorities and the adjustment of one or the other to achieve desirable effects and avoid undesirable ones (Gruber, 2007). Financing of government expenditures, with taxation as the central element of modern public finance, is one of the key elements of public finance theory. The autonomy for cities to raise local taxes (e.g. PVC tools such as property taxes) varies greatly among countries. Depending among other things on the restrictions to that autonomy, cities use other financing methods, including land sales and other PVC tools (e.g. developer obligations) to generate sufficient revenue to pay for infrastructure and other expenditures. Public finance theory helps to understand what are efficient and sustainable methods for cities to raise income and what are the distributional effects of these mechanisms. Theories of public finance, thus, also provide insight in the effectiveness of developer obligations vs. taxation policies.

5.3 *Communicative rationality in spatial planning*

Today, planning is not considered to be a process of merely seeking the means to maximize planning goals; rather, planning is moving towards identifying ways to merge/intertwine the interests of stakeholders and optimize the results of their decision-making through mediation, deliberation and negotiation (Samsura, 2013: 4). This implies a shift from direct control by a planning authority towards self-regulation by the stakeholders themselves. Moreover, it implies that the decision-making power and the behavior of multiple interdependent stakeholders must be acknowledged. Those collaborative strategies come in all kinds of forms, but have in common that responsibilities for the implementation of urban planning have become much more a joint responsibility for the public sector and private actors. A new *communicative* rationality (Healey, 1992) in planning is the result of this paradigm shift, emphasizing interactions and negotiations between stakeholders taking part in complex decision-making processes. The 'new' rationale also helps to understand the increasing willingness of public and private stakeholders to adopt negotiation processes with respect to developer obligations. The willingness of private and public stakeholders to collaborate is important for the effectiveness of developer obligations, and the effectiveness of the negotiation process can be crucial. Different variables might influence this effectiveness and the possible outcome of negotiations. First, there are studies that show that cultural conditions can play an important role in the potential success of negotiations (Samsura et al., 2010). Second, besides these cultural conditions, institutional and legal conditions are important as well, as Sections 3 and 4 of Chapter Conclusions show.

5.4 *Property rights theory*

Increasingly, studies of urban planning make use of 'property rights theory', based on the work by Ronald Coase (Coase, 1960), to analyze the impact of the way property rights over land are defined on resource allocation and, on the other hand, the existence of transaction costs (Alexander, 2001; Webster & Lai, 2003; Buitelaar, 2003; Lai & Hung, 2008; Van der Krabben, 2009). The extent to which individual property rights over land are secured – or, contrarily, the ambiguity over property rights – may affect urban development in three different ways. First, secure property rights over land can enhance investment incentives by limiting the risk of expropriation and by reducing the need to divert private resources to protect property rights. Second, well-defined property rights over land facilitate the transfer of assets and assists in efficient land resource allocation. Third, the possession of formal rights over land can improve the ability of landowners to use land as collateral increasing landowner access to credit markets. Introducing and/or adjusting negotiated or non-negotiated developer obligations obviously may have substantial impacts on property rights regimes and the positions of individual property rights holders, while at the same time reducing the ambiguity over property rights may add to the transparency of development practices and may thus help to increase a public body's income from value capture. Property rights theory also can offer insights into the relevance of transaction costs related to various value capture mechanisms and the extent to which value capture helps to internalize externalities.

Together with more practical considerations and sources presented in Chapter Conclusions, these theoretical lenses have contributed to the common list of relevant questions that authors have addressed in each country chapter. The theoretical lenses 'return' throughout the book in discussions of what can be seen as crucial aspects of a sustainable and effective system of both non-negotiable and negotiable developer obligations that enables cities to provide for better public urban infrastructure.

References

Alexander, E. R. (2001), 'A Transaction-Cost Theory of Land Use Planning and Development Control: Toward the Institutional Analysis of Public Planning', *Town Planning Review*, Vol. 72, pp. 45–75.

——— (2012), 'Institutional Design for Value Capture and a Case: The Tel-Aviv Metropolitan Park', *International Planning Studies*, Vol. 17, No. 2, pp. 163–177.

Alterman, R. (1988), *Private Supply of Public Services: Evaluation of Real Estate Exactions, Linkages and Alternative Land Policies*. New York: New York University Press.

——— (2009), *Can the "unearned increment" in Land Values Be Harnessed to Supply Affordable Housing?* Paper in Conference 'Financing affordable housing and infrastructure in cities: Towards innovative land and property taxation system', UN Habitat GLTN, Warsaw, 15–16 October.

——— (2012), 'Land-Use Regulations and Property Values: The "Windfalls Capture" Idea Revisited', in Brooks, N., Donangy, K. & Knapp, G. J. (eds.), *The Oxford Handbook on Urban Economics and Planning*. Oxford: Oxford University Press, pp. 755–786.

Amborski, D. (2017), *Tensions Regarding Developer Obligations in the Province of Ontario*. Paper in 11th Annual Conference International Academic Association Planning, Law and Property Rights, Hong Kong, China, February, p. 27.

Andelson, R. V. (ed.). (1971), *Land-Value Taxation Around the World (Studies in Economic Reform and Social Justice*. Wiley Blackwell.

——— (2004), 'Critics of Henry George: An Appraisal of Their Strictures on Progress and Poverty', *The American Journal of Economics and Sociology*, Vol. 63, No. 2 (supplement).

Bailey, S. J. (1990), 'Charges for Local Infrastructure', *The Town Planning Review*, Vol. 61, No. 4, pp. 427–453.

Bowers, J. (1992), 'The Economics of Planning Gain: A Re-Appraisal', *Urban Studies*, Vol. 29, No. 8, pp. 1329–1339.

Buitelaar, E. (2003), 'Neither Market nor Government: Comparing the Performance of User Right Regimes', *Town Planning Review*, Vol. 74, No. 3, pp. 315–330.

Burge, G. (2010), 'The Effects of Development Impact Fees on Local Fiscal Conditions', in Ingram & Hong (eds.). (2010), pp. 182–212.

Callies, D. L. & Grant, M. (1991), 'Paying for Growth and Planning Gain: An Anglo-American Comparsion of Development Conditions, Impact Fees and Development Agreements', *The Urban Lawyer*, Vol. 23, No. 2, pp. 221–248.

Christman, J. (1994), *The Myth of Property: Toward an Egalitarian Theory of Ownership*. New York: Oxford University Press, p. 219.

Clusa, J. & Mur, S. (2007), 'La experiencia británica 1973-2006 de JGB y el pago de una deuda pendiente´, in *ACE Architecture, City and Environment*, nr. 3, February 2007, p. 122–149, Barcelona.

Coase, R. H. (1960), 'The Problem of Social Cost', *Journal of Law and Economics*, Vol. 3, pp. 1–44.

Crook, T. (2016), 'Planning Obligations Policy in England: *de facto* Taxation of Development Value', in Crook et al. (eds.). (2016), Wiley Blackwell. pp. 63–114.

Crook, T., Henneberry, J. & Whitehead, C. (eds.). (2016), *Planning Gain. Providing Infrastructure & Affordable Housing*. RICS Research, Wiley Blackwell.

Fox-Rogers, L. & Murphy, E. (2015), 'From Brown Envelopes to Community Benefits: The Co-Option of Planning Gain Agreements Under Deepening Neoliberalism', *Geoforum*, Vol. 67, pp. 41–50.

García-Bellido, J. (1975), 'Gran Bretaña: *Community Land Act 1975*. ¿Hacia una socialización del suelo', in *Ciudad y Territorio*, Vol. 75, No. 4, p. 81–94, Madrid.

George, H. (1879), *Progress and Poverty*, 2006 edited and abridged edition. New York: Robert Schalkenbach Foundation, p. 210.

Gruber, J. (2007), *Public Finance and Public Policy*. New York: Worth.

Hagman, D. & Misczynski, D. J. (eds.). (1978), *Windfalls for Wipeouts: Land Value Capture and Compensation*. Washington, DC, Chicago, IL: Planners Press American Planning Association, p. 660.

Healey, P. (1992), 'Planning Through Debate: The Communicative Turn in Planning Theory', *Town Planning Review*, Vol. 63. No. 2, pp. 143–162.

Healey, P., Purdue, M. & Ennis, F. (eds.). (1995), *Negotiating Development: Rationales and Practice for Development Obligations and Planning Gain*. London: E & FN Spon.

——— (1996), 'Negotiating Development: Planning Gain and Mitigating Impacts', *Journal of Property Research*, Vol. 13, No. 2, pp. 143–160.

Ingram, G. K. & Hong, Y-H. (eds.). (2010), *Municipal Revenues and Land Policies*. Cambridge, MA: Lincoln Institute of Land Policy, p. 536.

——— (2012), 'Land Value Capture: Types and Outcomes', pp. 3–18, in Ingram & Hong (eds.)., *Value capture and land policies*. Cambridge, MA: Lincoln Institute of Land Policy, p. 466.

Kirwan, R. M. (1989), 'Finance for Urban Public Infrastructure', *Urban Studies*, Vol. 26, pp. 285–300.

Krueckeberg, D. A. (1995), 'The Difficult Character of Property: To Whom Do Things Belong?' *Journal of the American Planning Association*, Vol. 61, No. 3, pp. 301–309.

Lai, L. W. C. & Hung, C. W. Y. (2008), 'The Inner Logic of the Coase Theorem and a Coasian Planning Research Agenda', *Environment and Planning B*, Vol. 35, pp. 207–225.

Loughlin, M. (1981), 'Planning Gain: Law, Policy and Practice', *Oxford Journal of Legal Studies*, Vol. 1, No. 1, pp. 61–97.

MacIntyre, A. (1984), *After Virtue: A Study in Moral Theory*, 1st edition 1981, 2nd edition 1984. Notre Dame: University of Notre Dame Press.

Mathur, S. (2015), 'Sale of Development Rights to Fund Public Transportation Projects: Insights from Rajkot, India, BRTS Project', *Habitat International*, Vol. 50, pp. 234–239.

Monk, S. & Crook, T. (2016), 'International Experience', in Crook et al. (eds.). (2016), pp. 227–268.

Muñoz Gielen, D. & Lenferink, S. (2018), 'The Role of Developer Obligations in Financing Large Public Infrastructure After the Economic Crisis in the Netherlands', *European Planning Studies*, Vol. 26, No. 4, pp. 768–791, DOI:10.108 0/09654313.2018.1425376.

Muñoz Gielen, D., Maguregui Salas, I. & Burón Cuadrado, J. (2017), 'International Comparison of the Changing Dynamics of Governance Approaches to Land Development and Their Results for Public Value Capture', *Cities*, Vol. 71, pp. 123–134.

Nguyen, T. B., Van der Krabben, E., Musil, C. & Le, D. A. (2018), 'Land for Infrastructure' in Ho Chi Minh City: Land-Based Financing of Transportation Improvement', *International Planning Studies*, Vol. 23, No. 3, pp. 310–326.

O'Neill, P. M. (2010), 'Infrastructure Financing and Operation in the Contemporary City', *Geographical Research*, Vol. 48, No. 1, pp. 3–12.

Oxley, M. (2006), 'The Gain from the Planning-Gain Supplement: A Consideration of the Proposal for a New Tax to Boost Housing Supply in the UK', *European Journal of Housing Policy*, Vol. 6, No. 1, pp. 101–113, April.

Peddle, M. T. & Lewis, J. L. (1996), 'Development Exactions as Growth Management and Local Infrastructure Finance Tools', in *Public Works Management & Policy*, Vol. 1, No. 2, pp. 129–144.

Prest, A. R. (1981), *The Taxation of Urban Land*. Manchester: Manchester University Press, p. 190.

Pruetz, R. (2016), 'Transferable Development Credits Puts Growth in Its Place', pp. 142–154, in Leshinsky & Legacy (eds.). (2016), *Instruments of Planning: Tensions and Challenges for More Equitable and Sustainable Cities*, RTPI Library Series. London: Routledge, p. 258.

Samsura, D. A. (2013), *Games and the City: Applying Game-Theoretical Approaches to Land and Property Development Analysis*. Delft: Trail Thesis Series.

Samsura, D. A., Van der Krabben, E. & Van Deemen, A. (2010), 'A Game Theory Approach to the Analysis of Land and Property Development Processes', *Land Use Policy*, Vol. 27, No. 2, 564–578.

Sandroni, P. (2010), 'A New Financial Instrument of Value Capture in São Paulo: Certificates of Additional Construction Potential', in Ingram, G. K. & Hong, Y-H. (eds.), *Municipal Revenues and Land Policies*. Cambridge, MA: Lincoln Institute of Land Policy, pp. 218–236.

Smith, A. (1776), *The Wealth of Nations*. Wordsworth Editions Ltd.

Smith, J. J. & Gihring, T. A. (2016), 'Financing Transit Systems Through Value Capture: An Annotated Bibliography', *American Journal of Economics and Sociology*, Vol. 65, No. 3 (July 2006), pp. 751–786.

Smolka, M. O. (2013), *Implementing Value Capture in Latin America: Policies and Tools for Urban Development*. Cambridge, MA: Lincoln Institute of Land Policy, p. 72.

Spaans, M., Golland, A. & Carter, N. (1996), 'Land Supply and Housing Development: A Comparative Analysis of Britain and The Netherlands 1970-1995', in *International Planning Studies*, Vol. 1, No. 3., pp. 291–310.

Suzuki, H., Murakami, J., Hong, Y-H. & Tamayose, B. (2015), *Financing Transit Oriented Development with Land Values: Adapting Land Value Capture in Developing Countries*. Washington, DC: World Bank.

UN-Habitat. (1976), *The Vancouver Declaration on Human Settlements*, from the report of UN-Habitat: United Nations Conference on Human Settlements, Vancouver, Canada, 31 May–11 June.

——— (2015), *Municipal Financing in Developing Cities: Review of Land-Based Finance Training Package for Financing Sustainable Urban Development*. Expert Group Meeting Report. Kenya, Nairobi: UN-HABITAT.

Van der Krabben, E. (2009), 'A Property Rights Approach to Externality Problems: Planning Based on Compensation Rules', *Urban Studies*, Vol. 46, No. 13, pp. 2869–2890.

Vickrey, W. (1996), 'The Corporate Income Tax in the U.S. Tax System', *Tax Notes*, Vol. 73, pp. 597, 603.

Walters, L., du Plessis, J., Haile, S. & Paterson, L. (2016), *Leveraging Land: Land Based-Finance for Local Governments: A Reader*, United Nations Human Settlements Programme (UN-Habitat) Nairobi, Kenya, p. 223.

Webb, M. (2013), 'How a Levy Based on Location Values Could Be the Perfect Tax', *Financial Times*, 27 September. (23 March 2017).

Webster, C. J. (1998), 'Public Choice, Pigouvian and Coasian Planning Theory', *Urban Studies*, Vol. 35, No. 1, pp. 3–75.

Webster, C. J. & Lai, L. W. C. (2003), *Property Rights, Planning and Markets: Managing Spontaneous Cities*. Cheltenham: Edward Elgar.

1 Development obligations in Canada

The experience in four provinces

Eran S. Kaplinsky and David Amborski

1. Introduction

Canadian governments have used a variety of land value capture (LVC) tools for many years. Many of these tools were not specifically or even primarily designed for value capture, but sometimes captured land value inadvertently or incidentally to other policy objectives (Smolka & Amborski, 2000). In recent years, however, local governments facing fiscal pressures – mainly due to ageing infrastructure, mass-transit projects, and other growth-related costs – have begun to enlarge the use of developer obligations (DOs) and other policy tools to focus more explicitly on LVC objectives (Trillium Business Strategies Inc, 2009).

This paper provides an overview of LVC in Canada, followed by a summary of DOs in four of the 10 Canadian provinces comprising approximately 65% the total population: Ontario, Nova Scotia, Alberta, and British Columbia. DOs have long provided significant revenues for local governments, especially in high growth municipalities in Ontario and British Columbia (Amborski, 1988), and more recently in Alberta. A comparison of the policies across the four provinces follows, with discussion and conclusions.

2. Canadian experiences with LVC and DOs

In Canada's federal system, jurisdiction over land and property is reserved almost exclusively to the provinces (British North America Act, 1867). All LVC tools rely on provincial enabling legislation. Municipalities are legally "creatures of the province" and have only those powers delegated to them by provincial enactments. Moreover, Canadian municipalities have very limited capacity to raise revenues and are heavily reliant on property taxes, and to a lesser degree on shrinking capital/infrastructure grants from senior governments (Kitchen, 2003). Most LVC tools and DOs tend to be employed by local governments.

There has been significant Canadian experience with the application of land value capture tools, including Public Land Banking, Public Land Leasing, Density Bonuses, Tax Increment Financing, Joint Development or

Public Private Partnerships, and Developer Obligations (which are the focus of this paper), covering the full range of categories proposed by Alterman: macro, direct, and indirect land value capture tools (Alterman, 2011).

DOs in Canada include development charges, dedication of land for public purposes, and provision of infrastructure and amenities; their relative importance varies across different jurisdictions. DOs help finance (and shield local taxpayers from) growth-related capital costs, and in some cases provide for general needs of the community such as affordable housing. Development charges have a long history (over 50 years) in Canada, and in some jurisdictions their quantum is very high both relative to the cost of housing and in absolute terms. Development charges are typically not negotiable, but negotiations of the other two DOs are more common.

2.1 Development charges in Ontario

Development charges were first regulated by the Development Charges Act, 1989, but go back 60 years. Prior to that Act, municipalities relied on the Planning Act, but the vagueness of this legislation led to numerous appeals before the Ontario Municipal Board and the courts.

Development charges evolved from a range of obligations imposed by municipalities as a condition of development or subdivision approval, based on fiscal lessons learned in the years following WWI and the Great Depression, and especially during the post-WWII housing boom. The legality of subdivision agreements, too, was not established until 1960, when they were explicitly authorized by statute. By the 1960s, developers had been made to pay for the cost of the infrastructure internal to new subdivisions, but municipalities began to struggle with significant off-site growth-related capital costs. Local councils began levying additional costs on developers, which became known as municipal imposts, lot levies, or development charges. Over time the magnitude, scope, and popularity of these charges increased (Amborski, 1988).

As charges increased more rapidly than house prices, it also became obvious that the methodology for calculating charges often lacked fairness, consistency, and rationality, resulting in new legal challenges by the development industry. These challenges centred around the range of services to be funded by development charges, the calculation of the costs, and the apportionment of the costs between new and existing residents. Questions were raised as to whether charges could include "soft services", such as fire halls, recreation centres, police vehicles, and even conference centres (Kaplinsky, 2006). Some appeals challenged development charges calculated based on the average cost of roads and sewers across the jurisdiction, as opposed to the marginal cost of serving specific developments. Even if there was agreement that average cost calculations were appropriate, there could be questions about how the average is calculated, i.e. based on historic costs or projected costs.

Eventually, the province undertook background work in the late 1980s and prepared a discussion paper. The Development Charges Act, 1989, was passed and the charges were based on all growth-related capital costs, leading to increases in the quantum of the charges. The Act required that development charges be imposed by bylaw (to be renewed every five years at most), on the basis of a capital cost study taking into account growth projections and corresponding service needs indicated in the municipal (master) plan. The Act limited the service standards that used to compute the charges to the highest local standard that existed in the past 10 years. Payment was required upon the issuance of the building permit (meaning the homebuilder would pay the charge and not the land developer, where they were separate entities). A development charge could be appealed by any property owner in the municipality.

Typically in the Greater Toronto Area, there would be three components to a development charge: a local municipal charge for the capital cost of services provided by the local municipality, a regional charge for regional services, and a school board charge for contribution to the capital cost of new schools. The structure of the development charges is such that there are different charges applied to different types of housing and non-residential development. Since charges on residential development are calculated per capita, the charges are highest for single family detached units, as they have the highest number of persons per household, and lower for residential development associated with smaller households. The legislation attempted to hold municipalities more accountable by requiring development charges to be deposited in special reserve funds and earmarked for the specific purposes for which each was collected. Municipalities must report annually to the provincial government regarding the existing balance and use of these reserve funds.

Dissatisfaction with the application of the Development Charges Act by the development industry, lobbying, and changes in the provincial government led to the legislation being amended in 1997. The changes to the legislation restricted the range of services that could be funded by charges and required that for certain services; there was a mandatory reduction of 10% of the costs to reflect benefits from these services to existing residents. The service standard used to calculate the charge was changed from highest to the average locally provided during the preceding 10 years. The effect was to slow increases in development charges.

The other major change in the legislation was the opportunity to use area-specific basis for engineering services. This means that rather than using average costs across all new development, the charges are based on an approximation of the marginal costs in various areas of the municipality. This approach represents an increase in equity and economic efficiency over average-cost pricing (Kaplinsky, 2006). Not all municipalities opted to ally this approach, but several did in the Toronto area, including Markham and Richmond Hill.

The most recent changes to development charges came with the passing of the Smart Growth for Our Communities Act, 2015. This legislation is intended to help municipalities fund growth, as well as make the development charges system more predictable, transparent, and accountable. More specifically, increasing the funding for growth is facilitated by eliminating the 10% reduction in calculating the costs of transit infrastructure, and permitting municipalities to use development charges to help fund waste diversion, including recycling.

There are also provisions in the legislation to increase predictability, transparency, and accountability, including requiring better integration of land-use planning with development charges, clarifying reporting requirements for the collection and use of charges collected and in higher and denser developments including park land funds, and requiring payment when the first building permit is issued for a building to provide greater certainty for developers. Despite these changes, the new legislation didn't increase the funding opportunities for growth-related costs to the degree municipalities had hoped.

Currently, development charges in Ontario are among the highest in North America. In Brampton and Mississauga, the 2017 combined development charge, regional, local and school board, exceeds $83,000 CDN for a single family detached house (BILD, 2017). Recently, the City of Toronto – which has historically had some of the lowest charges in the Greater Toronto Area – has proposed dramatic increases in its development charges. For example, the single and semi-detached unit rate from $40,067 to $88,391 (121% increase) and multiples two plus bedrooms from $33,744 to $73,058 (117% increase) (Hemson Consulting Limited, 2018). The scope of development charges has been recently expanded to include a charge for transit services (in addition to roads), and in some cases, a contribution for affordable housing is also required. These two items have had a significant impact on the proposed increases in the Toronto development charge. The increase in the charges is at cross purposes with policies to encourage affordable housing.

In addition to development charges, the Planning Act requires a 5% land dedication for park land, or a payment in lieu based on the value of land, at the discretion of the municipality (or alternatively, based on calculations specified in the municipality's official plan).

2.2 Infrastructure charges in Nova Scotia

Of the four provinces discussed, Nova Scotia is the last jurisdiction to implement development charges, and only in its major city, the Regional Municipality of Halifax. The advent of capital cost charges in Halifax has been precipitated by sustained growth in the region since the 1980s. This growth also encouraged the creation of the Regional Municipality of Halifax in 1996, amalgamated of the municipalities of Halifax, Bedford, Dartmouth, and Halifax County. It is the largest municipality in Atlantic Canada, with a population of 420,000 and an area of 5,500 square kilometres. The Regional Municipality is responsible for the delivery of all municipal services within its jurisdiction. As the growth absorbed the available trunk infrastructure capacity, a study was undertaken in 1999 to assess the future needs of the Regional Municipality. The study identified a substantial need for new infrastructure to meet to serve growth in the core area of the municipality.

The municipality prepared a Multi-Year Financial Strategy to determine how to finance the necessary infrastructure. Legislative basis for development charges in Nova Scotia is found in the Municipal Government Act. It enables municipalities to impose an infrastructure charge to recover the capital costs incurred by a municipality to service new subdivisions. Prior to 2000, no municipality in Nova Scotia had exercised this power.

In 2000, Halifax undertook a study and consultation to develop a policy to impose infrastructure charges consistent with the legislation. This document provided a basis for the municipality to specify policies that set out a capital cost contribution policy. Although Section 274 of the Act authorizes infrastructure charges to recover capital costs associated with new development via a subdivision bylaw, the report anticipates that some changes were required to existing legislation. Based on this background work, Halifax's Capital Cost Contribution Policy was adopted in 2002. The policy is based on a charge that is applied to a specific area. A similar approach is used by the Halifax Regional Water Commission. The approach requires the designation of a master planning area within which a specific charge will be applied. For each master planning area, the developer's contribution is based on meeting the demand generated by the new development, and the municipality's cost is based on the demand and associated cost created by a specific development as determined by the municipality. The boundaries are defined based on the methodology set out in the Best Practices Guide (Halifax Regional Municipality, 2000).

In 2006, a Regional Municipal Planning Strategy (MPS) was approved by the Halifax Regional Council. The plan is significant in that it is the first regional plan for Halifax prepared since the mid-1970s. In addition to indicating that growth should be allocated among a hierarchy of centres, urban, suburban and rural, the plan forms the basis for the distribution of future growth, which in turn is used as the basis for future infrastructure and related capital cost charges. At this point, capital cost contributions (CCCs) were implemented for the Russel Lake Master Plan via a site-specific amendment to the subdivision bylaw. However, the use was limited. This suggests a need and motivation by local governments to increase the use of these types of charges.

In 2007, the regional sewer charge was transferred to the jurisdiction of Halifax Water. This was the precursor to the changes that took place in 2013, where the sewer charge was replaced with a development charge for wastewater. In addition to the power to levy this charge, all assets were transferred to Halifax Water.

Prior to the 2013 development charge for wastewater, the Regional municipality initiated a study in 2011 to review the current applications and legislative basis of charges, and to develop a methodology to apply capital cost contributions to a range of services including fire, parks and recreation, libraries and growth-related studies.

In 2014, as the concerns for financing the capital costs of infrastructure by Regional Council extended to transit, the Council approved a method for adopting charges for transportation and transit services. However, these charges were not implemented. Later, the Halifax Regional Municipality (HRM) Charter was amended to permit charges to be applied to a broad range of services. These services now include parks and recreation, fire, and library services.

More recently, in 2016, the Regional Municipality of Halifax engaged a consultant to undertake a comprehensive review of the approaches to infrastructure charges currently applied in the Halifax Region and elsewhere, and to recommend how the Regional Municipality should apply new charges for all eligible services. The review will also entail consultation with the development and building industry.

2.3 Developers' obligations in Alberta

Developer obligations may be imposed in accordance with the Municipal Government Act of Alberta (MGA) depending on the type of planning permission sought. Obligations fall into one of three categories: first, to dedicate for public purposes part of land proposed to be subdivided, or to make a cash tribute in lieu of land, as required by the subdivision authority; second, to make local improvements and provide or pay for on-site services according to the specifications of the development authority; and third, to pay an off-site levy or a redevelopment levy to defray certain capital costs as set out in the municipality's bylaw.

2.3.1 Land dedication

The MGA (Division 8, Section 661–670) requires the owner of land proposed to be subdivided to dedicate without compensation land as required by the subdivision authority (i) as an environmental reserve; (ii) for roads and public utilities; and (iii) as a reserve for municipal and school purposes.

The environmental reserve is set aside first and consists of all the lands that are deemed undevelopable for reasons of safety or environmental protection, or to provide public access to bodies of water. Ordinarily, an environmental reserve must be left in its natural state or used as a public park. The developer may elect to retain ownership of the land, subject to an environmental easement (a restrictive covenant) in favour of the municipality instead of dedicating it. Land thus retained is taxable and may be used for limited private uses, and the public is excluded from it. Of the land remaining, up to 30% may be required by the subdivision authority to be dedicated for roads and public utilities (as defined in the MGA), but no more than "sufficient" for these specific purposes. Additionally, land or cash in lieu of land may be required to be dedicated for school board purposes, or to the municipality for parks and recreation area, or as buffer between different land uses. The total contribution that may be required is specified in the municipal development plan, but it should not exceed 10% of the land developable or cash equivalent. In practice, 10% is almost always exacted (Laux, 2013).

2.3.2 Servicing agreements

A subdivision authority may require an applicant for subdivision approval to enter into a servicing agreement to provide or pay for access roads and public utilities necessary to serve the subdivision, as well as walkways and parking and loading facilities (MGA, section 655(1)). The construction and engineering specifications are usually standardized in municipal policies referred to in the servicing agreements. Near identical servicing agreement requirements may be imposed as conditions by a development authority on an applicant for a development permit if such conditions are authorized in a land-use bylaw (MGA, section 650). Recently proposed amendments to the enabling legislation would expand the scope of servicing agreement to include "inclusionary housing" obligations subject to the municipality's land-use bylaw and provincial regulations (yet to be promulgated).

2.3.3 Off-site and other levies

Levies may be imposed by a bylaw of the municipality in accordance with the MGA (Division 6, sections 647–651.2). The legislation contemplates three different levies. Off-site levies are the functional equivalent of Ontario's development charges and were first authorized by legislation in 1973. Off-site levies may be imposed by bylaw in respect of land proposed to be subdivided or developed to pay for all or part of the capital cost of the services enumerated in the legislation. Traditionally, off-site levies were authorized in respect of "hard services" only, including water (storage, treatment, and transmission), sewage (treatment, movement, and disposal), stormwater facilities, and new or expanded roads. More recently, the legislation was amended to authorize off-site levies to pay for the capital cost of community recreation facilities, fire halls, police stations, and libraries.

In developing their off-site bylaws, municipalities are subject to the principles set out in the Off-Site Levies Regulation (Alta. Reg. 187/2017). Each bylaw must establish a clear and consistent method for calculating the levy for each type of infrastructure. Importantly, a "correlation" is required between the levy and the benefit to new development. The regulation further requires that in designing levies for soft services, the municipality consider supporting statutory plans, policies or agreements, and any other relevant documents that identify the need for and anticipated benefits from the new facilities, the anticipated growth horizon, and the apportionment of the estimated costs between the levy and other sources of revenue. Finally, the regulation requires annual reporting of all levies received and utilized for each type of service in each benefitting area. Municipalities are otherwise given considerable latitude.

The magnitude of off-site levies varies across Alberta municipalities depending on the infrastructure provided in built up and greenfield areas and the method of apportioning costs. Current charges in Calgary range from $343,000–$385,927 per hectare in greenfield areas. In Edmonton, the weighted average off-site levy is $270,052 per hectare; based on a residential density of 35 dwellings per hectare (consistent with past practices), the levies amount to $7,716 per dwelling, up from $2,857 in 2014 (Urban Development Institute Edmonton, 2014, 2018). Across the Edmonton region, where densities are often lower and the per dwelling levy can be higher, levies range from $0–$384,979 per hectare. In Sturgeon County, for example, the off-site levy is assessed at $59,533 per residential lot.

Two other types of levies are authorized by the MGA. A redevelopment levy may be imposed in a bylaw adopting a redevelopment plan for any area of the municipality in respect of development in that area. A redevelopment levy may be used to pay for land for parks, school buildings, or new or expanded recreation facilities. Intermunicipal off-site levies may be imposed by the bylaws of two or more municipalities that have entered into an agreement for such purpose.

2.3.4 Negotiated and non-negotiated obligations

Whether obligations are prescribed or negotiated ad hoc depends not only on the legislative provisions, but also on the context in which development permission is sought. Subdivision approval is almost always discretionary, and the owner of the lands would often be unwise to contest a demand for land dedication or other contribution not strictly sanctioned by law.

Negotiated obligations are expected in the context of direct control zoning. Section 641 of the MGA authorizes council, subject to any applicable statutory plan, to designate any area of the municipality as a direct control district, and to exercise particular control over the use and development of land or buildings in that district. Direct control grants municipal councils the power to "spot zone" any parcel, and in exchange for a significant lift in the value of land, developers may be asked not only to mitigate negative externalities, but also to contribute public amenities such as public art, landscaping and streetscaping, heritage preservation, and affordable housing (City of Edmonton, 2017). The proponent may also be required to enter into a "good neighbour" agreement with the relevant Community League and to make a financial contribution to that entity toward an off-site amenity before a development permit can be issued.

In Edmonton, negotiated amenity contributions have often been guided by precedent and bargaining power, as determined by the real estate market. This practice has been criticized for its lack of consistency and transparency, and for adding delays to the rezoning process. Currently the city is developing a new policy that will establish a rate of amenity contributions based on a recent (2010–2017) average. Under the proposed policy, for each direct control rezoning, the actual required contributions will be based on that rate and the increase in development rights above the current zoning. (City of Edmonton, 2017; CityForum Consulting, 2017).

The courts in Alberta have resisted municipal attempts to exact from developers contributions other than those specifically enumerated in the legislation. For example, in *Prairie Communities Development Corp. v Okotoks (Town)*, the Court of Appeal held that the municipality could not rely on its so-called "natural person powers" to enter into agreements with developers to collect from the latter voluntary levies in respect of costs not expressly enumerated in the legislation.

2.3.5 Value capture in developer obligations in Alberta

DOs under the MGA are primarily intended to provide for the needs of the proposed development and to mitigate its effects on the community. Whether or not the obligations can be used to capture land value is a matter of statutory interpretation. In contrast to the US, where the courts held that the Constitution requires both nexus and proportionality in imposing obligations, in Canada, these are questions of *vires*. Based on the legislation and limited caselaw (most of which predates the current versions of the enabling legislation), different obligations may be subject to different nexus and proportionality standards. Off-site levies, for example, must fairly and reasonably apportion the costs of growth between existing and new residents (*Off-Site Levies Regulation*, 2017; *Urban Development Institute v Leduc [City]* [2006]; *Keyland Development Corporation v Cochrane (Town)* [2007]). But in *Canada Lands Company CLC Ltd v Edmonton (City)* (2005), the Court of Appeal concluded that while some statutory provisions authorizing developer obligations require a strict nexus, others disclose a "cost-spreading policy which must be balanced against the user pay principle".

2.4 Developers' obligations in British Columbia

2.4.1 Development cost charges

BC municipalities were granted the power to levy development cost charges in 1977, replacing an older arrangement grounded in land-use contracts that existed since 1971. Prior to that, there was no legal authority to impose charges, but planning authorities could refuse a subdivision application for lack of resources to provide the requisite services. The Local Government

Act (Part 14, Division 19, Sections 558–570) now authorizes local governments to impose by bylaw a development cost charge on every person who obtains a development permit or subdivision approval to defray the municipality's capital costs of servicing the development, directly or indirectly, by providing sewage, water, drainage, or highway facilities, or by providing and improving park land. Some types of development are exempt from development cost charges or eligible for reduced or waived fees.

Like the legislation in Alberta, the BC Local Government Act provides municipalities with some flexibility in designing their charges, but also some guidance. Charges may vary across the community depending on the use of land, the location, density, and similar factors, but must be "similar for all developments that impose similar capital cost burdens on the local government". The method by which the charges are computed is not specified, but the municipality must take into account the projected growth, the phasing of works and services, and whether the charges are excessive in relation to existing service standards in the municipality or regional district. The local government must also consider whether the charge will deter development (particularly affordable or "low environmental impact" development). Land dedication in lieu of charges may be accepted in some cases.

2.4.2 Development cost levies pursuant to the Vancouver Charter

The City of Vancouver is governed by the Vancouver Charter, which vests in the city distinct rights and responsibilities. Section 523D of the Vancouver Charter authorizes the City to impose a development cost levy for capital costs, which includes, in addition to the services referred to earlier, the cost of establishing day care facilities and acquiring property for such facilities, and the cost of "replacement housing" for persons expected to be displaced and unable to afford comparable accommodation in the area. Vancouver collects a city-wide levy, as well as an area-specific levy, which are calculated per unit or per square metre, and additionally a separate regional Development Cost Charge of $590–$1,731 per dwelling unit to pay for expanding sewage services. In December 2017, the Metro Vancouver Mayors' Council adopted a joint proposal for a new Regional Transportation Development Cost Charge (DCC), which is anticipated to come into effect in the future (2020) and raise $20 million annually. The charge would amount to over $1,200 per residential unit.

2.4.3 School Site Acquisition Charges

Similar to Ontario's education development charges, the Local Government Act (Division 20, sections 571–581) requires every person who obtains a building permit or subdivision approval, unless exempt by law, to pay according to a statutory formula a share of the local school board's costs of acquiring a school site, or provide land in lieu of the charge if the local and school authorities consent.

2.4.4 Subdivision servicing agreements and land dedication

Subdivision servicing requirements can be established by bylaw (Local Government Act, Division 11, sections 506–514) in respect of highways, sidewalks, boulevards, boulevard crossings, transit bays, street lighting or underground wiring. An owner of land proposed to be subdivided must also dedicate without compensation park land of an amount and in a location acceptable to the local government, or pay to the municipality an amount that equals the market value of the land that may be required for park land purposes. The maximum that may be required is 5% of the land. An owner of land being subdivided must also provide, without compensation, a portion of that land up 20 metres in depth for highway use.

3. Analysis and conclusions

Developer obligations in the form of development levies, land, and construction services comprise the primary vehicle for land value capture in Canada. This must understood in legal and historic context. Canadian municipalities bear the financial and political responsibility for providing local services – yet, as creatures of the province, possess no legal sources of revenue other than those enabled by provincial legislation. Canadian municipalities rely now more than ever on own-source revenue, and property taxes typically account for half or more of all local revenue sources.

The legislative arrangements which are now firmly established were intended to set out clear, standard principles for imposing obligations and to reduc the cost of negotiations. But experience in all provinces shows that ad hoc, project-specific negotiations have not been eliminated. In addition, while the schedule of payments in now set out in municipal bylaws, the development industry representatives are routinely consulted.

From the start, the impetus for DOs was primarily to shield the existing residents from the cost of growth, and more broadly from any adverse impact of development (Kaplinsky, 2006). An analysis of developer obligations in Canada today shows that shifting the cost of services away from the property tax continues to be of the greatest importance. The notion of value capture as a means of redistributing economic rents was secondary, although discussed from time to time (Hudec, 1980). Developers are expected to shoulder the capital cost of services to their buyers, including the cost of land. A proportionate share of all capital costs *generally* attributable to growth is also assessed against new development. In the four provinces surveyed here, as in most of Canada, the trend has been an increase in the scope of the services funded by charges and the magnitude of the charges.

The courts have insisted that in apportioning development levies, municipalities adhere in some measure to the user-pay principle advocated by public finance experts (Downing & McCaleb, 1987). Homebuyers are assumed, in other words, to pay for the services that benefit them. This is, however, a matter of statutory interpretation, and the courts in Alberta, for example, have given local authorities some leeway in using the subdivision approval process to exact contributions in excess of that which is needed for the development under consideration.

Value capture traditionally understood (Hagman & Misczynski, 1977) plays a limited instrumental role in Canada, generally speaking, in fast-growing municipalities. It is used to pay for services for which ratepayers have little appetite, such as affordable housing, public art, and transit. The rationale advanced sometimes is to transfer an unearned increment from the landowner to the public. This ignores the fact that in many Canadian metropolitan areas, most developable land is acquired or optioned decades in advance, and is not supported by studies of the economic incidence of charges.

Bibliography

Legislation cited

City of Toronto Act (Ontario) 2006, S.O. 2006, c. 11
Development Charges Act (Ontario) 1997, S.O. 1997, c. 27
Halifax Regional Municipality Charter, Chapter 39 of the Acts of 2008 (Nova Scotia)
Planning Act (Ontario) 1990, R.S.O.CP.13 1990
Local Government Act, RSBC 2015, c 1 (British Columbia)
Municipal Government Act, RSA 2000, c M-26 (Alberta)
Municipal Government Act, SNS 1998, c 18 (Nova Scotia)
Smart Growth for Our Communities Act, 2015 (Bill 73) (Ontario)
Vancouver Charter, SBC 1953, c 55 (British Columbia)
Off-Site Levies Regulation (Alberta), Alta Reg 187/2017

Cases cited

Urban Development Institute, Alberta Division v. Leduc (City), 2006 ABQB 952 (CanLII)
Keyland Development Corporation v. Cochrane (Town), 2007 ABQB 160 (CanLII)
Canada Lands Company CLC Limited v. Edmonton (City), 2005 ABCA 218 (CanLII)
Edmonton (City) v Edmonton (City) Subdivision and Development Appeal Board, 2016 ABCA 193 (CanLII)
Prairie Communities Development Corp. v. Okotoks (Town), 2011 ABCA 315 (CanLII)

Authorities

Alterman, R. (2011), 'Land Use Regulations and Property Values: The Windfalls Capture Idea Revisited', in Brooks, N., Donaghy, K. & Knaap, G. J. (eds.), *The Oxford Handbook of Urban Economics and Planning*. Oxford: Oxford University Press.

Amborski, D. (2016), 'Using Land Value Capture Tools in Canadian Municipalities', *Plan Canada*, Vol. 56, No. 2, Summer.

Amborski, D. (1988), 'Impact Fees Canadian Style: The Use of Development Charges in Ontario', in Nelson, A. C. (ed.), *Development Impact Fees*. Chicago: APA Press.

BILD. (2017), *Summary of Development Charges in the Greater Toronto Area*. Toronto.

City of Edmonton. (2017), *Developer Contributed Public Amenities in Direct Control Zoning*, 29 November. (Urban Form and Corporate Strategic Development CR_4814). http://sirepub.edmonton.ca/sirepub/view.aspx?cabinet=published_meetings& fileid=687103.

CityForum Consulting. (2017), *Amenity Contribution System Phase I Review*, October. http://sirepub.edmonton.ca/sirepub/view.aspx?cabinet=published_meetings& fileid=687104.

City of Toronto. (2016), *Implementation Guidelines for Section 37 of the Planning Act and Protocol for Negotiating Section 37 Benefits*.

Downing, P. B. & McCaleb, T. S. (1987), 'The Economics of Development Exactions', in Frank, J. & Rhodes, R. (eds.), *Development Exactions*, pp. 42–69.

Hagman, D. G. & Misczynski, D. J. (1977), *Windfalls for Wipe Outs: Land Value Capture*. Chicago, IL: American Planning Association.

Halifax Regional Municipality. (2016), *Density Bonusing for Affordable Private Rental Housing*. Halifax, Canada. pp. 1–6.

Halifax Regional Municipality. (2000), 'Infrastructure Best Practices Guide a Capital Cost Contribution Policy'.

Hemson Consulting Limited. (2018), *2018 Development Charges Background Study: City of Toronto*.

Hudec, A. J. (1980), 'Municipal Exactions and the Subdivision Process: A Legal and Economic Analysis', in *University of Toronto Faculty Law Review*, Vol.38, No. 1, 106.

Kaplinsky, E. S. (2006), *From Farms to Suburbs: Controlling Land Subdivision*, SJD Thesis, University of Toronto. [unpublished].

Kitchen, H. (2003), 'Municipal Revenue and Expenditure Issues in Canada', *Canadian Tax Paper*, No. 107.

Laux, F. (2013), *Planning Law and Practice in Alberta*, 3rd edition. Canada: Juriliber Publishers.

Smolka, M. & Amborski, D. (2000), *Value Capture for Urban Development: An Inter-American Comparison*. Lincoln Institute Working Paper, Cambridge, MA.

Steele, D. R. (1956), *Municipal Controls on Subdivisions*. Special Lectures of the Law Society of Upper Canada.

Trillium Business Strategies Inc. (2009), *Land Value Capture as a Tool to Finance Public Transit Projects in Canada*. Report submitted to the Surface Policy Directorate Transport Canada. Infrastructure Canada, Ottawa.

Urban Development Institute: Edmonton Region. (2014), *2014 Levies and Fees Report*. Edmonton, Alberta, Canada.

Urban Development Institute: Edmonton Region. (2018), *2017 Off-Site Levy Review*. Edmonton, Alberta, Canada.

2 Developer obligations in the US

Nico Calavita

Introduction

In the US, planning powers are conferred to the states by the Constitution. They, in turn, delegate such powers to localities. Central controls, found in most other countries, do not exist in the US. There is, then, a tremendous variety of ways in which planning is carried out, from no planning at all to extremely sophisticated systems of planning in certain states which provide uniform legal and regulatory frameworks. Depending on the state, these frameworks can be more or less rigid. As it can be expected, then, N-NDOs (development impact fees [DIFs] in the US) reflect this planning variety, with many places with no DIFs, and many others with highly sophisticated systems of N-NDOs and NDOs, all captured under the term 'exactions.' While there is great variety of N-NDOs and NDOs, and no centralized planning framework, they all have to meet legal requirements, as ultimately mandated by the courts.

1. Evolution of exactions in the US

Before the 1920s, development was largely unregulated. Public facilities, on- and off-site, where provided by the local government. During the 1920s, the necessity for the regulation of development became recognized, even by the real estate industry (Weiss, 1987). Zoning and subdivision regulations were established, and with them, the requirement that on-site facilities be provided by the developer. Gradually, as local governments realized that they lacked the resources to provide school or park sites, they started to demand the dedication of land for those facilities as part of the subdivision approval process (Nelson, 1991).

Development impact fees (DIFs) represent the latest stage in the process of increasing regulation of land use, and the shifting of development costs to developers. They are an enlarged version of the traditional in-lieu or hook-up fees, both in scope and area of application. Today, DIFs are used to charge to developers a portion of the capital facilities or infrastructure costs generated by new development to fund roads, water and sewer systems, parks, libraries, schools, fire stations, public cemeteries, police facilities and mass transit (Nicholas, 1991). A secondary function of DIFs is to "impose some discipline on new development"(Nicholas et al., 1991: xix). DIFs can be imposed to pay for the cost of public facilities miles away from a particular development. This shifting of development costs to developers can be attributed to changes in legal rulings, public finance, performance standards and increasing demand for, and higher quality of, infrastructure.

1.1 Law

Until the 1960s, the courts had taken inconsistent positions regarding DIFs. They looked at them either "with suspicion – as invalid taxation against new development," or they maintained a "hands off" approach, without much concern about the fairness of the fee, "considering them necessary corollaries to local land use regulations" (Stroud, 1988: 29). But by the late 1960s, courts started to apply a cost accounting approach, specifically tying exactions to the need created by the development. As this approach has evolved, a "rational-nexus" test has been established, by which the imposition of impact fees is evaluated on the basis of whether: 1) the new development creates the need for new or expanded facilities; 2) the fee charged is proportional to the need created (the "rough proportionality" test); and 3) the fee is used to reasonably benefit the feepayer (Stroud, 1988; Blasser & Kentopp, 1990).

1.2 Public finance

Starting in the 1970s, widespread changes at the federal level reduced government expenditures for capital facilities. For example, the Revenue Sharing Act of 1970 eliminated the grants-in-aid programs that had dedicated federal funds to the construction of specific public facilities at the local level – such as sewage treatment plants, for example. The federal retrenchment coincided with a 'taxpayer revolt' in several parts of the country, with California leading the way in 1978 with the passage of Proposition 13. That revolt, by limiting the taxation of real estate property and by rejecting new general obligation bonds for capital improvements, curtailed government's taxing authority at the local and state levels, further constraining the sources of revenue available to localities to pay for infrastructure and public facilities. The result was a search for "innovative" and "creative" sources of financing, i.e. finding somebody else to pay. That somebody is usually the developer.

1.3 Performance standards, demands and costs

As capital expenditures started to decline, the largest population cohort in American history, i.e. the "baby boomers," came of age. As they witnessed the environmental problems created by growth, they demanded new regulatory programs to ameliorate the destructive tendencies of new development. Higher standards governing the performance of capital facilities were established, as for example when the federal government mandated secondary treatment for all wastewater in the nation.

The consequences of these shifts was that, as a society "we increased the quantitative demands of our infrastructure, increased our qualitative expectations regarding it, and reduced the proportion of our resources that we were willing to invest in it" (O'Keefe, 1991: 3). Again, the developer was made to pay.

2. Direct or indirect rationale of DOs

As shown earlier, the impetus for the rise and expansion of exactions in the US was due to a combination of factors that came at the forefront in the 1970s. They include changes in law, public finance, performance standards, demand and cost, and a conservative anti-tax political climate. Following the tool categorizations in this volume, there are no direct public value capture instruments in the US.

Attempts at recapturing increases in land value resulting from planning changes is not part of the planning culture of the US. Indeed, the idea of 'unearned increments in land values' resulting from government actions and the appropriateness of 'recapturing' at least some of those increases, is not part of the American planner's lexicon. If certain planning regulatory programs do lower land prices, they are an unintended consequence resulting from the pursuance of other goals, such as having developers pay for the cost of infrastructure and public facilities or affordable housing.

3. Non-negotiable and negotiable developer obligations

It is localities that, within the more or less constraining prescribed legal parameters of individual states, establish locally binding regulations and N-NDOs. This ability of localities to control land use is based on the police power of the state, the power that restrict private activities in order to protect the health, safety and welfare of its residents.

States' controls vary tremendously. California courts have held that the police power of a city is as broad as that of the state, so long as its local laws are not in conflict with the state's general laws. This very broad grant of power provides the cities with the ability to impose fees when they have a real and substantial relation to public welfare. California, it seems, allows a great deal of freedom to its localities, as opposed to other states where the legislature has to specifically authorize practically everything, as in the case of the State of New York, for example. Because of such a tradition you have the odd situation of the City of New York, arguably the most powerful city in the world, subject to the whims of rural and suburban state legislators.

3.1 Types of N-NDOs

3.1.1 DIFs

As mentioned earlier, as the use of DIFs expanded, the courts set the standards for their application, including cost accounting approaches that specifically tie them to the need created by the development. As mandated by the US Supreme Court in the cases *Nollan v. California Coastal Commission*, 483 US 825 (1987), and *Dolan vs. City of Tigard*, 512 US 687 (1994), exactions must be directly related and roughly proportional to the impact that the project creates, the so-called nexus test. Many states have passed legislation to ensure that the basic constitutional principles embodied in the US Supreme Court decisions are applied locally. State courts apply the nexus test more or less broadly, with California being the most liberal. In that state, the fee will be upheld if the amount and location of land or fees bear a reasonable relationship to the use of the facilities by the future inhabitants of the development, and the fees are imposed on all developers as part of a land-use plan. If applied to a single developer, the relationship has to be more direct or "essential." Showing such a relationship is required in all cases in most other states.

3.1.2 Inclusionary housing (IH), or zoning

IH developed during the 1970s in certain areas of the US, especially California, New Jersey and a couple of the counties surrounding Washington, DC. With IH, developers are required to dedicate a small percentage of their development – usually between 10 and 20 percent – to affordable housing. IH had two goals; first, to provide affordable housing in situations of skyrocketing housing price increases and, second, to foster social integration in expanding suburban areas. IH has spread to many other areas of the country, including many large cities, from Chicago to San Diego to Denver, and most recently New York and Los Angeles. The legality of IH varies from state to state, and depends on whether it is considered legally an exaction or a land-use regulation. If a state considers it an exaction, then the legal requirements of exactions – establishing a strong relationship between the impact of the development and the affordable housing obligation become necessary. If considered a land-use regulation, no such relationship needs to be established. In California, after many years of uncertainty and lower-court cases, the state Supreme Court, in a unanimous decision, recently declared IH to be a land-use regulation and not subject to a rigorous analysis under the US Supreme Court's "exactions" doctrine (California Building Industry Association v. City of San Jose. *351 P. 3d 974* [Calavita, 2015]).

3.1.3 Commercial Linkage Fees

The notion of 'commercial linkage' is that commercial (non-residential) private development will generate affordable housing needs for those workers in the development who cannot afford market-rate housing. They are usually assessed per square foot and paid by the developer at the time of building, site or occupancy permit approval. In some states, localities have to obtain permission to adopt a linkage fee program. The 1987 Boston linkage program, for example, was placed on hold until specifically authorized by the Massachusetts Legislature.

3.2 Negotiated DOs and development agreements

Nowadays, while most development in the US follows the N-NDO model, large developments are more likely to be based on NDOs. With large developments, both the locality and the developer prefer to establish a generalized land-use plan which is flexible and action-oriented (the Specific Plan in California) and development agreements (DAs). With DAs, both the city and the developers are provided with security and certainty. Generally, localities can extract "far more in fees and/or infrastructure than they would have obtained under traditional processes" (Fulton 1999: 212). Is this a form of land value recapture? The former Director of the Planning Department of the City of San Diego and former President of the US American Planning Association, Bill Anderson, believes that while DIFs are not an LVR technique, DAs are (Anderson, 2018).

But DAs can be cumbersome and expensive for the city and the developers, both in time and money. In addition, while certainty is definitely a benefit, it can also be constraining, as when a developer needs to modify the specific master plan due to changes in the market. As most development in major cities is now occurring through infill and redevelopment, a shift is occurring from DAs towards new sorts of agreements in which negotiations take place in a very open political process, with different interest groups trying to extract more from the developers, be that more affordable housing or union contracts for workers – or stop the development altogether. But these agreements can be cumbersome and lengthy, as well. According to Bill Anderson (2018), "if there is growth in negotiated permitting, it may be because of its politics more than value capture objectives."

NDOs, however, in adding more time and costs and uncertainty to the development process, have come under fire for contributing to the skyrocketing housing costs in California, forcing the state legislature to intervene. A 17-bill package was passed by the legislature in 2017, with five bills dedicated to streamlining approval of development plans. One of the bills, Senate Bill 35, creates an optional pathway for developers to access a streamlined approval process for multifamily housing projects as long as the project meets certain labor, environmental and affordability standards. Even more radical in curtailing local planning powers is a proposed bill SB 50, which allows high densities in areas served by mass transit. At least in California, then, there seems to be an increase in NDOs, a practice that the state is attempting to curtail.

4. Decentalization, localism and the role of the courts

While in other countries N-NDOs are generally based on detailed legislation at the regional or national levels, in the US, it is localities that mostly regulate them. However, since localities are "creatures of the states" in which they are located, they are subjected to the states' control in various degrees. There are states were localities do not engage in land-use planning, let alone charging DIFs, and others such as California, with a legislative planning framework within which localities still have a tremendous freedom to engage in a variety of creative land-use planning controls. In all cases, however, whether there is a strict or loose state framework, both N-NDOS and NDOs are subject to court review, especially in relation to: 1) The "takings" clause of the Fifth Amendment of the Constitution of the United States that provides that "private property shall [not] be taken for public use without just compensation." What it means is that if a regulation 'goes too far,' that will constitute a taking. It is generally understood that a regulation has gone "too far" when all possible economic uses of a property have been extinguished by the regulation; and 2) Substantive due process, which is the principle allowing courts to protect certain fundamental rights from government interference. It requires that legislative bodies act in a manner that is not "arbitrary and capricious," and that a regulation is related to the promotion of health, safety and general welfare.

5. Land value recapture in the US? Signs of change

Something is changing. A few localities are engaging in approaches that attempt to recapture increases in land values resulting from certain land-use regulation decisions, most importantly higher densities (Bergen, 2012). In the rest of the chapter, I will focus on the new ways in which this approach is being shaped and implemented in a few cities in California. These programs have a variety of names, including Public Benefit Zonings, FAR Acquisition Programs, Amenity Bonus Programs and Community Benefits Programs, but not 'Land Value Recapture', term considered too 'radical.' There is a search for alternative terms. The Lincoln Land Institute, an advocate of LVR, has proposed 'Land Value Recovery.' Again, things are changing, but slowly and tentatively. I will argue that a new wave of LVR is emerging, characterized by two elements: reliance on economic analysis and utilization of extensive public participation processes (Calavita, 2015).

5.1 Economic analyses

Changes in land-use regulations, under appropriate market conditions, will lead to higher land prices. In order to calculate which DOs are economically feasible, it is necessary to compare the value of a project under existing zoning and its value after the plan change. This is done through economic analyses, such as land value residual methods that provide information about what the developer can pay. Comparing the residual land value before and after a rezoning, cities determine the 'uplift' (Vancouver, BC) or 'enhanced value' (Santa Monica, California).

5.2 Public participation and community benefits

When land-use regulation decisions that enhance developers' profits are exchanged for public benefits, it behooves planners to provide ample opportunities for transparency and accountability and for citizens to demand the same. As we shall see from the Santa Monica and San Francisco cases, value capture originated from citizen demands and was enacted under their careful watch. Citizen participation is especially appropriate for expressing preferences for possible amenities, and online participation is becoming common. Redwood City, for example, is making use of an online forum, in addition to community workshops, to define desired benefits and identify priorities.

5.1.1 Case studies

I will briefly describe the programs of two cities in California, San Francisco and Santa Monica, that have adopted 'value capture programs' in the past few years. Both cities already have DIFs, IH and commercial linkage fee (CLF) programs. The community benefits obtained through those value capture programs are in addition to those provided through DIFs, IH and CLF.

SAN FRANCISCO: A TIERED PROGRAM OF COMBINED FEES AND
HOUSING OPTIONS

The 2009 Plan for the Eastern Neighborhoods (ENs) came about as a result of the need for the city to guide the rapid increases in real estate values, gentrification and displacement of families and businesses in underutilized industrial areas east of Market Street – primarily the mostly Latino Mission District. The coalition fighting against displacement came up with the idea of 'Public Benefit Incentive Zoning' (PBIZ). They argued that increases in density create "greater value for property owners and sales or rental value for developers," and that PBIZ, could create "a mechanism to capture a portion of this increased land value in the form of public benefits that would mitigate the impact of the additional development." (MAP, 2005: 33).

The idea was eventually incorporated in the ENs plan by the city. It took the form of a 'Tier' system, whereby parcels designated for height increases would see fees increase accordingly, with alternatives such as on-site/off-site options and land dedication.

To fulfill the goal of increased affordable housing production in the ENs, this plan also requires that in areas rezoned from industrial to mixed uses (mostly residential), more affordable housing be produced than is required under the city's IH program.

Santa Monica has a long-standing tradition of achieving community benefits through development agreements, including parks and park improvements, community health access, childcare centers and low-income housing. In 2010, after many years of extensive community engagement, the city adopted the Land Use and Circulation Element (LUCE). A fundamental tenet of the LUCE program was that future development should fund a range of measurable public benefits, from open spaces and parks to affordable housing, in addition to existing requirements.

As part of the LUCE preparation, preliminary economic studies were undertaken that analyzed the extent of 'enhanced land value' resulting from higher densities. These analyses indicated for individual projects whether providing community benefits under LUCE was financially feasible. Consultants employed by the developer prepare an analysis that is then reviewed by consultants to the city in a give-and-take process referred to as a 'peer review' process that ends when both consultants agree on the soundness of the analyses.

LUCE established a community benefits tier structure for projects requesting an increase in the base building height of 32 feet (almost 10 meters). There are three tiers. In Tier 1, if the developer builds within the base height and FAR, no community benefits in addition to the existing ones are required, and the approval process is ministerial (not discretionary). Tier 2 allows additional height and FAR when community benefits are provided. Tier 3 allows even more height and FAR in exchange for higher levels of community benefits. It is when developers seek Tier 3 density increases that development agreements are required. This process requires additional public review and flexibility and encourages high-quality projects.

However, given the high costs of development agreements, the City has developed a ministerial approach with fixed-fees schedules as part of its zoning code update. When a developer chooses to exceed densities from Tier 1 up to Tier 2, he or she will be required to provide additional community benefits. The quantity (additional fees or affordable housing units) of these community benefits were defined in 2015 as part of the Santa Monica Zoning Update, which is legally binding. The benefits include:

- *affordable housing*: at least 50 percent more than the base fee as required under the IH programs. For non-residential projects, the housing mitigation fee is increased by 14 percent above the IH program 'Affordable Housing Fee for Commercial Development.'
- *transportation impact fee, open space fee and childcare facilities*: 14 percent above the base fee.

In Santa Monica, then, the move is from NDOs to N-NDOs.

5.1.2 Benefits and drawbacks of N-NDOs and NDOs

In the two cases, the LVR programs were based on plans: the Eastern Neighborhoods Plan in San Francisco, and the LUCE Plan in Santa Monica. The Santa Monica case is a hybrid between negotiated and not-negotiable. Tier 2 included benefits regulated beforehand, while Tier 3 – containing parcels with the highest potential density increases – requires negotiations with the city. The Eastern Neighborhood Plan, as a N-NDO, has the advantages of transparency and faster processing of projects. It minimizes, however, the captured value. The negotiated approach in Santa Monica, on the other hand, suffers from the possible lack of expertise of planners (there is only one Vancouver, BC!) and from transparency and accountability problems (Calavita & Wolfe, 2014).

7. Conclusions

LVR is not part of the American planning tradition. This rather unique state of affairs is probably the result of *American exceptionalism*, part of its entrenched suspicion of government interference in economic affairs. But such suspicion, while limiting federal and, to a large extent, states' intervention in urban planning, has not stopped localities from enacting widespread and detailed land-use regulations – especially when protecting single-use residential neighborhoods from other uses (Hirt, 2014). More recently, such regulations have been extended to exactions, to make sure that growth is accompanied by adequate public facilities and services. Exactions are not taxes, but 'fees' connected to needs created by new development. Their application may lead to LVR, but if that is the case, they do so surreptitiously and inadvertently. The idea of 'planning gain' to recapture 'unearned increments in land values' is not part of American planning culture or vocabulary. Such an understanding of the effects of planning decisions on land values is missing from the planning discourse, limiting the potential and scope of planning in the US. We might, however, be witnessing – in a very limited number of localities – the beginning of a shift where the recapturing of land value increases due to government actions becomes a conscious planning instrument. For now, the use of both N-NDOs and NDOs seem to be growing. The use of NDOs is expanding in areas experiencing growth problems as community groups and localities make demands – in addition to N-NDOs requirements – for additional community benefits.

References

Anderson, W. (2018), Email communication. 15 January 2018.

Bergen, M. (2012), 'How Can Cities Recapture Investment in Public Infrastructure?' *Forefront. Next American City*, Vol. 1, No. 18, pp. 1–17.

Blasser, B. & Kentopp, C. (1990), 'Impact Fees: The "Second Generation"', *Journal of Urban and Contemporary Law*, Vol. 38, No. 25, pp. 55–113.

Calavita, N. (2015), 'Practice Value Capture', *Zoning Practice*, American Planning Association No. 6.

Calavita, N. & Wolfe, M. (2014), *White Paper on the Theory, Economics and Practice of Public Benefit Zoning*. Sponsored by the East Bay Housing Organizations under a HUD-funded Sustainable Communities Grant provided to ABAG/Metropolitan Transportation Commission.

Fulton, W. (1999), *Guide to California Planning*. Point Arena, CA: Solano Press Books.

Hirt, S. (2014), *Zoned in the USA: The Origins and Implications of American Land-Use Regulations*. Ithaca, London: Cornell University Press.

MAP-The Mission Anti-Displacement Partnership. (2005), *The People's Plan for Jobs, Housing,and Community*. San Francisco: Asian Neighborhood Design.

Nelson, A. (1991), *Development Impact Fees as a Win-Win Solution*. Paper presented at the Conference of the Urban Affairs Association, Vancouver, BC.

Nicholas, J. (1991), *To Fee or Not to Fee? CUPReport 2:2*. Piscataway, NJ: Center for Urban Policy Research.

Nicholas, J., Nelson, A. & Jurgensmeyer, J. (1991), *A Practitioner's Guide to Development Impact Fees*. Chicago: Planners Press.

O'Keefe, P. (1991), *Impact Fees: Paying for the Sins of the Parents. CUPReport 2:2*. Piscataway, NJ: Center for Urban Policy Research.

Stroud, N. (1988), 'Legal Considerations of Development Impact Fees', *American Planning Association Journal*, Vol. 54, No. 1, pp. 29–37.

Weiss, M. (1987), *The Rise of the Community Builders*. New York: Columbia University Press.

3 Developers' obligations as a land value capture tool

Practice and lessons from Colombia

Juan Felipe Pinilla[1]

1. Introduction

Colombia has had a long tradition of implementing land value capture mechanisms. For instance, betterment contributions (*contribución por valorización*) are tools that have been used frequently used in Colombia to develop public infrastructure ever since 1921 (Smolka, 201).

Currently, there is a wide variety of land value capture instruments, of which developer obligations constitute an essential element. Said obligations are charges that landowners and developers must pay either in land or money as part of the procedure for obtaining approval for a specific development. After many judicial reviews of their implementation in different cities, and especially in Bogotá, court rulings have clarified the nature of these obligations as urban charges (not taxes) to landowners to compensate local governments for the increased land value generated by public authorization to develop the land (Pinilla, 2012), or, as is the case in its application in Medellín, as a measure to mitigate externalities of the development.

There is another important taxation tool which is known as *Participación en Plusvalías* (Capital Gains Sharing), which can be considered a sort of DO, too.[2] The basic notion is that as cities adopt development plans, they create land value as previously agricultural land is brought into the urban development sphere, or land use and densities for existing urban land are adjusted to accommodate future growth. Under the terms of the 1997 law, cities are required to capture 30–50% of this increased value through *Participación en Plusvalías*. Specifically, this is an explicit attempt to share in the unearned increments in land value created by public development authorization, making it a tool that is based on a direct rationale. However, implementing this

---

1 The drafting of this chapter involved Martín Arteaga Vallejo as research assistant.

2 Because *Participación en Plusvalías* is charged when a public body issues the development or building permit (*licencia de urbanización* or *construcción*; this permit constitutes thus a land-use regulation decision), and because it is charged on the one who asks for such authorization, it might be considered a sort of DO too, non-negotiable because of its regulated nature. However, when this chapter speaks of Dos, it doesn't refer to *Participación en Plusvalías*.

tool has proven both difficult and controversial, especially in Bogotá, where it was first implemented. It was not until 2004 that Bogotá began to receive any revenue from this source, and then only after several rounds of clarifying negotiations (Walters & Pinilla, 2014).

This paper seeks to describe the evolution of these instruments and the way in which its use has become consolidated, as well as the judicial discussions and disputes that have been taking place regarding its nature and scope. The Colombian experience clearly shows that the application of developer obligations is a fertile field for advances in constructing the bases and foundations of urban law. Given the judicial discussion that it has provoked, court rulings and legal debates have been the main source of analysis and comprehension of basic urban concepts. Some of said rulings include the effects of the transformation of private property and of the necessary evolution of land management in cities based on new regulatory frameworks. Despite the intensity of the judicial debate surrounding this legal figure, the academic interest in studying its history, evolution and concrete results is still very limited and precarious.

2. The evolution of developer obligations in Colombia

One of the particularities of the use of this instrument in Colombia is that its initial application was not the result of a robust, detailed legal framework defining the nature, scope and form of calculation. On the contrary, these obligations began to appear directly in the municipal norms that regulated urban planning processes in cities and defined the general conditions to which the land intended for urbanization should be subjected, with almost no basis from the national level.

Thus, for example, such norms began to be introduced in Bogotá starting in the 1930s,[3] establishing the different obligations regarding land transfer and construction of infrastructure that would be required in urbanization processes in the city (Galeano, 2011). The initial precedent even established the possibility that in certain cases, the transfer obligations were to be compensated by the delivery of land in a place different from that of the urbanization that generated the obligation.

As Rother (1990) has affirmed: "in general the transfer percentages required have been reasonable, or even timid." Therefore, although there were examples of this practice in other Colombian cities like Cucuta and Cali at that time, there was no clear and solid national legal rationale regarding its nature and scope (Rother, 1990). For this reason, it can be said that long before national regulation laid a legal framework for developer obligations, there was a consolidated practice in Colombia that served as a precedent for its legal formalization in the year 1989.

---

3 This refers to City Council Agreement No. 48 of 1934.

The most important precedent in Colombian urban law is Law 9 of 1989 (Pinilla, 2003). This law represented a very important conquest in the process of recognizing greater capacities of Colombian municipalities to face the challenges of the growing phenomenon of urbanization. This law, also known as "the urban reform law," laid the basis of modern urban law in Colombia. Despite not having been systematically applied, Law 9 of 1989 constituted the first step in the consolidation of a truly Colombian urban law. This law was enacted to serve as support for an integral policy of regional and urban development, based on reform of the use and ownership of urban land and its tax regime. It pursued the incorporation of land into urban development to promote social housing projects, and mechanisms to facilitate public procurement of land and the creation of reserves of well-located land through municipal land banks. Furthermore, Law 9 prescribed that one of the central topics that should be included in cities' plans were developer obligations, especially "free land transfers" (*cesiones gratuitas*). This law also defined the possibility that land transfer obligations would be the object of compensatory payment in money, in accordance with the specific conditions defined by each municipality.

This law formally recognized the possibility that the municipalities would regulate this matter directly through their development plans, thus establishing a national framework of these obligations and the competence of municipalities for imposing them. However, this law gave total autonomy to municipalities in fixing DOs' conditions and scope.

2.1 The debates on the constitutionality of developer obligations

Nonetheless, said law was soon severely questioned. A total of 14 lawsuits were presented against this law, which attacked around 70% of its content (Pinilla, 2003). One of these lawsuits was about the regulation relating to "free land transfers". On this occasion, the plaintiff argued that the requirement of free land transfers went against the protection of private property and constituted an expropriation without compensation, precisely because of its free nature. All the same, the court decision discarded this thesis, supporting the obligation of developers to give free land transfers.

What is fundamental in this decision, which constitutes the founding decision in the jurisprudence on this subject in Colombia, is the argument that the demand of transfers is essentially not free because it is closely related to the potential economic yield that authorization for urbanization represents. Clearly, by establishing the nature of transfers as compensation for public authorization to build, the jurisprudence takes the discussion out of the orbit of expropriation and dispossession positioning it in the logic of modern urban law, where land-use regulation decisions authorizing development are sufficient cause for the imposition of charges, duties and responsibilities on property (Pinilla, 2012; Alfonso, 2008).

A new political constitution was adopted in 1991 in Colombia. Among other things, this new constitution deepened the social function of property, recognized the collective right to public space, established the possibility of having public authorities recover increased land values produced by public decisions and recognized the autonomy of municipal authorities to regulate the uses of land.

Law 9 of 1989 was reformed in 1997, through Law 388, which updated it to the new constitution of 1991. As such, greater articulation was achieved between some new territorial planning instruments (POT, Partial Plans)[4] and the land management instruments established in Law 9. Once again, developer obligations where recognized and regulated in this law as a means of facilitating the equitable distribution of costs and benefits of urban development.

But then again, based on the new regulations established in Law 388, developer obligations were disputed as unconstitutional. This time, the argument was based on the idea that this instrument supposedly violated international agreements on human rights ratified by Colombia. Once more, the Constitutional Court ratified the constitutionality of this legal figure and its relation to the social function of property. On this occasion, the jurisprudence has also clarified that developer obligations constitute a form of municipal revenue source different from taxes.

2.2 The discussion on the scope and destination of developer obligations

Parallel to the whole judicial discussion regarding the constitutionality of developer obligations, there has been an intense debate in the administrative courts regarding the scope and destination of these obligations. Additionally, to land transfers for the infrastructure in an urbanization needed only for this urbanization and located within, Bogotá introduced in 1987 the "*Estatuto de Contribución de Valorización*"[5] that required that whenever a main road was projected within the area to be developed, provision had to be made to transfer 7% of the area for that infrastructure.

Said provision was the subject of a claim for annulment. In its appellate decision, the Council of State (*Consejo de Estado*) found that by imposing the obligation to transfer 7% of the gross area of plots affected by the works to be developed, through the system of betterment levy without considering whether such properties were subject to urbanization processes, was

---

4 Both the *Plan de Ordenamiento Territorial* (POT) and the *Plan parcial* (PP) can be understood as legally binding land-use plans.
5 Not to be confused with what is nowadays called "*Contribución de Valorización*" in Colombia, which is a sort of betterment charge, i.e. a financing mechanism for public works.

indiscriminately considering an obligatory transfer. According to the high court, such transfers were applicable only to plots intended for urbanization, and could not be extended to all types of land (Pinilla, 2012).

The last chapter in this history is a result of the establishment of an N-NDO system for partial plans (*plan parcial*) on developable land in Bogotá. This system was adopted based on the framework established through Law 388 of 1997 and through the city's POT of 2003. Partial plans are one of the new tools introduced by this new legal framework for improving the articulation between territorial planning and land management. Within this new framework, the partial plans are medium-scale planning and land management instruments aimed at developing or complementing the provisions of the POTs for certain sectors of urban land (urban redevelopment) and for all land intended for urban expansion. The application of this instrument has caused many difficulties and controversies in the country, in general, and in Bogotá especially. Ever since it began to be applied between 2002 and 2004, this instrument has given the administrations of Bogotá an opportunity to obtain a new source of financing for urban infrastructure, including the trunk network of road infrastructure, urban facilities and city parks. Nonetheless, this intention was questioned by builders and real estate developers, as well as by the Colombian Constructors and Developers Guild (CAMACOL, for its initials in Spanish).

Because of these criticisms, in 2006 the administration decided to regulate the whole system of developer obligations for partial plans of urban expansion. It determined the minimum contributions in terms of land and the building of parks and other facilities, the calculation of contributions required to have access to additional building potential, the procedure for payment and the rules relating to funds for compensatory payment of additional land transfers, among other things.

This regulation was severely criticized by CAMACOL. In its opinion, by establishing an obligatory regime of developer obligations as contributions for elements of trunk infrastructure, the city was exceeding its regulatory capacity and covertly creating a tax on land. Based on this argument, said guild demanded the annulment of this regulation. The *Consejo de Estado* decision put an end to the controversy by stating that it was clearly understood that the institution of land transfer in city planning serves as the compensation that the community in general receives, and must be assumed by whoever conducts a development project and exercises the right to private property, thus reasserting the direct rationale behind DOs.

This judicial ruling represented a clear triumph for the city of Bogotá and for the possibilities of establishing developer obligations related to backbone infrastructure. The argument that these obligations constituted the creation of a covert tax on land seems to be very common in other countries, and it could be said that it is a very recurrent argument in discussions of the nature and scope of these obligations. For this reason, in addition to representing a triumph for the city, this ruling also implied ascending one more step in the level of understanding of these obligations and in consolidating a complete and articulated corpus of jurisprudence of the high courts of Colombia that have clearly delineated the scope and nature of this instrument.

3. Contrast of negotiated and non-negotiated developer obligation regimes in Bogotá and Medellín

As mentioned earlier, the enactment of Law 388 of 1997 incorporated a set of urban planning and land management instruments, including the one known as partial plans, a land readjustment scheme, in which DOs are incorporated in different ways. Based on research carried out by Bogotá's Planning Secretariat (SDP, for its initials in Spanish), by 2015 a total of 43 urban extension partial plans had been adopted, through which a total of 13.6 million square meters of land for city expansion have been regulated. A total of 4.8 million square meters of this land (35%) has been ceded to the municipality. Another aspect to be considered is that the final DOs, as well as the land-use potential authorized by every partial plan, is made public through a local decree, thus serving as a means for transparency.

Nevertheless, less than one-fourth of developer obligations foreseen in these plans were actually built. This was because in most cases, the proper implementation of these obligations "depends on the execution of the usable areas and the delivery of the transfers to the city, which are operations with many complexities associated with the administrative processes that are required" (Contreras, 2016: 132).

Unlike city extension partial plans, whereby obligations have been regulated since 2006 and are thus a sort of N-NDO, urban renewal partial plans do not have any specific regulations that define city planning obligations and specific conditions for the distribution of burdens and benefits. This type of partial plans in the city of Bogotá thus represents a typical case of NDO.

Given this relative margin of discretion for determining and negotiating developer obligations that will be demanded of each partial plan in accordance with the constructive possibilities and the uses of land that are authorized, as well as the needs and conditions of the specific area where each plan is located, there is among these cases an extensive number of examples of types of obligations that range from the financing of the recovery of neighboring architectural patrimony (the Sabana Partial Plan), to the financing of public transport infrastructure (the Central Station Partial Plan), to the construction of replacement housing for current owners (the Fenicia Partial Plan).

These cases are just a sampling of the diversity and variety of financing objectives that have been achieved, thanks to the existence of an NDO scheme. It is probable that the wide variety of objectives to which these NDOs have been applied would not have been possible if there had been a complete, detailed framework for the regulation and assignment of these obligations. Given the complexity and variety of situations encountered in the city's urban renewal areas, this system has been adapted to such situations and has permitted more negotiation between the planning authorities and real estate developers than would have been possible otherwise.

Medellín has become a relevant case of study for similar developments in recent years. Several authors agree that the city is a leading example in these issues, not only because Medellín was the first municipality to adopt partial plans after Law 388, but also because of the successful experiences in generating social housing and public space. (García, 2010)

Also, since the adoption of its first POT, Medellín has had a complete system of urban development transfer obligations (exactions) applicable for developing or urbanizing vacant land and for building. Therefore, any construction project within the city has to comply with a set of N-NDOs. The precise obligations in any given location depend on the location and applicable land use. The main innovation provided by Medellín since the first POT adoption is the expansion of land transfer obligations to all kind of projects different of those of un-serviced land areas. Traditionally in Colombia, urban transfer obligations were applied systematically to the land included in urban extension projects, but not to building projects due to increasing densities resulting from the transformation of the city on a plot by plot basis. This expansion of transfers in practice, now used in cities like Manizales and Bucaramanga, began in Medellín (Walters & Pinilla, 2014).

4. Conclusions

The Colombian experience in relation to developer obligations shows the importance of studying the nature and scope of this instrument across time. As I have shown in this chapter, an understanding of this tool at different moments in time is very important for understanding the way in which its evolution can be characterized and the different tensions that its application can generate.

For the application of this instrument, and in accordance with the Colombian experience, it is fundamental at least to have clear ideas regarding the following aspects:

• Developer obligations as an exercise of the regulatory power of municipalities about land use.
• Developer obligations as compensation for the benefits generated by authorizations granted by municipalities in relation to land use.
• The not-for-free nature of developer obligations.
• Collection of the product of developer obligations as a municipal resource that is not of a fiscal or taxation nature.

On the other hand, as this chapter shows that based on the Colombian experience, it may be very useful and enriching for an analysis of the evolution of developer obligations to turn to the jurisprudence on the subject. As this case illustrates, the participation of judges can be crucial when it comes to facilitating the application of this tool and clarifying its characteristics and legal nature. Nevertheless, the position of judges can also become an obstacle that makes its application impossible. For these reasons, it can be very useful to study not only the evolution of the laws, but that of the relevant jurisprudence as well in the comparative studies done on this subject.

The practice of developer obligations in Colombia shows the level of impact that it can have on the ideas and concepts regarding private property. As illustrated in the first part of this chapter, much of the judicial discussion that took place before 2004 had to do precisely with the confrontation between this instrument and the protection of private property. This instrument may become a useful thermometer for measuring how landowners and real estate developers actually incorporate transformations in the private property regime in practical terms in the context of urban development.

The evolution of the NDO and N-NDO regimes in Colombia shows that there is a constant tension in relation to the impact they can have on the financial viability of real estate operations. This tension is greater in N-NDO cases and leads to the topic of economic valuation being a subject of constant discussion in the concertation processes. Although these analyses have been refined and are becoming more sophisticated within the framework of concertation of partial plans in Bogotá, they still depend very much on the civil servants in office at the time and on the levels of discretion that can be exercised in assigning the obligations on a case by case basis. The case of Medellín, on the other hand, is an example of how N-NDO regimes can require constant adjustments. In that city, the N-NDO regime has been modified three times within a period of less than 15 years.

Bibliography

Alcaldía Mayor de Bogotá, D. C. (2015), *Planes parciales de desarrollo: Evolución y práctica. Bogotá 2000–2015.* www.sdp.gov.co/imagenes_portal/documentacion/LibroPlanesParciales/PlanesParcialesDigital.pdf.

Alfonso, O. (2008), 'No hay suelo gratis. Un aporte desde la economía institucional urbana al desarrollo del principio de reparto equitativo de cargas y beneficios de la urbanización', *Revista Economía del Caribe,* Vol. 2.

Contreras, Y. (2016), 'Sistema urbanístico en Bogotá: reglas, prácticas y resultados de los planes parciales de desarrollo 2000–2015', *Cuadernos de Vivienda y Urbanismo,* Vol. 9, No. 17, pp. 122–141. Bogotá, Colombia. Pontificia Universidad Javeriana. http://revistas.javeriana.edu.co/index.php/cvyu/article/view/16856/13642.

Galeano, D. (2011), *El papel de las áreas de cesión en la configuración del espacio público en Bogotá. Documento de Tesis.* Maestría en Urbanismo, Universidad Nacional de Colombia, Bogotá.

García, J. C. (2010), 'Experiencias de gestión urbana reciente en Medellín: Iniciativas públicas', in *Las ciudades del mañana. Gestión del suelo urbano en Colombia.* Washington, DC: Banco Interamericano de Desarrollo, pp. 135–193, 137.

Pinilla, J. F. (2012), 'Las cesiones urbanísticas obligatorias en la jurisprudencia colombiana. Lecciones sobre su naturaleza y alcance', En *La ciudad y el derecho: Una introducción al derecho urbano contemporáneo*. Bogotá, Colombia: Universidad de los Andes.

Pinilla, J. F. (2003), 'Evolución legal y jurisprudencial del derecho urbanístico colombiano', En *Reforma urbana y desarrollo territorial: Experiencias y perspectivas de aplicación de las leyes 9ª de 1989 y 388 de 1997*. Bogotá, Colombia: Alcaldía Mayor de Bogotá, Lincoln Institute of Land Policy, Universidad de los Andes, y Federación Nacional de Organizaciones de Vivienda Popular, Fedevivienda.

Rother, H. (1990), *Derecho Urbano en Colombia*. Bogotá, Colombia: Editorial Temis.

Smolka, M. (2013), *Implementing Value Capture in Latin America. Policy Focus Report*. Cambridge, MA: Lincoln Institute of Land Policy.

Walters, L. & Pinilla, J. F. (2014), *Land Value Sharing in Medellín*. UN-Habitat Study Report.

4 Charging building rights as non-negotiable developer obligations
The case of Brazil

Marcio Alex Marcelino

1. Introduction

Brazil has long-time experience with public capture instruments, being together with Colombia the exponent country in Latin America to construct policy and legal frameworks in this field. This chapter addresses the Brazilian experience with the developer obligation (DO) "Sale of Development Rights" (SDR). Present in local legislations of 35% of municipalities, this tool is more visible in those with accelerated urban growth like São Paulo, Curitiba, Porto Alegre and Niterói (Smolka, 2013: 2; IBGE, 2016: 20; Furtado et al., 2006).

2. Public value capture in Brazil

Before detailing the SDR practice in Brazil, it is important to place this sort of DO among other public capture tools, including taxes, fees and other DOs. Brazilian municipalities can introduce charges and prescribe obligations on private land development supporting on three national laws: the 1966 National Tax Code, the 1988 Constitution and the 2001 *Estatuto da Cidade* (City Statute).

2.1 Public value capture through taxes

Three main tributes generate revenues from private land. First, the annual property tax (*Imposto sobre a propriedade predial e territorial urbana*), used by 95% of municipalities, follows a direct rationale and is charged on a recurrent basis, independent from modifications in land-use regulations. National laws determine the exchange value of land as base for its calculation, while every city details its implementation, stablishing tax plans, exemptions and price adjustments. As tax plans are frequently outdated, it is considered an underused instrument, generating less than 10% of municipal budgets, on average (Furtado et al., 2006: 7; Afonso et al, 2013: 24; IBGE, 2016: 23).

Betterment contributions (*Contribuição de melhoria*) are levied on landowners benefiting from urban improvements made by public investments, but their implementation encounters many difficulties. It is applied mostly in Brazilian south and southeast regions, generating an equivalent to 0.1% of cities' budgets (Pereira, 2012: 13–17).

The third tribute is the tax upon transfer title (*Imposto sobre a transmissão "intervivos" de bens imóveis*). It charges between 2% and 3%, depending on local regulations, of the highest exchange value of land (real transaction price or value the government calculates). This tax is extensively used, and provides around 4% of total municipal budgets (De Cesare, 2005: 52, IBGE, 2016: 23).

2.2 Public value capture through developers' obligations

Brazil presents mixed approaches to the governance of urban development. The government frequently provides the infrastructure, but mostly land is developed by private parties while public bodies regulate the land use. Under this predominant passive form of governance, municipalities prescribe negotiable (NDO) and non-negotiable (N-NDO) developer obligations.

The subdivision of land, i.e. creation of new building plots, is generally regulated by a national law (*Lei do parcelamento do solo urbano*) and detailed by local plans. These plans establish N-NDOs (*Diretrizes Básicas*) such as infrastructure provision and donation of from 10% up to 50% of land for public facilities and open spaces.

Besides meeting the requirements of the *Diretrizes Básicas*, developers must submit studies concerning traffic, environment and neighborhood impacts (*Estudo de impacto ambiental e de vizinhança*). Based on these studies, municipalities condition the building permit to NDOs (*Medidas mitigadoras e compensatórias*), usually in kind like improvement of accessibility, streets and donation of land. These obligations follow an indirect rationale, i.e. that developments must internalize their negative externalities. Still, these NDOs are introduced heterogeneously across the country. Curitiba and Belo Horizonte, for example, lack regulations concerning the amount of obligations, and special urbanization chambers (composed by members of the government and society) do the negotiations. The absence of technical and legally binding standards results in a variety of obligations ranging from simple road improvements to creation of parks, minor contributions being the most frequent. In São Paulo, the local government develops impact studies and releases a document prescribing obligations (*Certidão de Diretrizes*), mostly focused on traffic congestion. Local legislation states that these NDOs can charge up to 5% of the development's cost, but often obligations are lower.

2.3 DOs in exchange for additional building rights

Brazilian municipalities with active real estate markets introduced another two sorts of DOs. The first modality is the transfer of development rights

(TDR). This instrument permits landowners to sell unused development rights among them, transferring building rights from one property to another. TDRs are normally prescribed to allocate density and compensate landowners that have legal limitations to develop their properties, like environment restrictions or the obligation to preserve and renew historical buildings (Smolka, 2013: 42–44; Walters et al., 2016: 87).

The second modality is the sale of development rights (SDR), which allows local governments to levy for changes in land use – from rural to urban, or from housing to commercial; and for permission to build beyond predetermined basic limits (Furtado et al., 2006: 17–18; Walters et al., 2016: 86–87). From an international point of view, Brazil is one of the few countries which has popularized this tool to capture increments in land value. This chapter focuses further on this experience.

3. The evolution of SDRs

The SDR follows direct rationales (the economic value increase belongs to the community) and an intrinsic redistributive logic: finance unprofitable services with windfalls from profitable developments.

The public manifesto in 1976 called *Embu* Chart inspired the introduction of SDRs. This manifesto advocated that diverse allocation of building rights in the city causes unequal and unearned valorization of land and disclosed the "Created Land" concept: all landowners should have the same basic building rights, equivalent to one time their land area (floor area ratio [FAR] = 1). Every additional building above this ratio would need virtual new land to accommodate it. This virtual land belongs to society; therefore, the developer should pay for it (Azevedo Netto, 1977: 46; Furtado et al., 2006: 17–18).

3.1 The first experiences with SDR as NDO

The first city to adopt the concepts of the *Embu* Chart as an NDO was São Paulo through the local law 10,209 in 1986 (Brazilian municipalities at that time had large autonomy to legislate about anything inside their jurisdiction, including urban policies). The instrument "Linkage Operations" allowed improvement of building rights in certain areas in exchange for social housing construction. The regulation was very basic, and demanded the creation of specific plans to be approved by the local government. Negotiations between developers and government defined the final plans stating the amount of building rights' increase and the consequent obligations (Cymbalista & Santoro, 2006: 10; Maleronka & Furtado, 2013: 13–14). The regulation evolved until 1995, when the local law 11,773 accepted the DOs to be monetarily fulfilled. The instrument, nevertheless, started to be accused of causing negative effects in the urban environment, attending only market demands and lacking transparency in decision-making. Further investigations revealed irregular authorizations, poor generation of resources and misuse of funds. The city of Rio de Janeiro, which started in 1992 using the same NDO, experienced equal problems. These findings discredited the instrument, and in 1998 São Paulo ceased its use, after it had provided 13,000 social housing units (Cymbalista & Santoro, 2006: 6–9; Smolka, 2013: 35–36).

These first controversial experiences helped though to create in developers the culture to pay compensations in exchange for building rights (Maleronka & Furtado, 2013: 15), opening the way not only for the legal consolidation of the separation of property rights from development rights but also for enlargement of the scope of obligations.

3.2 The experience with SDR as N-NDO and evolution of scope of obligations

Other Brazilian municipalities started their experiences with the SDRs shaping them as non-negotiable. Density indexes, form of calculation and resources' earmarking were pre-determined. The first cities to introduce the tool as N-NDO were São Bernardo do Campo in 1977 (before São Paulo's negotiated SDR), Florianópolis since 1989, Curitiba since 1990, and Natal and Porto Alegre from 1994 (Maleronka & Furtado, 2013: 10). These cities successfully prescribed obligations with redistributive logics and without clear links with the development, like provision of social housing, environment protection and construction of public facilities.

3.3 The consolidation of SDRs' scope and non-negotiable status

Based on these first experiences, the public opinion linked negotiable SDRs with arbitrariness and corruption, and perceived the non-negotiable ones as more successful. In 2001, the national law *Estatuto da Cidade* prescribed the social function of property and separated property rights from development rights, allocating these last to the public. It named the SDRs "Onerous Concession of the Right to Build" (*in Portuguese*, OODC) and regulated them so as to make N-NDOs of them.

The instrument was then required to be embedded in local land-use plans: minimum and maximum density parameters (floor area ratio, or FAR) should be prescribed by local law, as well as the form of calculation and locations where additional rights could be purchased (Cymbalista & Santoro, 2006: 10–18; Smolka, 2013: 36). Additionally, the *Estatuto* prescribed that the resources from the OODC could only be allocated to regularization of informal settlements, financing of social housing, public land banking, urban development steering, public facilities construction, creation and protection of preservation areas, and conservation of historical buildings. This legal shaping of SDRs as a N-NDO disclosed parameters and obligations. Standard procedures avoid – theoretically – special treatment to one developer over the other. This enhanced the social acceptability of SDRs and diminished discussion regarding its application (Maleronka & Furtado, 2013: 15).

3.3.1 CEPACs

The *Estatuto* also introduced the new instrument "Urban Operations" (*Operações Urbanas – OU*). This tool allows cities to improve urban areas through a detailed plan of intervention, changing the zoning, upgrading development rights and charging for them through the Certificates of Additional Potential Construction Bonds (*in Portuguese*, CEPACs). The CEPACs stand for building rights which are sold by the government (which owns them, thus a direct rationale) through bids in public auctions. The revenues can only be spent providing infrastructure to support new development inside the OUs, since the objective is urban renewal within these boundaries. So, despite its initial direct rationale, this obligation additionally supports on an indirect rationale (internalization of urbanization impacts). So far, the CEPACs have been used only in São Paulo, Rio de Janeiro and Curitiba.

3.3.2 Policy base of, and conditioning development to, obligations

National and local legal frameworks provide municipalities with statutory powers to condition modifications in land-use regulations to the developer's payment of obligations. Cities approve legally binding land-use plans (*Planos Diretores and Leis de Zoneamento e Uso do Solo*) ruling their whole territories and stating which building rights are free to landowners (basic FAR) and which are subject to payment (additional FAR, only possible in specified zones). Further decrees and neighborhood plans (*Planos Regionais*) detail the procedures for modification of the basic FAR, like calculation of obligation and earmarking of revenues. Only if developers fulfill the obligations, i.e. the payment for the development rights, do they receive the building permit (*Alvará de Construção*). This administrative document certifies the modification of the land-use regulation (additional building area) and is prerequisite for starting to build.

3.4 Variations of SDRs

As each municipality is required to detail locally the obligation's parameters, the efficiency in capturing land value increase depends on a careful construction of these local regulations, considering particular conditions. This local autonomy resulted in diverse models of SDR implemented across the country (see Furtado et al., 2006).

3.4.1 Modifications in the basic building rights

Due to strong resistance from the real estate market, several cities like Porto Alegre, Natal and Curitiba were not able to reduce the basic FARs according to the principles of the *Embu* Chart and adopted high and heterogeneous indexes. São Paulo approved its 2002 land-use plan with a gradual reduction, during two years, of the basic indexes to one or two FARs (depending on the zone) (Sandroni, 2011: 4–6). In 2016, São Paulo passed a new revision of its plan homogenizing the FAR for the whole city as one time the size of land.

3.4.2 Economic appraisal of obligations: land values, flat rates and auctions

The calculation of non-negotiable SDRs is based on how much land area is necessary to accommodate development above a baseline, and how much this virtual area costs. Assessing land values is imprecise because it involves many variables, and every piece of land is unique. The difficulties in appraisal led several municipalities like Goiânia, Campo Grande and Niterói to take shortcuts, using fixed prices or calculating the obligations based on tax plans. These shortcuts affect the amount of contributions: tax plans are usually inaccurate and not updated (Furtado et al., 2006; Smolka, 2013; Maleronka & Furtado, 2013), and levying fixed prices means that plots with different values and history of valorization pay the same price for building rights. Despite the difficulties, cities like Curitiba and Blumenau legally bind a methodology for market values appraisal, and they use it to calculate obligations for each development. Since this method considers particular conditions, it captures more land value increments than those based on fixed prices or tax plans (Marcelino, 2017: 69–72).

In the case of CEPACs, the final price of the obligation is defined in the open market through transparent auctions. The municipality assigns the initial price, based on feasibility studies concerning land values and development's costs, profits and risks. CEPACs were used for the first time in São Paulo in 2004. The two "Urban Operations" (OUs) which successfully sold certificates were created in areas where the real estate market was traditionally active. In those areas, additional construction limits allowed by the land-use plan were sold out. Once CEPACs were auctioned in these two OUs, new additional building rights were created in those areas where building possibilities were first limited. This fulfillment of the market's interest, plus the scarcity of options in other "market significant areas," created a big demand in which the initial price of the CEPACs was not even questioned, but sometimes far exceeded (Maleronka & Furtado, 2013: 25–26; Maleronka & Hobbs, 2017: 44, 49, 53–55).

CEPACs in Curitiba has not yet skyrocketed as in São Paulo. Curitiba has a conservative real estate market and plenty of areas still available for construction through other SDR models than CEPACs. Moreover, the OU *Linha Verde* was implemented in an area with poor market interest. The bonds' initial price was questioned, leading developers to build in other areas and impairing the instrument's implementation (Maleronka & Hobbs, 2017: 54; Marcelino, 2017: 52–53).

4. Outcomes of the SDR and conclusions

4.1 The economic incidence of SDRs

The prescription of non-negotiable SDRs in legislation makes obligations' parameters available to developers beforehand. In this case, theoretically, developers should pass the cost of obligations to landowners (Muñoz Gielen, 2010: 48, 201). As happens in many countries, there is also in Brazil little evidence of the economic incidence of SDRs. Gross values of obtained obligations by CEPACs are available online, but more detailed information and data regarding the OODCs are difficult to obtain. Current research findings present diverse results, not allowing conclusive evaluations. Therefore, they should be cautiously analyzed.

In São Paulo, the implementation of the OU *Faria Lima* increased land prices at least 15% in the area (Biderman & Sandroni, 2005: 11–14). A further study demonstrated that the CEPACs captured big part of increments coming from this OU's implementation (Biderman et al., 2006: 11–12). Considering that new developments emerged absorbing this increase in land price, the CEPACs and the additional construction's costs, it is possible to infer that the profit of developers was high enough to cover these expenditures. The *Faria Lima* is an area with extreme high demand. Those previous studies found that, after the approval of the OU, the price of real estate units sold and the average population's income increased. Therefore, in this case the value increase was large enough to afford both a land price increase and some public land value capture, i.e. the CEPACs did not result in lower land prices but might have moderated their increase.

In Curitiba, the use of non-negotiable SDRs since the 1990s allowed a similar analysis, but with more data supporting it. A comparison between the increments in land values between 1996 and 2016 and the intensity of use of these SDRs (Figures 4.1 and 4.2) reveals that prices of land increased less in central areas, where the prescription of these obligations was more intensive. It cannot be excluded that prices in the periphery increase proportionally more than in central areas due to city expansion, but it is reasonable to conclude that charging obligations must have also moderated land price's increases in central areas. This suggests that the cost of SDR were passed to landowners.

4.2 Amount of obligations obtained through the non-negotiable SDRs

Comparing obtained obligations and cities' earnings from property tax, amount of capital investments and increments in land values clarifies the financial relevance of DOs. Data consolidated from reports of São Paulo and Curitiba allowed some conclusions regarding the importance of non-negotiable SDRs for these cities' local budgets.

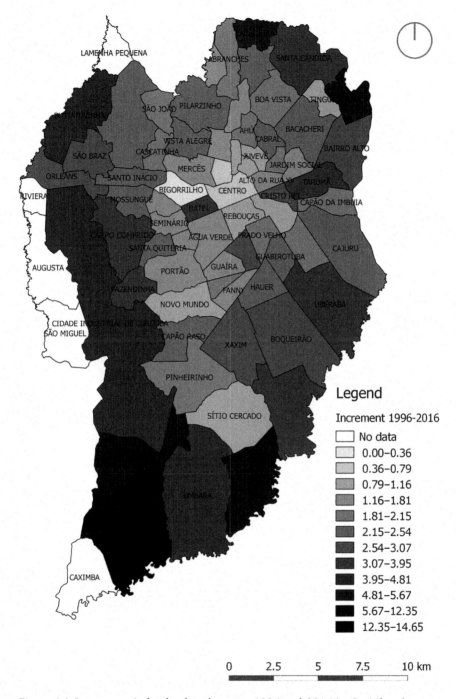

Figure 4.1 Increments in land values between 1996 and 2016 in Curitiba. Average land values per neighborhood

Note: The legend of the map states how many times the land value of 1996 increased.

Data source: INPESPAR (Paraná Institute of Research and Development of the Real Estate and Condominium Market).

Map: the author.

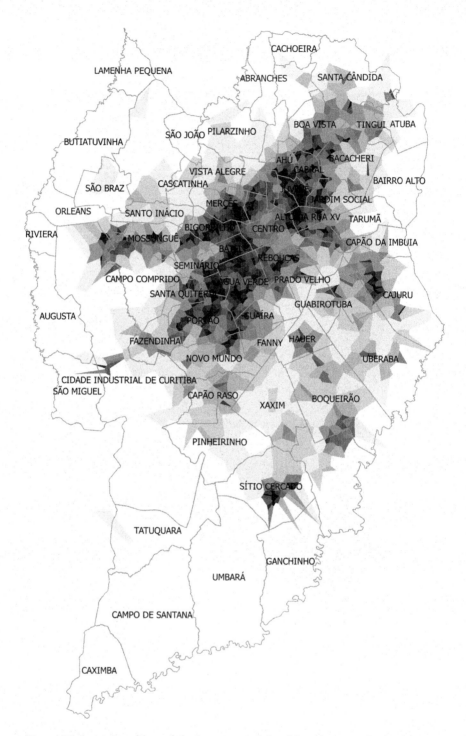

Figure 4.2 Intensity of use of the instrument Sale of Development Rights between 1992 and 2016

Note: The darker the shading, the more developments in the area purchased additional building rights through the SDR.

Data source: Municipality of Curitiba.

Map: the author.

4.2.1 Comparison with property tax

The annual property tax in Curitiba obtained R$2.4 billion between 2011 and 2016 (6.30% of the city's budget). In the same period, four OODC models and the CEPACs generated R$180 million, equivalent to 7% of the annual property tax (Marcelino, 2017: 56). In São Paulo, between 2005 and 2015, the property tax generated around R$45.5 billion (14% of the municipal budget). In this period, the OODC captured R$1.8 billion (4.0% of the property tax) while two operations with CEPACs (*Agua Espraiada and Faria Lima*) captured more than R$4.4 billion (9.6% of the property tax).

Urban instruments develop differently along time; therefore, consolidated data must be cautiously interpreted. For example, between 2005 and 2006, the revenues from the CEPACs in São Paulo were equivalent to 3% of the property tax. But in 2008, a very successful sale of certificates made this instrument generate revenues equivalent to 22% of the property tax (2005–2008).

Curitiba also in 2012 registered its highest revenue generation through non-negotiable SDRs. In this year, while the property tax levied on 605,000 properties captured on average R$570.00 per property, the SDRs charged from 272 developments captured on average R$181,676.00 per property: 318 times more. Although SDRs obtain revenues only one time (property tax generates resources every year), these data indicate the instrument's high potential to capture land values (Marcelino, 2017: 56).

4.2.2 Comparison with capital investments

Public capture tools aim at financing capital expenditures; so how much do the obtained obligations represent in the amount of capital investments (construction and improvements) of a city?

During a six-year period (2011–2016), Curitiba invested a total of R$1.8 billion in capital investments. The models of OODC studied generated equivalent to 7.6% of this investment and the CEPACs, 2.4%. São Paulo invested in 10 years (2005–2015) R$58 billion, and the OODC generated an equivalent to 4% and the CEPACs to 7.5% of those investments.

4.2.3 Comparison with increments in value of land

In Curitiba, between 2011 and 2016, the CEPACs captured the equivalent of 20% of increments in land value from the previous 20 years (1996–2016), while the OODC's captured 8.5% (models using market land values) and 5.5% (models using flat rates).

As mentioned in Section 3.4, the way the non-negotiable SDRs are designed impacts the amount of obtained obligations. When considering only areas where the basic building rights are one time the land size (FAR = 1) and developers purchased all additional building rights available, the collected obligations raises to 55% of the estimated land value increase for the OODC (models using market values) and 51% for the CEPACs (Marcelino, 2017: 78). Therefore, a fine tuning of parameters according to local conditions is crucial for a successful implementation of the non-negotiable SDR.

5. Conclusions

The Brazilian experience with a variety of models of the selling of development rights (a DO based on direct rationales and operating under passive forms of governance), provides interesting conclusions for the academic debate. The presence of direct rationales in all levels of legislation, plus the poor transparency of the first negotiable SDRs, contributed to evolving the instrument to a statutory non-negotiable status. This increase in regulation provided the developers beforehand with certainty about the requirements and about the goals of the obligations, which facilitated acceptance by the market. Additionally, the possibility for municipalities to condition the building to the payment of the development rights sold by the government effectively guarantees fulfillment of these obligations. The way SDRs are regulated influences their effectiveness, however, which largely varies across the country. The collected resources are relevant for many cities' budgets, especially considering that they are collected from only a part of the real estate market operators. In this context, the CEPACs stand out as a powerful and transparent tool for appraisal and capture of land values.

References

Afonso, J., Araújo, E. & Nóbrega, M. (2013), *IPTU no Brasil: Um Diagnóstico Abrangente*. Brasília: Instituto Brasiliense de Direito Publico and FGV-Projetos.

Azevedo Netto, D. (1977), 'Experiências similares ao solo criado', *C.J.Arquitetura*, Vol. 4, No.16, pp. 44–54. São Paulo.

Biderman, C. & Sandroni, P. (2005), 'Avaliação do Impacto das Grandes Intervenções Urbanas nos preços dos Imóveis do Entorno: O Caso da Operação Urbana Consorciada Faria Lima'. *XXIX EnANPAD*, Brasília.

Biderman, C., Sandroni, P. & Smolka, M. (2006), 'Large-Scale Urban Interventions: The Case of Faria Lima in São Paulo', *Land Lines*, Vol. 18, No. 2, pp. 8–13.

Cymbalista, R. & Santoro, P. (2006), 'Outorga onerosa do direito de construir no Brasil: entre a regulação e a arrecadação'. Seminário Projetos Urbanos Contemporâneos, Universidade São Judas, São Paulo, pp. 1–20.

De Cesare, C. (2005), 'O Cadastro como Instrumento de Política Fiscal', in: Erba, D., Oliveira, F. & Lima, P. (eds.), *Cadastro Multifinalitário como Instrumento de Política Fiscal e Urbana*. Rio de Janeiro: Ministério das Cidades.

Furtado, F., Rezende, V., Oliveira, T. & Jorgensen Jr, P. (2006), Outorga onerosa do direito de construir: panorama e avaliação de experiências municipais. . Cambridge: Lincoln Institute of Land Policy.

IBGE. (2016), *Perfil dos Municipios Brasileiros: 2015*. Rio de Janeiro: IBGE.

Maleronka, C. & Furtado, F. (2013), *A Outorga Onerosa do Direito de Construir: A Experiência de São Paulo na Gestão Pública de Aproveitamentos Urbanísticos*. Cambridge: Lincoln Institute of Land Policy.

Maleronka, C. & Hobbs, J. (2017), *Operações Urbanas: o que podemos aprender com a experiência de São Paulo?* Washington: Interamerican Development Bank.

Marcelino, M. (2017), *How Investments in Urban Services Can Be Financed by the Land Value Capture Instrument "Sale of Development Rights" – The Case of Curitiba.* Master Thesis. Erasmus University Rotterdam.

Muñoz Gielen, D. (2010), *Capturing Value Increase in Urban Redevelopment.* Doctoral Thesis. Radboud University Nijmegen.

Pereira, G. (2012), *Recuperação de mais valias urbanas por meio de contribuição de melhoria.* Curitiba: Lincoln Institute of Land Policy.

Sandroni, P. (2011), *Urban Value Capture in São Paulo Using a Two-Part Approach: Created Land and Sale of Building Rights.* Cambridge: Lincoln Institute of Land Policy.

Smolka, M. (2013), *Implementing Value Capture in Latin America: Policies and Tools for Urban Development.* Cambrdige: Lincoln Institute of Land Policy.

Walters, L., du Plessis, J., Haile, S. & Paterson, L. (2016), *Leveraging Land: Land Based-Finance for Local Governments: A Reader.* Kenya, Nairobi: UN-Habitat.

5 The progressive acceptance of developer obligations in Chile, 1990–2017

Pia Mora and Vicente Burgos Salas

1. Context: national Chilean Planning System

The prevalent perspective in the Chilean Planning System and DOs legislation is that property rights can only be limited by law. The social function of the property recognized by the Chilean National Constitution is regulated as a *limit* to the enjoyment of property. Neither the doctrine nor legislation have recognized explicitly direct rationales, differently from other countries of the region like Brazil or Colombia.

DOs are regulated mostly in the General Law of Urbanism and Construction (LGUC, *Ley General de Urbanismo y Construcciones*) introduced originally in 1976, and its General Ordinance. LGUC rules nationally the conditions for obtain construction permits and the procedures of legally binding zoning plans (PRs, *Planos Reguladores*). Through PRs, local administrations can designate roads and parks of public interest (Designation of Public Utility), which become thus obligatory for developers, a sort of N-NDO. LGUC also classifies urban development into *new urbanization* and *densification*. Developers of *new urbanizations* are required to transfer a maximum of 44% of the development land for public equipment and green spaces. Until 2016, when the Public Space Contributions Act (LAEP, *Ley de Aportes al Espacio Público*) was enacted, densification projects only were responsible for transport mitigation measures (see Section 3).

In addition to the LGUC, successive modifications of the 1994 Regional Zoning Plan of Santiago (PRMS, *Plan Regulador Metropolitano de Santiago*, a legally binding zoning land-use plan covering the entire metropolitan region) included several additional N-NDOs for new urbanizations. The next section focuses further on these additional obligations.

2. Developer obligations in Santiago: trial and error

This section describes and evaluates the main DOs created and implemented in Chile. First, it describes DOs in new urbanizations in the outskirts of Santiago. Second, DOs in urban densification.

2.1 DOs in new urbanizations

Successive modifications of the PRMS included, additionally to those prescribed in the LGUC, three different sorts of N-NDOs:

- Conditioned Urban Development Zones (ZUDCs, *Zonas Urbanizables con Desarrollo Condicionado*): introduced in 1997, they allow the developers to increase the density and constructability of land plots on the condition to pay for hard infrastructure to connect the developments to the rest of the metropolitan area and to use a 5% of the total development area for high-density developments (with no deadline to develop them), trying to induce in this way the construction of social and economic housing.
- Conditioned Urban Development Projects (PDUCs, *Proyectos de Desarrollo Urbano Condicionado*): very similar to ZUDCs, introduced in 2003, they prescribe the contribution to social housing. They suffered considerable delay in their approval.
- Conditioned Building Zones (ZUCs, *Zonas Urbanizables Condicionadas*): introduced in 2006, they are similar as ZUDCs and PDUCs, but include the obligation of maintaining new green areas.

Chilean legislation prohibits urban development outside the city limits, but these N-NDOs offer landowners the possibility of developing outside these limits (Cordero, 2008: 57, 103). Accordingly, the Explanatory Memorandum of the 1997 PRMS established that the required contributions "do not constitute a limitation of the normal urbanistic faculties that the owners have, but a possibility to improve these ones" (p. 57). Although formally, these DOs are non-negotiable, in practice they leave large room for negotiating the exact location of the development and the infrastructure, budget allocation, the way of its expenditure and the interpretation of other regulations. Negotiation processes have not always been transparent. Private developers identify many difficulties related to reaching fluid communication with the public sector, related to the institutional fragmentation of urban policy (Tello, 2013: 2). The length of time between the planned extension, the interest and investment of private developers and the actual approval of the different public organisms has reached, in some cases, more than 15 years.

2.1.1 Conditioned urban development zones, ZUDCs

ZUDCs were introduced in 1997 by an addition to the PRMS, responding to private pressure of real estate developers who owned land located in the outskirts of Santiago (in Chacabuco province). Developers were allowed to develop 15,242 hectares in the municipalities of Colina, Lampa and Til-Til, on the condition of building social and economic housing, but this requirement was very vague and became largely eluded.[1] Another condition was to pay for hard infrastructure to connect the development. Hitherto, there are five activated ZUDCs in Santiago and four expected to be approved. As a whole, they add up to 6,414 and 3,049 hectares, respectively, of urban land (Transsa, 2013).

Negotiations between the private developers and the authorities were crucial. The initial transport plan designed by the Ministry of Public Works (MOP, *Ministerio de Obras Públicas*) to connect all those ZUDCs required an investment of USD 312 million, of which 59% should be paid by 14 private projects (USD 184 million). Most developers dropped the negotiations, arguing as arbitrary that the roadworks looked to solve transport problems which were distant from their developments. An arrangement was reached with the three remaining private developers, who paid USD 70 million. This agreement demonstrated the viability of demanding private contributions, and made it possible to reach later in 2001 another agreement between representatives of nine private developers and the Regional Branches of the Transport Ministry (MTT, *Ministerio de Transporte*), the MOP and the Ministry of Housing and Urban Planning (MINVU, *Ministerio de Vivienda y Urbanismo*) (Poduje, 2006). This Framework Agreement established the general basis and principles for the execution of roadworks inversions in order to mitigate ZUDCs' transport impacts. It included contributions for road infrastructure needed for the developments projected until 2010 (USD 55.5 million) and for road infrastructure needed for developments constructed after 2010 (see Table 5.1).

The perception of the consulted civil servants of the regional branch of MINVU is that road mitigations and local hard infrastructure have been achieved successfully, but social housing has not. In fact, its construction has not been generalized in all private projects, with Valle Grande and Santo Tomás being an exception. This case, presented ahead, illustrates the working of ZUDCs.

VALLE GRANDE – SANTO TOMÁS[2]

This is an urban development located in El Alfalfal ZUDC, at Lampa Municipality, oriented to middle and middle-low income households. Housing prices range from USD 40,385 to USD 156,133. At the end of 2017, there were 8,605 housing units with issued or almost issued construction permits (of a total of 24,236 units). This project included 9% of affordable housing oriented to low income groups – linked to its location and potential

---

1 The Explanatory Memorandum of the PRMS is not entirely clear about the obligation of social housing. On page 51, it says: "when dividing into plots, a 5% of total surface must be destined to social housing". Then, on page 56, it states: "mentioned conditions (related to density zoning) intend to induce the construction of social and economic housing". Later, the PRMS expressed this requirement more ambiguously, only referring to high density instead of social housing.

2 www.ivallegrande.cl/inicio.html [Consulted: 20 December 2017].

Table 5.1 Projected contributions of ZUDCs according to the Framework Agreement

Real estate project	Homes projected to 2010	Initial contribution (total amount)		Future Mitigations (payment per house)	
	N°	UF	USD	UF	USD
Pan de Azúcar	1,853	161.456	6,657,979	37	3,533
Huertos Familiares	401	6.110	251,959	20	825
El Chamisero	3,294	294.313	12,136,619	90	3,711
Ciudad Chicureo	5,727	506.421	20,883,340	39	3,670
Santo Tomás	3,310	135.606	7,653,356	52	2,144
Valle Grande	3,934	191.636	7,902,515	52	2,144
Total	19,024	1,345.542	55,436,263		

Source: Own elaboration based on Framework Agreement (2001). All USD values are converted using current exchange value as of 11 December 2017 (1 UF = USD 41,237).

demand, with a higher urbanization standard in comparison with traditional social housing developments. The reason that the developer included affordable housing was more related to the location and potential demand than to the 1997 PRMS. According to the developer, Valle Grande has contributed USD 26,008,495 to roadworks mitigation. Several problems have appeared in the implementation of this ZDUC: other investments necessary besides the contributions agreed in the 2001 Framework Agreement have not been made; for example, health and education facilities, and the operation of road infrastructure and public transport.

2.1.2 Conditioned urban development projects, PDUCs

In 2003, the Regional Zoning Plan of Santiago (PRMS, *Plan Regulador Metropolitano de Santiago*) incorporated PDUCs. These were not tied to a specific territory as ZUDCs were, but applicable in any rural agroforestry area in 10 municipalities of the metropolitan region (EM PRMS, 2003: 7). PDUCs objectives were to internalize costs and impacts, reduce infrastructure and equipment deficits and produce new affordable and social housing (EM PRMS, 2003: 3). The experience with ZUDCs showed the need of including affordable housing, which was made explicit this time: a 30% of subsidized housing was demanded, with a 40% of it for the lowest-income households.[3] Private developers also had to contribute to infrastructure to mitigate mobility and environmental impacts.

---

3 In Chile, housing policy subsidizes households belonging to the 70% of the lowest income, with higher vouchers amounts at lower income. The so-called "social housing" corresponds to residential units destined to the lowest-income households, which contribute very little savings and do not have to contract debts in private banking.

Figure 5.1 Valle Grande and Santo Tomás, Lampa. Selected photos of green spaces, roads and housing

Source: Images provided by María José Balmaceda, Valle Grande's Commercial Manager.

Figure 5.1 (Continued)

Fourteen years have passed since the introduction in 2003 of PDUCs' in the PRMS, but no project has been implemented yet. On March 2018, two PDUCs – Urbanya and Praderas – were finally approved by the Comptroller General of the Republic (CGR, *Contraloría General de la República*).[4] Thus far, each developer has already spent around USD 7 million, considering administration, studies and roadworks, among other items. The developers expect that these PDUCs will contribute around USD 124,120,811 due to transport mitigations. They faced important obstacles to get the PDUCs approved, being the necessary support of different involved public bodies an especially complex obstacle. Under the eyes of the affected companies, an intersectorial approach is needed, whereby different public entities, lead by a powerful leader, must collaborate with private parties to provide services. According to some interviewees, PDUCs are not a permanent governmental policy, and is not based on a solid consensus among different public entities that need to approve different aspects of PDUCs.

2.1.3 Conditioned building zones, ZUCs

In December 2006, MINVU's Regional Branch announced the "modification n°100" of the 1994 PRMS. This modification added to the Metropolitan Area of Santiago 10,262 hectares of new urban land, belonging to eight municipalities, and created the figure of ZUCs. New ZUCs developments could reach 150 inhabitants per hectare if they contributed to roadworks, green areas implementation (included maintenance for five years), 6% of the development area for urban amenities, and 8% for social housing. Nowadays, nine ZUCs projects have been presented, and three of them approved, faster than PDUCs. On the whole, ZUCs' expected land contributions for roads, green areas and social housing would be around 74, 285 and 35 hectares, respectively.

2.2 DOs in urban densification

Inside its urban boundaries, Santiago has experienced an important rise in the rhythm of building, and consequently, the externalities of density projects have increased. The central government and some local administrations have proposed to introduce fixed obligations and mitigation measures to urban developments. This section analyzes the proposed DOs and their indirect rationale: to obtain revenues to mitigate externalities.

2.2.1 Local NDOs: filling the gaps

Local NDOs share some common features. First, they are used in municipalities with a significant real estate activity, large budgets and a comparatively high standard of technical and human resources. Second, they are if not

4 CGR ruling 4987–2018. The CGR is an independent and autonomous control organ that rules and dictates the actions of public organisms and safeguard the use of public funds.

illegal, at the margins of the rule of law. No legislation gives municipalities the power to negotiate contributions in exchange for construction permits, as the Comptroller General of the Republic, CGR has repeatedly argued.[5] Finally, they depend on the negotiation capacity of municipalities with the private developers of the projects.

A first illustrative case is "Parque Araucano'" in Las Condes municipality. The development area had poor transport infrastructure in 2006. In agreement with the local administration, a group of interested developers commissioned a transport study that established and budgeted the infrastructure needed. Then, the local administration established a contribution per unit.[6] This group of developers agreed with the local administration a total investment of USD 1.5 million, divided in quotas per developer.

A second case is "Lo Barnechea" municipality. At the beginning of the 1990s, this municipality faced an incipient interest in developing residential suburbs in areas with bad connectivity.[7] The municipality approved an "Urban Street Network Capacity Study" and a zoning plan (PR), and created a public local infrastructure development corporation in charge of promoting, planning, designing and building the road infrastructure needed for Lo Barnechea. The study anticipated the needed infrastructure and the corporation started to ask developers to voluntarily contribute USD 3,155 per housing unit or USD 41.8 per square meter of other uses. The payment was done through agreements, using the corporation as guarantor, recipient and implementer of the funds for building the road capacity. The total amount of infrastructure investment reached more than USD 33 million until 2015.[8]

In contrast, there are examples that show that the lack of proper legal base forms a constant threat for these instruments to succeed. This is the case of modifications of land-use regulations allowing more building in exchange for developer contributions. In Pudahuel Municipality, a developer agreed with the local administration on a contribution for transport infrastructure and parks in exchange of an increase of density. However, local communities filed a motion at CGR against the project and won the case.[9] Other contributions agreed in Providencia and Las Condes municipalities for several

---

5 CGR Rulings 1.101–2011, 67.330–2013, 85.958–2013, 82.539–2014, among others: "*in this context, it must be pointed out that LGUC . . . does not contemplate the possibility that planning instruments regulate the land according to the verification of conditions outside its legal precepts, such as the situation that is being reviewed . . . it is not proper that PRC stablish benefits nor conditions as the ones projected in the article that is being reviewed.*"

6 The contribution per each parking slot is USD 1,654 for commerce, USD 546 for offices, USD 605 for housing and USD 1,443 for hotels.

7 According to statements of the Lo Barnechea Municipality's representatives in the discussion of the Public Space Contribution's Act (LAEP, *Ley de Aportes al Espacio Público*, Legislative History of LAEP, p. 14).

8 *Ibid.*

9 CGR Ruling 14.711–2006.

years also suffered from recent rulings of CGR, which argued that there was no legal support in the competences of local administrations to require contributions in exchange for better building conditions included in the PR.[10]

2.2.2 Impact study on the urban transportation system, EISTU

Since 1992, subsequent national laws and decrees have given municipalities different competences to request from developers the execution of new transport infrastructure in the surrounding of the development. Until 2001, municipalities were able to require studies and adjustments to constructions permits without much specification. However, its unprecise wording failed in producing a clear and effective procedure (Santa María, 2009). In 2001, a decree streamlined the procedure by requiring a study on the impact of a new development in the transportation system (EISTU, *Estudios de Impacto sobre el Sistema de Transporte Urbano*), and by prescribing that developers must build the needed infrastructure. However, EISTUs were mandatory only for urban developments with more than 150 and 250 parking slots for commercial and residential use, respectively. Consequently, many projects artificially limited the number of parking slots just to avoid the study.[11] Some developers claimed an unfair and inefficient system, whereby the lack of coordination between many administrative actors made the system very unpredictable and nontransparent.[12] Hearing these claims, the involved Ministries modified the 2001 decree,[13] but this modification was ruled unconstitutional in 2002.[14] An attempt to repair the 2001 decree with a bill failed in 2007 due to disagreements between the Transport and Housing & Urban Development Ministries. Thus, EISTU and its problems remained untouched for more than 15 years until the approval in 2016 of the LAEP.

2.2.3 Most recent attempt to improve DOs in urban densification: the LAEP

The approval of the Public Space Contribution´s Act (LAEP, *Ley de Aportes al Espacio Público*) in 2016 was the result of addressing through the legislative process the mentioned experiences with all different sorts of DOs, instead of the piecemeal approach in the previous decennia of approving ad hoc decrees. According to the President of the National Council of Urban Development, the LAEP is the "first urban reform that went through the

---

10 CGR Ruling 4987-2018.
11 As a consequence, only 4.6% of densification projects had to prepare an EISTU (Legislative History of, p. 14).
12 Legislative History of LAEP, p. 14.
13 Supreme Decree MTT/111–2002 and Decree DDU 114, Ord. 367 of MINVU, 2002.
14 Ruling of the Process 370–2002 from the Constitutional Court.

legislative process, since the LGUC in its actual form".[15] The process of approval included a failed act in 2007 and a long parliamentary discussion (2012–2016). The original bill intended to new densification projects to transfer a maximum of 44% of the development land value for public equipment and green spaces, similarly to urbanization projects. However, after the legislative process the final text went further by combining different DOs instruments meant for developers solving the development impacts in their surroundings and for them contributing too other needs of the city. Accordingly, The LAEP contains two sorts of obligations:

- Direct Mitigations (Mitigaciones Directas): N-NDOs which require mitigation of mobility problems in their influence area; they replace the EISTUs.
- Public Space Contributions (*Aportes al Espacio Público*): N-NDOs which require the payment of a fee equivalent to a percentage of value of the development land. When the development is located in a city with a Regional Development Plan, the revenues of the fee will be divided: 70% for a Municipal Infrastructure and Mobility Investment Plan, and 30% for a Regional Infrastructure and Mobility Investment Plan.

The LAEP transformed many DOs based on weak regulations with "rules of thumb". EISTUs were reformed into a generic approval of transport impacts required for any urban project that increases density, no matter how small. PRs are now allowed to prescribe DOs in exchange for new use or building possibilities. The LAEP demands from any densification project to contribute to the municipality or the regional government. The use of the collected funds will be spent based on an Investment Plan developed by local governments. For the first time, contributions can be spent on "social infrastructure" that aim "social cohesion" and "urban sustainability", which opens the door for an enlargement of the scope of contributions. The LAEP also regulated the urban expansion through conditions as the old N-NDOs ZUDCs, PDUCs and ZUCs (see Section 3.1).

During the legislative process, there were significant political discussions that shaped the LAEP. Real estate developers (CCHC, *Cámara Chilena de la Construcción* and ADI, *Asociación de Desarrolladores Inmobiliarios*) opposed the bill. They argued that contributions could rise housing prices and disincentive investment. The bill included a limit of 44% of the cadastral value of the land as a limit to the contribution.[16] A second discussion

---

15 Interview in National Television Channel, 24.09.2016, available at www.youtube.com/watch?v=frAXJJTp4Jg&t=503s [Consulted: 20 December 2017].
16 The original draft of the LAEP stated a commercial value instead of the cadastral value. The limit of the cadastral value, which is used as base for the property tax, was incorporated to give certainty to real estate developers.

regarded whether DOs were a tax or not. The first draft of the LAEP explicitly argued that contributions were not a tax but a "compensation" from the developer for the surplus received[17] that needs to be spent in the area of influence. However, next drafts included the possibility of using the funds for infrastructure located in the Region of the project, with an indirect relation to the project, which led some legislators to qualify it as a "tax".[18] The organizations of real estate developers resisted with the argument that contributions were now meant to remedy historical infrastructure deficits.[19] However, the bill was approved by the Congress Financial Committee and the Constitutional Court did not object on constitutional grounds. A third discussion that the LAEP had to overcome was the argument that some private developers were paying for the externalities that all projects were producing, not only theirs. LAEP included the principles of universality (all developments must mitigate their impact), proportionality (there must be a relation between the externality and the DO, so to avoid charging for the "historical deficit" of urban infrastructure) and predictability (contributions must be calculated with objective and standardized methods; these will be published to guarantee that they are measurable ex-ante in order to include them in the costs calculation of the investment). These principles will guide in the future, in case of controversy around the application of the LAEP, the interpretation of MINVU, the Courts and CGR.

During the writing of this chapter, the regulation decree of the LAEP was being approved by CGR. The implementation of this regulation, therefore, will start during 2019.

3. Lessons from implementing DOs in Chile: learnings and challenges

The implementation of DOs in Chile has been possible without an optimal legal framework. This was one of the biggest weaknesses of DOs. Processes have normally been longer than expected, and anticipated results have not always been obtained. The support of the legal system has proven to be critical for the security of private developers and the public actors to get the planned results. The 2016 LAEP represents, at least initially, a great progress to make easier DOs implementation.

The Chilean legislation has been historically reactive to the use of direct rationales to support public value capture tools. The arguments of the private sector against the LAEP (mentioned earlier) were also against the *direct rationales* perceived in its objectives. However, some direct rationales have been used without much opposition, especially in the outskirts of Santiago

---

17 Legislative History of LAEP, p. 37.
18 Ibid., p. 304, 305, 359, 454–456.
19 Ibid., p. 300.

de Chile, where the development expectations of landowners are lower than in central areas. In general, it has been easier to base DOs on indirect rationales, mainly on the idea that development must mitigate externalities, especially considering transport infrastructure and green areas.

The degree of negotiability of DOs existent in other countries is hardly achievable in Chile. DOs in Chile (as almost any other urban planning provision) are based on a strict interpretation of the rule of law, where competences, rights and duties are regulated. Any contribution of real estate developers must belong to the public knowledge and must be formally non-negotiable. In fact, private actors also oppose legal modifications to make DOs more negotiable, which is against the idea of a general and predictable rule. At the same time, public actors have no capacity to lead negotiations. However, bargaining processes exist, related to the creation, interpretation and implementation of the rules. These negotiations, which have not been completely transparent for the public, have resulted into relatively successful DOs outputs. However, the LAEP does not foresee explicitly the possibility of negotiations.

In the coming years, DOs will face several challenges in the light of the new LAEP. First, it will be critical to visualize and include civil society. LAEP includes the formulation of new local investment plans, and during their elaboration and/or implementation, municipalities should call civil society to develop solutions to manage building projects externalities. This element could give more transparency to the negotiation processes. But transparency is also needed in the implementation and results. The lack of data and literature regarding implementation of DOs is problematic. Most information collected in this chapter was provided by private actors. Despite the existence of transparency legislation, most public authorities simply do not collect the data regarding the implementation of DOs. This hinders their evaluation and is a threat for successful reforms in the area. To measure the implementation and results of LAEP and Dos, it is required that the state become actively involves in the accountability of transport mitigation and public space contributions.

Bibliography

Balmaceda, M. (2014), *¿Qué son las ZUDC? Zonas Urbanizables con Desarrollo Condicionado*. Presentación power point elaborada en contexto de seminario organizado por la Universidad Mayor.

Cámara Chilena de la Construcción:

—— (2014), 'Aprobación PRMS-100, Análisis y Alcances', *Minuta CTR n° 04*.

—— (2010), 'Modificación al Plan Regulador Metropolitano de Santiago (PRMS)', *Fundamenta*, Vol. 39. ISSN 0718-3240, Santiago, Chile.

—— (2004), 'Las ZODUC y el Crecimiento de la Ciudad: ¿Llave Maestra o Candado?' *Revista En Concreto n°21*, Santiago, Chile.

Congreso Nacional de Chile. (2016), 'Historia de la Ley N', *Revista de Derechos Fundamentales*, 2, Viña del Mar, Chile, pp. 91–112.

Cordero, E. (2008), 'El Derecho Urbanístico Chileno y la Garantía Constitucional de la Propiedad', *Revista de Derechos Fundamentales*, 2, Viña del Mar, Chile, 91–112.

Poduje, I. (2006), 'El globo y el acordeón: planificación urbana en Santiago, 1960–2004 from the Book', in Galetovic, A. (ed.), *Santiago, Dónde estamos y hacia dónde vamos.* Santiago, Chile: CEP, p. 256.

Sabatini, F., Mora, P., Polanco, I. & Brain, I. (2014), 'Conciliando integración social y negocio inmobiliario. Seguimiento de proyectos integrados (PIS) desarrollados por inmobiliarias e implicancias de política', *Documento de Trabajo del Lincoln Institute of Land Policy*, 2013.

Santa María, M. (2009), 'Legislación sobre impacto vial: una necesidad urgente e inevitable', *Dirección de Asuntos Públicos*, Año 4, N° 29, Santiago, Chile: Pontificia Universidad Católica de Chile.

Secretaría Ministerial Metropolitana de Vivienda y Urbanismo, Ministerio de Vivienda y Urbanismo:

——— (1997), 'Modificación del Plan Regulador Metropolitano de Santiago, Incorporación de las comunas de Colina, Lampa y Til Til'.

——— (2003), 'Memoria Explicativa Modificación del Plan Regulador Metropolitano de Santiago. Incorporación artículo 8.3.2.4, correspondiente a los Proyectos con Desarrollo Urbano Condicionado'.

——— (2008), 'Memoria Explicativa Modificación PRMS 100. Actualización áreas de extensión urbana y reconversión'.

——— (2013), 'Modificación Plan Regulador Metropolitano de Santiago'.

SEREMI RM MINVU, SEREMI RM MTT y SEREMI RM MOP. (2001), 'Acuerdo Marco que establece las bases y principios sobre mitigación de impacto vial en la Provincia de Chacabuco, de la RM'.

Tello, C. (2013), 'Institucionalidad para la Integración Social Urbana', *Documento de referencia.* Espacio Público.

Transsa. (2013), 'Estudio de inserción en mercado de PDUC xx xxxxx. Comunas de Colina, Lampa, Til Til y Pudahuel', Código informe Y27016–13–13.

Interviews

Alejandro Magni, Praderas, 28 November 2017
Cristián Cominetti, Piedra Roja, Inmobiliaria Manquehue, 6 December 2017
María José Balmaceda, Valle Grande, 29 November 2017
Rodrigo Poblete, Inmobiliaria Avellaneda, 29 November 2017
Vicente Domínguez, ADI, 27 November 2017
Pablo Contrucci, DDU MINVU y ex gerente general Urbanya, 23 November 2017
Fabián Kuskinen y Mathias Koch, DDU SEREMI MINVU, 31 October 2017

Press

Plataforma Urbana. (2012), *Organizaciones Ciudadanas y Colegio de Arquitectos se manifiestan ante PRMS100.* Press reléase. Plataforma Urbana available at webpage [Consulted].

6   Poland

Ban on conditioning the land-use plan to developer obligations diminishes their effectiveness

Demetrio Muñoz Gielen, Tomasz Ossowicz and Tomasz Zaborowski

1. Overview of public value capture instruments in Poland other than developer obligations

Poland is rich in other sorts of PVC instruments than DOs. Because most of these other PVC tools are ineffective, practice has developed some informal tools without however providing satisfying results. Here, first the formal and then the informal ones (i.e. those associated with some acting not deriving directly from legal empowerment of public bodies):

- Land-lease of urban land: many Polish public bodies own large pieces of urban land and lease them (*użytkowanie wieczyste*), which provides important financial sources, especially for municipalities (Marmolejo Duarte & Plocikiewicz, 2012).
- Property tax (*podatek od nieruchomości*): provides significant revenues (often around 10% of the total municipal budget), even though it is not *ad valorem*, i.e. not based on the real market value of properties but on plot and building surface area, regardless the location, and even though there is a national maximum rate fixed by law which is relatively low (Zaborowski, 2018).
- Planning levy (*opłata planistyczna*): based on a direct rationale, it is charged on the transfer of the property of land made within five years after the land-use plan (*miejscowy plan zagospodarowania przestrzennego*, MPZP, translated as 'local development plan') becomes legally binding. Its payment is widely avoided because landowners deliberately wait to transfer the property until the five-year period has expired, and because it is complex to collect. Many Polish municipalities deliberately give up on exacting any (significant) levy rate (Nelicki & Zachariasz 2008; Rumińska, 2015).
- Statutory betterment charge (*opłata adiacencka*): this levy (a share of the land value increase) may be charged on the owners of land and buildings that benefit from public investments in infrastructure. This charge is not effective in practice because of several limitations (Nelicki &

Zachariasz, 2008), and the political sensitiveness of charging existing homeowners (Rumińska, 2015).

- Informal (negotiated) betterment charge: sometimes municipalities make clear to the developer, after the land-use plan is approved, that the municipality is not able to construct the necessary public infrastructure. Municipalities are formally responsible for the public infrastructure, but no sanction exists for not constructing it. Municipalities then also make it clear that they wish for the developers to agree to construct the infrastructure themselves. Sometimes municipalities offer, depending on the public interest of the infrastructure, a contribution to the costs. Thus, developers might just wait and nothing happens, or construct the infrastructure, possibly with a public contribution. This is thus a sort of non-statutory betterment charge, i.e. a voluntary and negotiated contribution in exchange for public investment in infrastructure.

- Informal conditions to development: there are contributions negotiated as conditions to administrative decisions that cannot be characterized as land-use regulation decisions. Hence, they cannot be defined as DOs, as defined in this book. For example, a municipality prescribes one-way circulation in the only road that connects the city to a large shopping centre so long as its owner does not voluntarily contribute to improving this road. Another example is when developers must compensate cut down trees by planting new trees in public spaces; therefore, developers must ask to the greenery department of the municipality for a permission to plant new trees in public spaces; then, the greenery department asks the developer to pay for other improvements in these public spaces.

2. Overview of developer obligations (DOs) in Poland

Besides those PVC tools, there are some formal DOs:

- Formal NDOs (traffic infrastructure): developers, in order to obtain the building permit (*pozwolenie na budowę*), are obliged to commit in a contract with the road traffic authority (*zarządca drogi*) to (re)construct those public roads necessary for the development.[1] If there is an MPZP, this land-use plan prescribes the need for road infrastructure, which leaves still some room for negotiation. If there is no MPZP, there is no

---

1 The formal sequence is that the road traffic authority must certify first the connection to a public road, and that this road authority will only certify this provided it has an agreement with the developer. The negotiations and the sealing of the contract might take place before the issuing of the planning permit (*decyzja o warunkach zabudowy*, DWZ) in case there is no MPZP, or after it but before the issuing of the building permit. In any case, the certification of the road authority is needed to obtain the building permit, which implies that the contract must be signed before.

policy base prescribing the road infrastructure, but only the vague and too-flexible legal requirements about connection of the building to public infrastructure that govern the issuing of planning permits (*decyzja o warunkach zabudowy*, DWZs). In most cases, if this form of NDO is applied, municipalities require just a minimum package of infrastructure (only the connection to the public road, or improvements in the public road directly needed because of the development, although sometimes, in larger developments, the improvements do also serve other developments). A common practice in smaller developments is to give a permit without a real access to the infrastructure (no sewage, no road). The road may be just a theoretical one (not paved, just drawn on a plan) (Zaborowski, 2018). In order to 'repair' this, municipalities must pay themselves the infrastructure, or try to obtain a contribution from landowners through the previously mentioned betterment charge.

- Formal N-NDOs (*opłata adiacencka*): this levy can be used to charge owners that profit from two sorts of public decisions on land-use regulations: decision on plot subdivision and on land readjustment. First, this *opłata* can be charged in case of an administrative decision on land subdivision (*podział nieruchomości*), requiring a payment of at most 30% of the value increment due to this decision. This sort is somehow effective, but has many limitations[2] and often municipalities just avoid their application (Rumińska, 2015). Second, this *opłata* can be charged in case of a public decision of the local council on land readjustment (*scalenie i podział nieruchomości*), which does almost never occur (see next section for more details about LR in Poland) (Jędraszko, 2005).

- New formal N-NDOs: in 2015, a new Act on Revitalisation (*ustawa o rewitalizacji*) enlarged the possibility, in prescribed revitalization areas with a land-use plan (*miejscowy plan rewitalizacji*, MPR, a special sort of MPZP) to require contributions from developers: the land-use plan may impose the obligation of a contract between the municipality and the developer (*umowa urbanistyczna*) in which he commits to contributions. This contract is a condition for the issuing of the building permit. The contracts with the road authority mentioned before also can formally condition the building permit to contributions, but now the scope of contributions can be larger (more than road infrastructure, also indirectly related). Thus far, we have no notice of application of this new provision. The contributions must be prescribed in the land-use plan, so in theory there is no room for negotiation, which makes of it a N-NDO. However, probably the practice will show, if the provision is applied,

---

2 It can be levied only in case of a land subdivision made according to a valid land-use plan (MPZP), and only if landowners apply for it. So, the municipality has to wait passively for their initiative. The levy is due only if the subdivision occurs within three years from the adoption of the MPZP.

that before or during the approval procedure of the land-use plan, the contributions, along with other development conditions, will be the subject of some form of negotiation (which will lack any legislative base in public law, the same as the informal NDOs nowadays). Practice might also show that developers, instead of conforming with higher contributions in these revitalization areas, will prefer cheaper developments elsewhere, leaving this 2015 Act unemployed (Zaborowski, 2018).

Most of the formal DOs mentioned earlier are not very effective, which has stimulated informal negotiated DOs:

• Informal NDOs: there is no formal room for negotiating DOs in Polish public law. Polish municipalities cannot, formally speaking, condition the approval of legally binding land-use regulation decisions on the developer performing any kind of contribution. The only exception to this are the traffic road's contracts mentioned before, which can be an indirect condition to issue the building permit and the *opłata adiacencka* as a condition to plot subdivision and land readjustment. In practice, there is sometimes some discretional room for negotiating DOs in exchange for approval of the land-use plan (MPZP), so municipalities sometimes use this, often at the edge of legal possibilities, to try to obtain some contributions. Sometimes municipalities refuse to modify this plan if the developer doesn't voluntarily undertake the initiative of constructing some infrastructure. This is a sort of informal NDO. Here problems arise when municipalities include such contributions in contracts because they easily can be fought at the courts (Prejs, 2017), so developers must provide the infrastructure before the approval of the MPZP or municipalities must approve the MPZP and trust that the developer will indeed construct the infrastructure afterwards. This means that often these NDOs are not agreed on paper, but only orally or in a unilateral letter of intent of the developer. Further, the relevance of these informal NDOs must be relativized because most of new buildings in Poland are not erected in areas covered by land-use plans, but are made possible with ad hoc planning permits (DWZs). These permits are issued both in urban areas as well as on agricultural or natural land; in 2012, 80% of all new buildings were erected with such permits (Kowalewski et al., 2014: 9). These permits have thus become the main regulatory mechanism of the Polish land-use control (Izdebski et al., 2007). The decision of granting such DWZ leaves in practice no room for municipalities to informally negotiate any contribution, because applications for DWZs cannot easily be rejected.[3]

3 The tool of the DWZ was theoretically envisaged to be issued only in consistently built-up areas that do not require any land-use plan because they have an easily recognizable

3. Embedment of DOs in forms of governance in urban development

The predominant form of governance in Poland is private land development. Public bodies, especially municipalities, do only develop land if they own it already and are willing to develop it.[4] Instead, municipalities more frequently prefer to sell the land (full property or land-lease) to developers. Buying land to develop it is often financially not feasible for Polish municipalities, and when this is feasible, municipalities avoid it because of transparency and corruption risks.

Municipalities can exercise a pre-emption right to acquire the land (the price is established by the market), but pre-emption is only possible in a limited number of cases (buying back leased public land, historical monuments, land needed for public uses and especially land in designated urban regeneration areas) (Zaborowski, 2018). If public bodies want to expropriate land for public infrastructure, there are two cases. The first case is 'soft' infrastructure (e.g. schools, green, public facilities) for which necessary land can be expropriated only through the normal procedure, which is long, complex and expensive because the compensation due is based on the future use and building possibilities. The only alternative is thus to negotiate with the landowners and pay high prices. The second case is road infrastructure which, the same as railways and airport infrastructure, follows a special expropriation procedure, much faster than the first.

Public-private land development is not common. Poland disposes of a land readjustment regulation (*scalenie i podział nieruchomości*), but it is almost not used in practice.[5] So, DOs in Poland, in so far as used in practice, are used in private land development.

---

pattern of development that can easily be continued by all new buildings. The requirements to obtain these permits are, in theory, the presence of neighbouring buildings, of an access to a public road and technical infrastructure, as well as conformity with agricultural and forest land protection rules. In practice, due to permissive legislation (both national agricultural and forest protection legislation, and secondary legislation – governmental orders), judicial interpretation and lack of official standards of infrastructure equipment, issuing these ad hoc permits without an access to a paved road, sewage system and public amenities, and located on greenfield land not adjoining buildings, is common (Izdebski et al., 2007).

4 In the western parts of the country after WWII, much land was distributed among the state, municipalities and public institutions. Until now, public institutions possess here vast amounts of land (e.g. Wrocław), which makes much easier to conduct an active planning policy. To the contrary, in the central and southern parts of the country, the majority of the land is private (e.g. Cracow). A special case is Warsaw, where because of the destruction of about 80% of the city during the war, a special governmental decree was introduced (s.c. *dekret Bieruta*) that nationalized all inner-city land (but not buildings). However, owning the land does not automatically mean that municipalities deploy active land policies, as the case of Warsaw shows.

5 Land readjustment (*scalenie i podział nieruchomości*) may be implemented only in areas covered by a binding land-use plan (MPZP). It may be ordered by local authorities or by the

As mentioned before, a dichotomy exists in Poland between developments with land-use plans (MPZPs) and with ad hoc planning permits (DWZs). Most new buildings are authorized through the second option; in 2012, 80% of all buildings (Kowalewski et al., 2014: 9). Polish municipalities are in general in a weak negotiating position (if compared with municipalities in other countries that can formally condition land-use regulation decisions to DOs). This is for sure the case in developments outside land-use plans, because here municipalities cannot easily refuse issuing the ad hoc planning permits. But also in building projects within legally binding land-use plans (MPZPs), the negotiation position of Polish municipalities is weak because the approval of these plans cannot formally speaking be used as leverage in the negotiations. Most of the time, municipalities approve the land-use plan before there is any specific development initiative (i.e. before the developer submits an application for a building permit), so when municipalities and developers come to speak, land prices have already capitalized value increases. At that time, only negotiations are allowed with the traffic road authorities to provide a basic package of road infrastructure in exchange for the building permit, and if municipalities want to realize other public infrastructure, they must pay it themselves (buying the land and paying the construction costs). Expropriation is not an alternative because municipalities can only expropriate land needed for public uses (and not the entire development area), and the fast special expropriation procedure is reserved for traffic authorities in charge of constructing roads, railways, airports or anti-flood installations.

There is thus a strong interdependency between landowners and municipalities that does not stimulate development: landowners are comfortable with waiting because the land-use plan is already approved (or, in areas without land-use plan, because they are certain about obtaining an ad hoc planning permit), and high expectation values are already capitalized in the market and serve as collateral. As a consequence, most of the time, developers of privately owned land only provide a minimum package of the most indispensable road infrastructure. In small developments made possible through ad hoc planning permits (DWZs), the situation is even worse: local access roads are often not even paved.

---

landowners of at least 50% of the land (LR then becomes obligatory for the rest, although in the case of a built-up area, all owners must consent). However, despite the fact that there is the possibility of compulsory LR, in practice LR is almost not used because the procedure is hard to impose on landowners. Another important problem is financing. Local authorities may recover their overhead costs only if the land readjustment was initiated by landowners. Landowners have to pay the statutory betterment charge mentioned before (*opłata adiacencka*), which cannot charge much. But the municipality must pay 100% compensation for the land acquired for public uses, in compliance with the expropriation regulations (see earlier). In sum, LR is not advantageous for municipalities, and landowners prefer a piecemeal urban development in which they obtain a maximum price for their land and do not need to coordinate actions with other landowners (Zaborowski, 2018).

4. Evolution and dynamics: NDOs vs. N-NDOs

As mentioned in previous sections, the ineffectiveness of almost all PVC tools in Poland (including DOs), and the resulting lack of public infrastructure and facilities, is stimulating the introduction of more informal tools, which imply some degree of negotiations.

Regarding DOs, we saw that there exists in Poland only the formal possibility to condition minor land-use regulations (but not the land-use plan) to some sorts of contributions. This makes DOs in Poland less effective, because public bodies cannot easily threaten to refuse development and developers are more certain about their development rights. Of the few actually used DOs, the most effective one is actually the only formal NDO, i.e. the possibility for traffic road authorities to negotiate the construction of a basic package of roads in exchange for a building permit. Of the two other formal DOs (*opłata adiacencka* in plot subdivision and in land readjustment, sort of N-NDOs), the only actually applied in practice is the first. And finally, although the approval of the land-use plan (MPZP) does, formally speaking, not offer room for negotiating contributions, sometimes some form of negotiations take place that end in some forms of contributions. However, the limitations are large, as up to now there is no legal basis for such negotiations in public law.

The 2015 Act on Revitalisation introduced the possibility for the municipality in urban revitalization areas of conditioning the granting of the building permit to a contract. The previously mentioned traffic roads contract is similar, but here it is the traffic authority, and not the municipality, that seals the contract (although in practice, often both fall under the authority of the mayor). Another new element is that the new contributions can be larger (they can go further than only a basic package of access roads, and do not need to be directly connected to the development). In theory, these contributions must be prescribed in the land-use plan and are not negotiable, but in practice, this might end up into negotiating DOs previously to the approval of the land-use plan. The chances are, however, also high that developers will prefer cheaper development sites outside these revitalization areas and leave the new provision un-used (Zaborowski, 2018). So far, this provision has not been applied in practice.

Although, in general, a more critical stance against the effects of laissez-faire is heard in politics, there seems not to be in Polish governments enough understanding of the deficiencies of free markets in urban development. Therefore, we don't dare to predict radical changes in the near future.

5. The scope of obligations, its evolution in time and the rationales behind it

As far as used, DOs in Poland do sometimes provide some income which is not earmarked and is freely expendable for any goal, both 'hard' and 'soft' or 'social' infrastructure, even if there is no connection with the development (for example, the only formal N-NDO which provides some results in practice, the *opłata adiacencka* in plot subdivision). More often, however, DOs (formal and informal) only provide some 'hard' infrastructure directly related to the development, mostly roads. The generated sources must thus serve a public purpose, be connected to the development and be earmarked. The new N-NDOs introduced in the 2015 Act on Revitalisation in the future might offer the opportunity of requiring contributions towards 'soft' and off-site infrastructure as well.

In general, DOs are not proportionally allocated among all developments because their use is irregular, depending on whether and how the municipality deploys them in practice.

6. Transparency about the use of DOs and possible negotiations

Of all DOs in Poland, the only somehow effective ones (the formal N-NDO *opłata adiacencka* in plot subdivision and the formal NDOs negotiated with the road traffic authority in exchange for the building permit) are to a certain extend transparent. In both the contributions are known beforehand (the *opłata* fixes the rate beforehand for the whole municipality, and the requirements of the road traffic authority must be strictly connected to the development). They are, however, not fully transparent (the appraisal of the value increase in the *opłata* is often questionable, and traffic authorities have some room of interpretation of what is strictly connected to the development). Development possibilities are transparent when there is a valid land-use plan beforehand, MPZP (always the case with the *opłata* and sometimes with the contracts with traffic authorities, but not when these contracts are made pursuant to a planning permit, in areas without MPZP). In both cases, the final contributions are public (both the paid *opłata* and the contract with the traffic authority are public). So we could conclude that at least in areas covered with a land-use plan, the main parameters surrounding the application of both DOs and the possible negotiations around them seem to be quite transparent, at least compared with other countries.[6]

The findings thus suggest a certain causal relationship between transparency and effectiveness of DOs. However, we must be nuanced about this conclusion, because DOs in general – even those two somehow effective DOs mentioned earlier – do not provide much results (generally the *opłata* provides modest revenues and the traffic roads contract only a basic package of road infrastructure, and the rest of DOs almost nothing). This is because of two variables. First, that transparency might be only apparent,

---

6 In many countries, there is not even a land-use plan approved before DOs are deployed, contracts are not public, etc. See Chapter Conclusion.

not truly transparency, because DOs are not 'certain', in the sense that it is not certain whether municipalities will apply them. As a matter of fact, municipalities often do not apply DOs (or apply them with minimum rates), even though in theory they should. In other words, if DOs are applied, they might be applied in a relatively transparent framework, but as they are 'evitable' they send a wrong message to the developers and landowners, who often anticipate on the possibility of not having to contribute at all. The second variable explaining the poor results of DOs is that Polish municipalities are not allowed to condition the land-use plan to obligations (see earlier).

7. Conclusions

In a country where since the fall of the Berlin Wall in 1989, private land development is the predominant form of urban governance, municipalities do depend largely on agreement with landowners to capture land value increase and finance public infrastructure. The planning levy (*opłata planistyczna*), based on direct rationales, prescribed a generous public capture of land value increase, but little attention seems to have been paid to its effective implementation, which has led to its general failure. Municipalities must therefore support on other PVC tools that are generally not effective because legislation took much care in avoiding any link between the contributions and the public decisions on land-use plans, and does not offer in public law any legal base for negotiations. Municipalities, therefore, cannot threaten to refuse developments – and hence have neither much leverage to offer nor the formal possibility to engage in negotiations with developers. This has very much limited the deployment of DOs. Landowners have often much certainty about their development possibilities without the obligation to commit to much contributions, which results in land speculation (many empty urban plots, despite the high demand for urbanization) and poorly provided urban development. Many Polish cities still rely on the public infrastructure constructed during the socialist times, without private developments since then having significantly contributed to public urban quality. Since 2015 the legal possibilities to obtain obligations in urban regeneration areas are larger, but it is uncertain whether this will provide many results in practice.

References

Izdebski, H., Felicki, A. & Zachariasz, I. (2007), *Zagospodarowanie przestrzenne – polskie prawo na tle standardów demokratycznego państwa prawnego*. Warszawa: Ernst & Young.

Jędraszko, A. (2005), *Zagospodarowanie przestrzenne w Polsce – drogi i bezdroża regu-lacji ustawowych*. Warszawa: Unia Metropolii Polskich.

Kowalewski, A., Mordasiewicz, J., Osiatyński, J., Regulski, J., Stępień, J. & Sleszyński, P. (2014), 'Economiczne straty i społeczne koszty niekontrolowanej urbanizacji w Polsce – wybrane fragmenty raportu', *Samorzad Terytorialny*, Vol. 4, pp. 5–21.

Marmolejo Duarte, C. & Plocikiewicz, M. (2012), 'El derecho de superficie sobre suelos públicos: el caso polaco', *Ciudad y Territorio-Estudios Territoriales*, Vol. XLIV, No. 172, pp. 299–313.

Nelicki, A. & Zachariasz, I. (2008), 'Planowanie przestrzenne a udział podmiotów prywatnych w budowie infrastruktury publicznej. Rozwiązania polskie a wybranych krajów UE i USA', *Samorząd Terytorialny*, Vol. 10, pp. 29–41.

Prejs, E. (2017), Presentation in 11th Annual Conference International Academic Association Planning, Law and Property Rights, Hong Kong, China, February.

Rumińska, M. (2015), *Skuteczność poboru opłat planistycznych i adiacenckich jako skutków planowania miejscowego w subregionie ciechanowskim* (*The Effectiveness of Planning and Betterment Levies Collection as Result of Binding Local Planning in Ciechanów Subregion*), Master Thesis at the Faculty of Geography and Regional Studies, University of Warsaw, 28 October.

Zaborowski, T. (2018), 'Land Acquisition and Land Value Capture Instruments as Determinants of Public Urban Infrastructure Provision: A Comparison of the Polish Legal Framework with Its German Counterpart', in *Geographia Polonica*, Vol. 91, No. 3, pp. 363–379.

7   The Netherlands

Developer obligations towards cost recovery

Demetrio Muñoz Gielen

1. Introduction

In the Netherlands, the Civil Code prescribes full enjoyment of owned property, and there is no legislation giving to the public the land value increase caused by a change to the permitted land use or otherwise (Needham, 2007: 154–155). Besides tax legislation (capital gains tax and property tax), the Dutch legislature has regulated several times in planning law (the last one through the 2008 Physical Planning Act, *Wet ruimtelijke ordening*) the possibility of capturing land value increase, but only for the sake of 'cost recovery', i.e. the recovery of those costs of public infrastructure and facilities that benefit the owner and are necessary because of the building on his property, thus an indirect rationale. As a consequence, PVC tools (except perhaps the property tax, *onroerende zaak belasting*, OZB, which provides presently around 8% of the total municipal incomes) support only on this indirect rationale.

Besides developer obligations (DOs), capital gains tax and property tax, there are also two other PVC tools: the property tax in Business Investment Zones and a betterment contribution. The first is based on the Experimental Act on Business Investment Zones (*Experimentenwet BI-zones*), which allows the property tax to be increased in a specific area and the extra revenues to be earmarked for public infrastructure in that area. So far, it has not been applied often, maybe because it requires majority support of the business in the area (Schep, 2012: 305–306, 499). Municipalities can also charge a betterment contribution (*Baatbelasting*) on landowners when public infrastructure is constructed that directly serves their properties. It covers the costs of local, site-specific, on-site public infrastructure. Large public infrastructure, especially if located off-site, cannot be charged through this tax. It does not consist thus of charging the land value increase, but only a share of the infrastructure costs. There is no connection with land-use regulations decisions; all landowners which profit from the public infrastructure must pay, whether their properties regard consolidated urban uses or become developed into new real estate. This betterment contribution is used only very rarely. It is unanimously characterized as too complex, risky and an insufficient way of financing public infrastructure, even local infrastructure (Sorel et al., 2014: 40–41).

So besides capital gains tax and property tax, the only other relevant PVC tools in the Netherlands are developer obligations.

2. Non-negotiable developer obligations

Non-negotiable developer obligations (*exploitatiebijdrage* prescribed in the development contributions plan, *Exploitatieplan*) were introduced in the Netherlands in the 2008 Physical Planning Act. In case land-use regulation decisions rezone land (e.g. from agricultural to any urban use, or from industrial to housing) and/or increase the building possibilities (e.g. from single family dwellings to an apartment building), and provided that there are costs to be made for public infrastructure which have not yet been secured,[1] the municipality *must* approve a development contributions plan together with the land-use regulation decision (*bestemmingsplan*, or in some cases, *omgevingsvergunning* and *ontheffing*). The 2008 Act and the 2008 Physical Planning Decree (*Besluit ruimtelijke ordening*) regulate in detail the costs that can be included in a development contributions plan and charged to landowners: mostly local, site-specific, on-site public infrastructure. Large public infrastructure, especially located off-site, can only to a limited extend be charged to the landowners. There are examples of municipalities charging this off-site infrastructure to landowners through a development contributions plan, but judicial scrutiny is limiting this practice so as to allow only charging a relatively small share (Buitelaar et al., 2012: 63–65). Besides, especially in urban regeneration areas, the appraisal methods of land prescribed in the 2008 Act and Decree often further diminish the amount of costs that can be charged to landowners and might even end up forcing municipalities to grant subsidies to the landowners.[2]

Once the costs that can be charged to landowners have been calculated, and once the development contributions plan is approved together with

---

1 Costs are 'secured' when there is certainty that there is, or will be, financial means available to pay them.
2 These appraisal methods presuppose that landowners bought their land for the market value of the future, more profitable building and use possibilities. This translates to the presumption that landowners already made large investments in land, even though they actually bought the land long beforehand for a much lower price. Through the residual calculation method, the development contributions plan concludes then that there is a deficit, even though in reality the landowners paid much less for the land and have a considerable profit. As municipalities are not supposed to pass financial losses to the landowner, they must subsidize the deficit. Thus, municipalities may be forced to subsidize while landowners collect a substantial share of the land value increase.

the new land-use regulation, municipalities can make granting the building permit conditional on a contribution. This is the first time in the Netherlands that a land-use regulation decision (only the granting of the building permit, not the previous modification of the land-use plan) can formally be made conditional on paying a contribution. After a landowner receives a building permit, he must pay the contribution; otherwise, the municipality can withdraw the building permit. In this sense, municipalities can compulsorily charge these costs on landowners: if landowners ask for a building permit but do not pay, they cannot build. Because municipalities can unilaterally impose this charge, which is not negotiable, this contribution is a N-NDO.

Besides the statutory N-NDOs, there are the more popular negotiated DOs.

3. Negotiated developer obligations

Dutch municipalities have the legal possibility of negotiating developer obligations (*exploitatiebijdrage* and *bijdrage ruimtelijke ontwikkeling*) in a development agreement (*anterieure overeenkomst*). Here, the municipality and the developer agree who is going to pay for the public infrastructure. This contract is voluntarily negotiated and sealed before the approval of the new land regulation (*bestemmingsplan*, or in some cases, *omgevingsvergunning* and *ontheffing*). In case this contract indeed secures all costs to be made for public infrastructure, it is not necessary anymore to prescribe N-NDOs in a developer contributions plan. A development agreement (*anterieure overeenkomst*) securing all costs excludes thus the possibility of charging N-NDOs. If a development agreement does not actually secure all costs, it is actually not considered an *anterieure overeenkomst*, and there is thus still the legal obligation for municipalities to prescribe N-NDOs through a development contributions plan.

3.1 Larger value capture through NDOs than through N-NDOs

A development agreement supports mainly on private law, but its contents are to some extent also regulated in public law: the 2008 Act and Decree provide rather vague indications about the scope of NDOs and about which sort of policy the municipality should introduce to support these NDOs. In addition, during parliamentary approval of both Act and Decree, some discussions took place that made clear that the meaning of the law was not to negotiate contributions towards maintenance and operational costs of public infrastructure. But this legislative and parliamentary framework still leaves much room for negotiation, so there are larger possibilities to charge public infrastructure through negotiated development agreements than through the N-NDOs (those prescribed in a development contributions plan). Until now, jurisprudence has only confirmed that there is indeed larger room through negotiations, but it does not clarify the limits, and further, there are no governmental directives. Interpretations of the jurisprudential, legislative and parliamentary framework state that local policy should at least prescribe in a transparent way which infrastructure is charged, why and how these costs are allocated in an equal way to each development (e.g. Muñoz Gielen et al., 2016: 535–536). However, there are many other unclear aspects, and there is neither much writing nor unanimity on what the contents should be of this policy and how far municipalities should negotiate (Muñoz Gielen & Lenferink, 2018: Section 3.2.4).

As a consequence of this, provided that municipalities introduce specific policy that properly underpins the contributions (although it is not entirely clear what 'properly' means), they are allowed to negotiate with property developers a contribution for public infrastructure far more generous than allowed through a development contributions plan. For example, municipalities can negotiate a much more generous contribution for large infrastructure located off-site (for an overview of which costs can be charged through development agreements that cannot be charged through development contributions plans, see Muñoz Gielen, 2010: 228–234). This is one of the reasons that explains why in practice municipalities approve so few of these plans (in total, 120 from July 2008 to July 2011, Buitelaar et al., 2012: 62) and instead prefer to use development agreements.

3.2 Conditioning land-use regulations to NDOs is not allowed

Although municipalities are allowed to negotiate contributions, following the Dutch rule of law, property developers cannot be obliged to negotiate an agreement. Public bodies do not have the statutory powers to refuse modifying the land-use regulations only with the argument that the developer is not willing to negotiate. Dutch municipalities have thus no statutory powers to formally condition land-use regulation decisions to the developer signing a development agreement. Because of this Dutch particularity, in the Netherlands, municipalities do not dare to modify land-use regulations in an early stage because once they are modified, municipalities have no leverage anymore – so municipalities wait first until the development agreement has been negotiated and sealed. In practice, thus, municipalities do often condition the land-use regulation decisions to the developer agreeing to contribute through this contract. Up to the moment in which the land-use regulations are brought into the public decision-making process, not much – if any – publicity is given to the details of the developer's initiative and the negotiations (Muñoz Gielen, 2010: 241–242; Buitelaar et al., 2011: 938–940). This behaviour is sometimes explained as the consequence of Dutch municipalities pursuing public control of urban development more than in other countries (e.g. Buitelaar & Sorel, 2010), but the mentioned Dutch legal peculiarity might play a more relevant role.

3.3 Lack of transparency

As mentioned, municipalities and developers negotiate developer obligations prior to the moment in which the land-use regulations are brought into the public, formal decision-making process. So, until that time, not much – if any – publicity is given to the details of the developer's initiative and the negotiations. After the negotiations, municipalities must publish a summary of the development agreement, but not the full document itself. In practice, the legal framework leaves room for municipalities to avoid disclosing important details.

4. Rationales behind the scope of obligations

In case of N-NDOs, contributions must fulfil three criteria: the development must profit from the infrastructure (*profijt*), there must be a causal connection between the development and the infrastructure (*toerekenbaarheid*) and the costs of this infrastructure must be allocated proportionality to all profiting developments, included the existing urban fabric (*proportionaliteit*). These criteria limit the possibilities of charging off-site infrastructure through a development contributions plan – and of course, all contributions are earmarked: they can be spent only for this infrastructure, not for other goals.

In case of NDOs, the rationales are less clear, as there is almost no legal framework limiting their scope. There is some agreement about that judges, based on the 2008 Physical Planning Act, the Civil Code and administrative law (*Algemene wet bestuursrecht*), if confronted with such cases, will at least require that the infrastructure is needed, has a public purpose, is somehow related to the development and is somehow proportionally allocated among developments, and that contributions are earmarked so they cannot be spent for other purposes. Further, there is the expectation that judges will require some degree of transparency from municipalities. So, there is with NDOs much more room than with the three criteria governing N-NDOs mentioned earlier. For example, there is no need of a direct connection or of a causal relationship between development and infrastructure. Jurisprudence has, however, so far not clarified very much.

5. Economic appraisal feasibility obligations

In the case of N-NDOs, there is detailed legislation that prescribe whether contributions are economically feasible. As mentioned earlier, N-NDOs are prescribed in a development contributions plan. The municipality must prepare and approve this plan, which includes a residual calculation of all development costs and profits. The municipality must prove that the landowner can pay the contributions, taking into account all costs and profits. The municipality must thus appraise, among other things, the value of the land, which is considered as part of the costs. The basis for the appraisal of the land value is the market value, not the real price paid by the developer. The expropriation law (*Onteigeningswet*) and related jurisprudence prescribe appraisal methods of the land value. In general, it could be said that developers are quite confident with these methods, probably in the first place because these methods tend to appraise a high value for the land, and thus limit the amount of contributions (if costs are higher than profits, municipalities cannot charge contributions).

In case of NDOs, there are no legal prescriptions about whether and how contributions should be economically feasible. This is left to the negotiations. Although the Netherlands has a well-developed profession of land appraisers, the wide range of possible departing points (mainly the question whether the value of the actual or the future use should serve as basis) frequently leads to diverging appraisals and disagreement in the negotiations.

6. Embedment of DOs in passive governance approaches

In the Netherlands, DOs are most of the time deployed in private land development, thus when developers own the land and develop it. Both N-NDO and NDO depend here on some form of agreement. In order to be able to charge N-NDOs, the developer must be willing to ask for a building permit, and in order to charge NDOs, the developer must be willing to negotiate them and sign a development agreement. There is thus interdependence among municipalities and developers, and this interdependence is high because there are no efficient land policy instruments to avoid it.

If a developer does not cooperate, municipalities can only threaten with expropriating the land. The sequence of events is than as follows: if a developer does not agree to negotiate NDOs, the municipality can approve a development contributions plan and prescribe in it the contributions to be paid in exchange for a building permit. If the developer does not apply for a building permit, or does it but does not pay, the municipality can expropriate him and must end up paying a high compensation. Compensation sums following the expropriation law (*Onteigeningswet*) and its jurisprudence are high. They include all possible damage suffered by the owner (e.g. the damage of ceasing business activities, or of having to move the business to other location), but also the value of the most profitable use of the land: the actual or the future use possibilities. Land must be appraised based on land transactions in the surroundings or in similar contexts, transactions which most of the time internalize the future development possibilities and often even include a surplus price (developers often pay high prices for development land as a way to guarantee a negotiation position). With other words, compensations are based on real market prices that internalize speculative expectations, and not on theoretical or modelled prices.

If landowners sell their land, municipalities also have pre-emption rights (*voorkeursrecht*) that allow them to buy it first. Compensation sums are based, the same as expropriation, on the most profitable use possibilities of land, but do not include other damages, so compensation can be cheaper than expropriating that land.

Expropriation is used very rarely, mainly because it is expensive for municipalities (but also because, from a political point of view, it is not a very popular instrument). It is used only in very specific cases, mostly in public or in public-private governance approaches, when after years of negotiations, only one or a couple of landowners still refuse to agree. Preemption rights are more popular in these approaches, when municipalities develop land alone or together with developers. Both expropriation and pre-emption rights are rarely used in private land development.

7. Scope of obligations, and evolution with time

In the Netherlands, private land development has a relatively short history. Until the end of the 1980s, most land development was undertaken by public bodies, and since then the share of private land development, and thus the use of DOs, is gradually increasing. Until 2008, there were no legal means of unilaterally enforcing obligations on private developers (so there were no N-NDOs), and the possibilities of negotiating contributions were not always clear. In case municipalities asked for contributions *in pecunia*, i.e. payments, the scope was limited to on-site, 'hard' public infrastructure like roads, urban green spaces, etc. For example, payments towards off-site hard infrastructure, or for any kind of social housing or facilities, were not allowed. There was more room in case municipalities negotiated contributions in kind, i.e. that the developer constructs the infrastructure. The little available evidence suggests that municipalities were negotiating a barely minimum amount of on-site, hard infrastructure (Muñoz Gielen, 2010: 227–228, 265–271). It is possible. however – but again, there is no much evidence on this – that in public-private land development, municipalities were negotiating larger contributions from developers (both *in pecunia* and in kind).

Since the introduction in 2008 of the Physical Planning Act, it is possible to unilaterally prescribe hard, on-site infrastructure, social housing on-site or a share of off-site hard infrastructure. Regarding negotiated contributions, they can include a larger share of off-site infrastructure and some sorts of social infrastructure besides social housing; for example, cultural facilities. However, maintenance and operational costs of public infrastructure are excluded.

8. Moment prescription obligations: the economic 'incidence' of developer obligations

In case of local, on-site hard infrastructure, contributions are usually prescribed quite late in the process: mostly, after developers submit a plan and the municipality studies its impact. At that time, developers usually already bought the land, or at least agreed on the land price with the landowners. Also, at that time, the future use and building possibilities are most of the time quite clear because municipalities use non-legally-binding policy documents for approval in early stages that give an idea where and what will be possible to build in the future.

In the case of large, off-site infrastructure, the situation is diverse. About one-fourth of all Dutch municipalities do approve local non-legally-binding policy documents that prescribe contributions for large infrastructure to be paid by all developments in certain areas or in the whole municipal territory (Muñoz Gielen & Lenferink, 2018: Sections 4.1–4.2). Thus, here these contributions usually are prescribed before developers buy the land, submit a plan and start to negotiate with municipalities.

There are no available data about the economic incidence of DOs. It is reasonable to conclude that when municipalities prescribe contributions beforehand, developers tend to internalize their contribution into land prices and/or their profit margins. For sure, developers are more willing to contribute when contributions are prescribed beforehand.

9. Empirical evidence of actually obtained obligations

In practice, development contributions plans (*Exploitatieplan*) are not providing significant resources for financing public infrastructure. First because, as said earlier, the possibilities of charging the costs of off-site, not site-specific large infrastructure are very limited. Second, because the appraisal methods of land can in some cases lead to the need for public subsidization. And third and most importantly, because this instrument is not used frequently: the last available figures show that up to July 2010, municipalities used it in only 3% of all building plans (Buitelaar et al., 2012: 62). No signs since then suggest any significant increase in their use. Actually, many municipalities show disappointment with their results, which suggest that their use might actually even diminish. Instead, municipalities prefer to recover the costs of public infrastructure through negotiated development agreements.

Regarding the negotiated DOs, there is some agreement about that municipalities are succeeding in capturing the basic package of on-site, site-specific hard local infrastructure (Buitelaar et al., 2010: 63, 2012: 62–63). Development is not possible without this infrastructure and its costs can often be compulsorily charged through a development contributions plan, so it seems reasonable to conclude that development agreements are including at least this minimum. Regarding large public infrastructure, often located off-site, it seems that only one-fourth of municipalities are negotiating and obtaining contributions. Its seems, however, that their relevance, although growing, is not large (Muñoz Gielen & Lenferink, 2018: Sections 4.1–4.2), at least when compared with countries with larger traditions of negotiating contributions, e.g. England.

References

Buitelaar, E., Bregman, A., Van den Broek, L., Evers, D., Galle, M., Meijer, T. & Sorel, N. (2012), *Ex-durante evaluatie Wet ruimtelijke ordening: tweede rapportage*. The Hague, The Netherlands: Planbureau voor de Leefomgeving, p. 126.

Buitelaar, E., Bregman, A., Van den Broek, L., Evers, D., Galle, M., Nieuwenhuizen, W. & Sorel, N. (2010), *Ex-durante evaluatie Wet ruimtelijke ordening*. The Hague, The Netherlands: Planbureau voor de Leefomgeving, p. 133.

Buitelaar, E., Galle, M. & Sorel, N. (2011), 'Plan-Led Planning Systems in Development-Led Practices: An Empirical Analysis into the (lack of) Institutionalisation of Planning Law', *Environment and Planning A*, Vol. 43, pp. 928–941.

Buitelaar, E. & Sorel, N. (2010), 'Between the Rule of Law and the Quest for Control: Legal Certainty in the Dutch Planning System', *Land Use Policy*, Vol. 27, pp. 983–989.

Muñoz Gielen, D. (2010), *Capturing Value Increase in Urban Redevelopment*. Leiden, The Netherlands: Sidestone Press.

Muñoz Gielen, D., & Lenferink, S. (2018), 'The Role of Negotiated Developer Obligations in Financing Large Public Infrastructure After the Economic Crisis in the Netherlands', in *European Planning Studies*, Vol. 26, No. 4, pp. 768–791.

Muñoz Gielen, D., Nijland, H. & Van der Heijden, T. (2016), 'Openbaarheid en verantwoording onderhandelingsresultaat gebiedsoverstijgende kosten', *Tijdschrift Bouwrecht* 2016/79, afl. 10, pp. 534–542.

Needham, B. (2007), *Dutch Land-Use Planning: Planning and Managing Land-Use in the Netherlands, the Principles and the Practice*, Den Haag: Sdu Uitgevers, p. 299.

Schep, A. W. (2012), *Naar evenwichtig bijzonder kostenverhaal door gemeenten*. Delft: Eburon, p. 539.

Sorel, N., Tennekes, J. & Galle, M. (2014), *Bekostiging van publieke voorzieningen bij organische gebiedsontwikkeling*. The Hague, the Netherlands: Planbureau voor de Leefomgeving.

8 The influence of politicization on the implementation of developer obligations in a federalist country

Evidence from Switzerland[1]

Sébastien Lambelet and François-Xavier Viallon

1. Introduction: a federalist framework favouring diversity of implementation

Switzerland is a federal state composed of three governmental levels: the Swiss Confederation, the cantons as member states, and the municipalities. Federal laws are elaborated and decided by the national parliament, but their implementation remains in the hands of cantons and municipalities. Such decentralized enforcement has often allowed subordinated authorities to interpret federal laws in a way defending their regional and local interests, even if such interpretation contradicted the initial will of federal authorities (Delley, 1982; Rieder et al., 2014).

In matters of land-use planning, the Confederation had no competence until 1969, when the federal government was granted a general planning competence to ensure an economic use of the land (Article 75, Swiss Constitution). Economic and federalist milieus perceived this new article as a necessary evil to tackle urban sprawl, but conditioned their political support on the joint adoption of a constitutional guarantee of ownership (Art. 26, Swiss Cst.) (Nahrath, 2003). The cornerstone of constitutional Articles 26 and 75 is the 'tax on added land value' created by zoning (*taxe sur la plus-value/Mehrwertabgabe/compensazione del plusvalore*), defined in the Federal Spatial Planning Act (FSPA) of 1980 (Nahrath, 2005). This instrument, a sort of N-NDO, is based on a direct rationale, as it aims to tax landowners benefiting from favourable planning measures, in order to compensate landowners suffering from economic losses due to unfavourable planning measures. However, its implementation faced strong opposition in numerous cantons and municipalities. Out of 26 cantons, only Basel and Neuchâtel

1 Research work for this publication has been funded by the Swiss National Science Foundation (Grant numbers 143057, 140366, and 162157, p3.snf.ch). Alphabetical order reflects equal contribution of both authors.

have implemented this compensation mechanism in their cantonal legislation prior to the 2010s. At the local level, municipalities, which are in charge of adopting land-use plans in most cantons, either zoned land without defining value recovery mechanisms, or negotiated local development plans with contextually defined negotiable developer obligations (NDOs).

Besides federalism and the extensive protection of property rights, the opposition of local and cantonal politicians to anchor N-NDOs in federal legislation, such as the tax on added land value, can also be explained by the 'consociational' nature of Swiss politics (Sciarini, 2014). Neo-corporatist arrangements between authorities, interest groups and political parties, a widely spread culture of negotiation and the possible use of the referendum against laws and land-use plans result in consensus-driven solutions tailored to the local context. However, local authorities often lack the resources and political will to demand substantial financial compensation from developers. For instance, in canton Bern, municipalities negotiate obligations with developers (infrastructure contracts), but often have trouble getting more than the standard financial participation in basic infrastructure, such as roads, water supply and sewers (Viallon, 2017: chap. 4). In canton Vaud, some municipalities which have been pioneers in levying infrastructure taxes beyond those defined in federal legislation (Berta, 2016), were suddenly challenged by a developer in 2007, with the argument that there was no cantonal legal basis for such practice. To solve this problem, Canton Vaud became in 2011 the first, and so far, only canton, to create an 'extended land service tax' (*taxe sur les équipements communautaires*). The instrument is legally defined as an N-NDO charged with modification of land-use regulation, and includes financial contributions to school buildings, public transport infrastructure and green spaces. However, this N-NDO is implemented by local authorities which may in practice negotiate the tax amount with developers, as shown in one of our cases.

2. The revised Federal Spatial Planning Act (FSPA) of 2014

The previously mentioned examples of negotiated obligations in Bern and Vaud show how the N-NDO introduced in the federal law of 1980 (the non-negotiable tax on added land value) has been either implemented through more flexible NDOs, or simply ignored by local actors. In the absence of nationwide studies or statistics, the phenomenon remains difficult to quantify precisely. During recent decades, several cantons and municipalities have continued to create new constructible areas instead of sparing land resources, as required by the federal constitution. As a result, about one-fifth of the country's constructible areas are not effectively constructed (Federal Council, 2013: 27).

This led to a substantial revision of the FSPA aiming to preserve agricultural land and stop urban sprawl. This revision was accepted by 62.9% of the Swiss voters in March 2013, and entered into force in May 2014.

Since then, the FSPA has slightly moved towards a logic of direct rationale. It made the tax on added land value compulsory when rezoning agricultural areas into urban, and stipulated a minimum taxation rate of 20% of the land value increase. In case of other land-use regulation decisions (e.g. upzoning in existing constructible areas), the federal law encourages a rate of 20%, but cantons are free to set their own taxation rate (see Figure 8.1). Finally, tax revenues can also serve to protect agricultural land and fund urban renewal, rather than only compensate wronged owners. Cantons have to adapt their legislation by 2019, as otherwise the moratorium on the extension of building zones introduced by the new FSPA remains in force.

Figure 8.1 reveals an interesting phenomenon: 15 cantons out of 26 do not set any minimum taxation rate in existing constructible areas, and explicitly grant in their legislation the possibility for municipalities to negotiate the taxation rate through ad hoc contracts signed with developers. In doing so, these cantons encourage their local authorities to continue within a framework of NDOs, despite the 2014 federal act, which encourages cantons to set up a minimal taxation rate of 20% within constructible areas. Basel and Neuchâtel, which have implemented the tax on added land value for decades, are the only cantons exceeding the 20% threshold. So, in a nutshell,

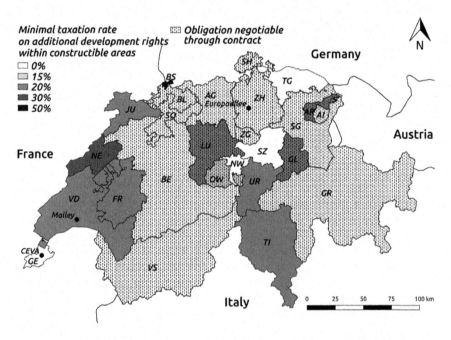

Figure 8.1 Minimal taxation rate collected through the tax on added land value on additional development rights within existing constructible areas per canton (as of September 2017)

Source: ASPAN (2017) Own representation.

Figure 8.1 clearly demonstrates that despite a strong federal will to apply the same N-NDO over the whole territory, diversity of implementation and NDOs contracted at the local level remain the rule in Switzerland.

3. The impact of politicization on the implementation of DOs

Given the wide spread practice of negotiating DOs with developers through contracts, we argue that the type of compensation mechanisms and the amount of land value obtained by local governments – if there is any – strongly depends on the local political context. In particular, we claim that, in the presence of a high level of politicization, i.e. when the project generates conflicts between authorities and developers, as well as debates in the public arena, local authorities are empowered to constrain developers to accept more DOs. On the contrary, in the absence of conflicts and public debates, local authorities are in a weak position for negotiating with developers.

To test our argument, we investigate three major urban renewal projects conducted by the Swiss Federal Railways (*Schweizerische Bundesbahnen*, SBB) in the agglomerations of Zurich, Lausanne and Geneva (see Figure 8.1 for their locations). Focussing on the SBB allows us: a) to isolate the impact of the local context, as the same developer is present within different projects, and b) to study a developer who is constrained by the federal government to generate profit. Indeed, since 1999, federal authorities have transformed the SBB into a state-owned limited company and require them to generate a minimal annual real estate profit of 150 million CHF (130 million EUR),[2] in order to finance national railway infrastructure. As a result, the real estate division of the SBB seeks profitability, similarly to any private developer. Moreover, since the FSPA aims to densify around public transport axes where the SBB owns most of its land, this federal law reduces the ability of cantonal and municipal governments to negotiate DOs with SBB. In this context, let us see what the outcomes of the negotiations regarding DOs in three major SBB projects were.

3.1 Europaallee *in Zurich (Canton Zurich, ZH)*

The first project is called *Europaallee* and aims to create a new central business district (CBD) next to Zurich's main train station. By 2020, the site will host 6,000 workplaces, a high school with 2,000 students, 300 dwellings and other public facilities. The SBB has invested around 1.5 billion CHF (1.3 billion EUR) in the project, but this amount will already be amortized

---

2 The exchange rate used in this chapter is 1.15 CHF per EUR. It is based on the average exchange rate fluctuation between August 2017 and July 2018.

at the end of construction work, thanks to the Municipality of Zurich, which increased the density rate of the area by 22% compared to the highest density zone of the municipal zoning law. This special measure generated an added land value of approximately 320 million CHF (278 million EUR), and the city government forwent the opportunity of taxing it.

The main reason that pushed the city government to offer such a good deal to the SBB was its delight to finally achieve urban renewal around the main train station, after several renewal projects had failed since the 1970s. The only concern of the city government was to guarantee the attractiveness of the new CBD. It gave the aforementioned zoning exceptions to the SBB on the sole condition that a specific international architectural competition should be organized for each building, with members of the municipal administration seating in the jury. Based on this guarantee, the City Council accepted the land-use plan. The far-left party in the local council was the only one opposing the project, and launched a referendum against it. After a rather timid campaign, 65.5% of the local voters approved the new CBD in September 2006.

Significant opposition against *Europaallee* emerged only after the inauguration of its first buildings in 2012. In response, other sites planned by the SBB in cooperation with the city government included one third of affordable housing or comprised participatory processes with inhabitants. However, the SBB still makes comfortable profit with these projects.

3.2 Malley *in Lausanne (Canton Vaud, VD)*

The second project deals with the redevelopment of *Malley*, an industrial backyard in the agglomeration of Lausanne, located in the suburban municipalities of Renens and Prilly, in canton Vaud. By 2025, the site is due to host about 2,700 new inhabitants and 5,000 new workplaces.

More than half of the land plots of *Malley* belong to the SBB, and the remaining to the Municipality of Lausanne. This peculiar situation led to tensions between Prilly, Renens and cantonal authorities, acting as planners on the one hand, and Lausanne and the SBB, acting as developers on the other. The first tensions appeared in 2008 around the density rate of the area. After tough negotiation, Prilly and Renens gave a substantial increase of the overall density rate to compensate use restrictions next to the railways, in accordance with legal requirements on the transportation of dangerous goods.

Other tensions appeared a couple of years later, when Renens introduced the extended land service tax mentioned in the introduction. Lausanne and the SBB heavily contested the use of this new instrument, arguing that their public status exempted them from this taxation. Legal expertise was collected on both sides, but, in the end, both parties agreed on the payment of a lump sum to avoid going to court. The landowners agreed to pay 50% of the costs related to infrastructure (12 million CHF, 10.5 million EUR) and part of the construction costs of public buildings (700,000 CHF, 609,000 EUR), which amounted to 20–25% of what the extended land service tax (in theory a N-NDO) would have obtained.

Finally, the City Councils of Prilly and Renens, while debating on the land-use plan, increased the pressure on previously negotiated DOs and decided to increase the total number of dwellings and to introduce a minimal amount of social dwellings (15% subsidized dwellings and minimum 35% dwellings with controlled rent prices). Then, the City Council of Prilly proposed a referendum on the project's land-use plan. This strategy was successfully used as a mean to fix definitely the required DOs, and to confront the opposition of some inhabitants directly in the public arena, as the referendum ended up in November 2016 with 58% of local voters supporting the project.

3.3 CEVA *in Geneva (Canton Geneva, GE)*

The third project aims to construct a 16-kilometre suburban railway line in Canton Geneva and to create new neighbourhoods around its main stations by 2019. Called *CEVA*,[3] this project has received the support of the Swiss Confederation since 1912, but the two world wars and the golden age of the automobile delayed it until the 1990s. When it reappeared on the agenda, the project became highly politicized, as parties strongly disagreed on the route of the future railway line.

To decrease the level of politicization, the cantonal government engaged in tripartite negotiations with the federal government and the SBB. After tough negotiation, the cantonal government managed to reactivate the convention of 1912, stipulating that the Confederation assumes 57% of the 1.6 billion CHF (1.4 billion EUR) costs of the railway line. Moreover, for each *CEVA* station, Canton Geneva, the municipality where each station is located and the SBB created a public-private land corporation to jointly elaborate the land-use plans around the stations. The Canton and the SBB, which owned the land around the future stations, made the following deal. The Canton created high-density zones above the future underground stations, thereby generating an added land value of 178 million CHF (155 million EUR) on its own land plots and on the ones of the SBB. Then, the cantonal government urged the SBB to reinvest the entire land added value in the railway infrastructure. The SBB accepted on the condition that the Canton transferred all his plots of land to the SBB free of charge.

Surprisingly, the cantonal parliament did not discuss these land arrangements when it approved the funding of *CEVA* and its related zoning modifications. This matter was also absent from the highly ideological referendum

---

3 This acronym comes from *Cornavin–Eaux-Vives–Annemasse*, which are the names of some stations that will be served by the suburban train.

campaign of 2009, which ended up with a 61.2% popular support for *CEVA*. However, we expect that criticism might come when public opinion notices that public infrastructure in the new neighbourhoods, as well as the annual exploitation deficit of *CEVA* (30 million CHF, 25 million EUR) will be at the expense of the Canton, whereas the SBB will benefit from very profitable rents generated by hundreds of dwellings and thousands of workplaces on plots given by the Canton.

4. Discussion and conclusions

The comparison of the three cases in Table 8.1 shows a clear trend regarding the effect of the projects' degree of politicization on the amount of DOs contracted with the SBB. In line with our hypothesis, *Europaallee* is the project with both the lowest politicization and the fewest DOs, whereas *CEVA* is the exact opposite. *Malley* fits in the middle of the continuum on both variables. Thus, it seems that, despite a federal legal framework pushing for more non-negotiable compensation mechanisms, case-by-case contract negotiations remain the standard way of elaborating land-use plans in Switzerland. As the example of the extended land service tax in *Malley* shows, developers can even negotiate N-NDOs during the elaboration of these contracts.

Therefore, city governments still need to be challenged by their City Council or by other local actors to constrain developers to contribute more. In the absence of such public debate around projects, city governments tend to consider that realizing projects increasing the attractiveness of their municipality and maintaining good relations with developers for future projects is more important than obtaining a substantial share of DOs. More than a lack of ability to constrain developers, we thus observe a lack of political willingness of local authorities to do so. This trend is not specific to our cases and has been observed in several other projects in Switzerland. The strategy of public bodies to use their land property to generate new revenues that we observe with the SBB and the Municipality of Lausanne, is also increasingly used all over the country since the turn of the millennium (Nahrath et al., 2009; Viallon, 2017).

In this context, the public-private land development approach of *CEVA* has to be considered as an exception linked to the very high politicization of the project. It led to a short-term deal whereby the entire added land value was used in one shot to finance *CEVA* and prevented the negotiation of any other DOs. This case shows that a high politicization can also be counterproductive for the implementation of DOs, since local authorities use land added values in the short term to finance projects at the top of the political agenda, without contracting any other DOs in the longer term.

In sum, our study shows that negotiations between local elected officials and developers within a moderately politicized environment (as in the *Malley* case) seems to be the most accurate solution for implementing DOs in Switzerland. However, this method is mostly project-based, and prevents

Table 8.1 Comparison of three SBB projects on key variables of the analysis

Project	Europaallee – Zurich	Malley – Lausanne	CEVA – Geneva
Total gross floor area allowed	322,300 m^2	52,500 m^2	196,000 m^2 (in three different locations)
Land added value, in million CHF	320 (estimation)	24[4]	178 (estimation)
Level of politicization (independent variable)	Low	Middle	High
Negotiation between local authorities and developers	Quick, leading to a 'carte blanche' for the SBB	Long and enduring	Tough and multi-level
Intensity of debates in the public arena	Low, even with the referendum	Under control of local authorities (self-activation of the referendum)	Very high concerning the railway infrastructure, but rather low regarding densification around stations
Obtained obligations (dependent variable)	Very few NDOs: – guarantees regarding architectural quality – part of basic infrastructure paid by the SBB	The SBB and Lausanne pay: – through NDOs: 50% of basic infrastructure – through an a priori N-NDO: 20 to 25% of the extended land service tax Social housing: 15% subsidized and 35% with fixed rental prices	The entire added land value is captured by a public-private land assembly to finance the railway infrastructure, but Canton Geneva relinquishes part of its properties and assumes other infrastructure costs in the area

local authorities from generating long-term land rents to compensate wronged owners as required by the FSPA, or to cover maintenance costs of public infrastructure.

4 As it was the result of a land exchange between the SBB and the Municipality of Lausanne, this land added value does not reflect the development potential of the Malley area, and cannot be compared to the two other projects.

Moreover, if local authorities can mobilize N-NDOs, like the extended land service tax in the case of *Malley*, they can enhance the amount of value recovered from a development project. Yet, the implementation of N-NDOs remains rare and highly controversial (see the minimal rates of Figure 8.1). As a result, most local governments avoid the use of N-NDOs and generally negotiate case-specific DOs bilaterally with developers, together with the amount of development rights. Then, they reinvest the tax proceeds directly on the site of the same development project, thereby making developers the primary beneficiaries of the obligations they pay.

The use of DOs in Switzerland has to be further analyzed by future research, especially after 2019, when all cantons will have adapted their cantonal legislation to the prescriptions of the 2014 FSPA. Our research reveals that so far, the way of implementing DOs remains weak and flexible in most parts of Switzerland, since local governments lack resources and political will to use policy instruments to constrain developers to more obligations. However, several city governments (e.g. Biel and Bern, BE, and Nyon, VD) elaborate a more active and enduring governance approach. They adopt land banking strategies, mobilize public landownership and use time-limited property rights such as emphyteutic leases to reverse the balance of power. By doing so, they gain additional control on future land uses and benefit from the land value induced by their zoning policy (see Lambelet, 2016; Gerber et al., 2017).

References

ASPAN. (2017), *Prélèvement de la plus-value dans les différents cantons. Comparaison des réglementations cantonales (état au 21.9.2017)*. www.vlp-aspan.ch/sites/default/files/comparaison_reglement_cantonales_a3_170921_0.pdf.

Berta, E. (2016), 'Nyon ou la recherche de l'équilibre par les conventions', *Collage*, No. 3, pp. 16-20.

Delley, J-D. (1982), *Le droit en action*. Saint-Saphorin: Georgi.

Federal Council. (2013), *Explications du Conseil Fédéral. Votation populaire du 3 mars 2013*. www.bk.admin.ch/themen/pore/va/20130303/index.html?lang=fr.

Gerber, J-D., Stéphane N. & Hartmann, T. (2017), 'The Strategic Use of Time-Limited Property Rights in Land-Use Planning', *Environment and Planning A*, Vol. 49, No. 7, pp. 1684–1703.

Lambelet, S. (2016), 'Le déclin comme atout et la croissance comme handicap', *Métropoles*, No. 18. https://metropoles.revues.org/5320.

Nahrath, S. (2003), *La mise en place du régime institutionnel de l'aménagement du territoire en Suisse entre 1960 et 1990*. Lausanne: Université de Lausanne. http://doc.rero.ch/record/501.

———— (2005), 'Le rôle de la propriété foncière dans la genèse et la mise en œuvre de la politique d'aménagement du territoire', in Da Cunha, A., Knoepfel, P., Leresche, J-P. & Nahrath, S. (eds.), *Enjeux du développement urbain durable*. Lausanne: PPUR, pp. 299-328.

Nahrath, S., Knoepfel, P., Csikos, P. & Gerber, J-D. (2009), *Les stratégies politiques et foncières des grands propriétaires fonciers au niveau national*. Cahiers de l'IDHEAP 246 et 247. Chavannes-près-Renens: Swiss Graduate School of Public Administration. https://serval.unil.ch/notice?pid=serval:BIB_2FB6FC5EF27C.

Rieder, S., Balthasar, A. & Kissling-Näf, I. (2014), 'Vollzug und Wirkung öffentlicher Politiken', in Knoepfel, P., Papadopoulos, Y., Sciarini, P., Vatter, A. & Häusermann, S. (eds.), *Handbook of Swiss Politics*. Zürich: NZZ, pp. 563–598.

Sciarini, P. (2014), 'Processus législatif', *Handbook of Swiss Politics, op. cit.*, pp. 527–562.

Viallon, F-X. (2017), *Redistributive Instruments in Swiss Land Use Policy*, Lausanne: Université de Lausanne. https://serval.unil.ch/notice/serval:BIB_E738FB9AFB2A.

9 Developer obligations for public services

The Italian mix

Laura Pogliani

1. Introduction

In Italy, non-negotiable and negotiated developer obligations (N-NDOs and NDOs) are both in use, but with a conspicuous variation in their quantity and in the emphasis on their justification over the years.

In the boom years of the 1960s and 1970s, the improvement of urban life and compensation for the existing severe social inequalities were the main planning aims. The capture of increased land value from public actions and decisions was a strong political issue that influenced the introduction of a specific taxation and of an N-NDO (Falco, 2016), although the argument of direct rationale was not included in the legal framework that admitted them only as a compensation of social costs (Campos Venuti & Oliva, 2010). More recently, the housing markets crisis and the shrinkage of public national finances have seriously limited public works. Accordingly, local plans have introduced the possibility of negotiating extra funds for urban facilities, negotiations that are often poorly regulated in the regional framework. These NDOs support on an indirect rationale, too.

This chapter investigates first the integration of N-NDOs and NDOs into the Italian planning system, with the international debate on urban development practice as background (Ingram & Hong, 2012; Crook et al., 2016). Then, it presents two cases in the Milano metropolitan area that integrate different types of obligations added with an exploratory introduction of direct rationales in value capture.

2. Developer obligations and urban planning

The relation between developer obligations and urban planning is rooted in the national Planning Law n.1150/1942, still in force, which sets up the *Piano Regolatore Generale* (PRG, General Regulatory Plan), a legally binding land-use plan covering the whole municipality. This law gives local authorities the faculty to expropriate land, with the state initially providing the funds, to locate public infrastructure and facilities prescribed in the plan. After expropriation, municipalities elaborate detailed land-use plans (the

Piani Particolareggiati Esecutivi, PPE, executive detailed plans) to implement the general plans. Both expropriation and detailed plans were seldom
applied.

Institutional contradictions and pressure to change in the boom years
opened the door to mandatory land and monetary contributions in urban
developments. Their rationale originated from the 1948 Italian Constitution, which acknowledges property ownership provided it fulfils substantial
public purposes (as a mixed set of rights and responsibilities). Their rationale also drew from the 1942 Planning Law, which claims no compensation
for zoning regulations and allows land expropriation for the use of social
services.

2.1 Mandatory non-negotiable developer obligations in
local planning

Following a long public and political debate, parliament passed the law
n.765/1967 and the decree 1444/1968 to introduce two paramount inno-
vations: *i.* a new planning tool, the *Piano di lottizzazione convenzionato*
(PLC, private agreed allotment plan), which acts as a Land Readjustment
Plan in the case of fractioned ownership; *ii.* N-NDOs, named *aree per standard urbanistici e attrezzature di interesse generale* (compulsory dedication
of land for infrastructure and urban facilities at neighbourhood and urban
scale). These N-NDOs were extended to the whole municipality and were
prescribed in the PRG.

Standard urbanistici consist of land earmarked for public uses and for primary services in all residential, offices, production and retail developments,
for present and future needs. Giovanni Astengo, an influential scholar and
expert town planner, defined them as the "minimum level of urban civili-
zation" (Astengo, 1967: 4), the answer of the social state to the primary
needs of society. *Standard urbanistici* were mainly implemented through
expropriation (except some through PLC, see further) and consist of a
minimum 18 m²/inhabitant for public services (parks and public gardens,
schools, libraries, religious sites, parking lots, etc.) and an additional minimum 17.5 m²/inhabitant in larger urban centres (more than 20,000 inhabitants) for higher education, health centres and large scale public parks.
Some recent regional laws have recognised a larger and more varied range
of public facilities, including social housing, residential units for university
students, cycle and pedestrian paths and start-ups. Non-residential functions must likewise contribute with parking lots, green areas and special
facilities. This being a minimum quantity, regional legislation has the faculty
to raise it, and some regions did. Also, local authorities are allowed to ask
for a higher share, without any need to compensate landowners.

The PLC is a detailed local land-use plan, consistent with the mandatory
PRG regulations for development areas. It covers mainly private buildings
and tends not to include much of the public infrastructure and facilities

prescribed in the PRG (which follow the *standard urbanistici*). Landowners must sign a formal agreement with the municipality that allocates development rights and requires a proportional quantity of land dedication and monetary charges to pay the urbanisation costs and to contribute to the construction of public infrastructure and facilities (for so far as they are included in the PLC). Most buildings prescribed in PRGs (but not so much the public infrastructure and facilities) have been successfully implemented through PLCs and agreements.

National law 10/1977 further strengthened private contributions by establishing the *concessione edilizia onerosa* (recently renamed as *permesso di costruire*), a building authorisation subject to payment of fees (*oneri di urbanizzazione*), proportionally to the volumes, uses and to the location. Any private intervention, included or not in a PLC, for new construction, renovation or modification of use, must obtain such authorisation. Regional regulations and criteria prescribe these fees, which are thus N-NDOs. In some cases, reduction or exemptions are provided to support urban regeneration (as opposed to urban sprawl) or to supply social housing.

An additional fee (*contributo sul costo di costruzione*), which is also non-negotiable, is proportioned to the construction costs of the private building itself and is paid before the construction begins. At the beginning, it was aimed to contribute to public infrastructure, but for more than a decade, local authorities are allowed to use it (better: misuse it) to meet a large range of municipal costs and to cover general budget deficits.

All three N-NDOs (*standard*, *oneri* and *contributo*) have effectively produced a betterment in the urban welfare in the boom years up to the 1980s, albeit more successful policies have been accomplished in Northern and Central Italy (INU, 2016).

See Table 9.1 for the legislative base of these N-NDOs and role of national, regional and local public bodies.

Table 9.1 Responsibilities for N-NDO at the three levels of government

	State	Region	Municipality
Land dedication *(aree a standard urbanistico)*	National minimum quantity areas Decree 1444/ 1968	Regional minimum quantity areas (can increase national minimum)	Local minimum quantity areas in comprehensive Plans (can increase regional minimum)
Urbanisation charges *(oneri di urbanizzazione)*	General requirement Law 10/1977	Criteria for municipalities	Local ordinance (paid when the building permit is issued)
Construction charges *(costo di costruzione)*	General requirement Law 10/1977	Criteria for municipalities	Local ordinance (paid when the construction starts)

The crucial problem lied with expropriation that remained as the prevalent way for public bodies to obtain land for public uses. Since the expropriation values were progressively paired to market values, a significant number of areas dedicated to urban facilities and planned in the PRGs were not implemented. One important point is that, outside expropriation, there were no compensation mechanisms for those landowners who had to deliver their land. Therefore, in the mid-1990s, the Istituto Nazionale di Urbanistica (an association of professional and academic experts) proposed the introduction of the *perequazione* tool into the planning system, to grant equal building rights to all landowners and significantly reduce the need of expropriating land. *Perequazione* consists of a sort of transfer of development rights: owners of land that has been zoned for public infrastructure and facilities (and has not been obtained through PLC or expropriation) are given some development rights, and owners of land that has been zoned for building who want to build above a certain basic threshold must buy development rights from landowners who must deliver their land for public uses (Micelli, 2002; Scattoni & Falco, 2011). *Perequazione* is regulated in regional legislation and prescribed by municipalities, which sign agreements with the developers who want to build. In these agreements, the free delivery is secured of the land meant for public infrastructure and facilities, and sometimes additional obligations are negotiated. At present, the unavailability of a clear mandate in national legislation has not prevented a broad use of the *perequazione* tool in large and medium-size cities, mostly in northern and central Italy.

2.2 Negotiated developer obligations

Minimum N-NDOs are in force in a good part of the country, but they are insufficient because they are generally modest, especially in urban regeneration that usually needs costlier public investments in infrastructure and facilities (Pasqui, 2017). Therefore, NDOs were considered a good solution at a certain time, consistent with new trends in the Italian planning system. Since the 1990s, the top-down, comprehensive plan-led approach is progressively shifting towards a 'planning by agreement' approach, a project-led development (Urbani, 2000). Before the 1990s, negotiations made on a voluntary basis to change planned zoning were officially not permitted, even though they often occurred in practice (Mazza, 1997). Following the real estate market boom between the mid-1990s and mid-2000s, which affected all Italian cities, the 'agreement' procedure has been used more frequently, and partially supported in the context of decentralisation and diminishing local fiscal revenues. Both planning approaches (plan- and development-led) are in use because of the variety of regional regulations, but the attitude towards negotiation has deeply changed.

In accordance with the new trends, few regions prescribed a set of additional negotiated obligations, in order to meet the 'public interest'. In some appreciable cases, city councils (the political board) have approved urban plans that introduced *ex ante* negotiations. Plans give developers incentives (such as higher densities and/or reduction of the non-negotiable monetary contributions) in order to comply with priority planning aims. The 'public interest' consists sometimes of a reduction of the redevelopment times in urban regeneration, other times as additional provision of public infrastructure and amenities. The Lombardia Region – capital city Milano – has actively promoted and practised the integration of negotiation and planning, with controversial outcomes (Pogliani, 2006; Healey, 2007; Arcidiacono & Pogliani, 2013). This region introduced in 1999 a specific planning tool, called *Programmi Integrati di Intervento PII*, to empower local authorities to bargain with developers for both in-kind and monetary additional contributions in exchange for a modification in land-use regulations. In the late 2000s, the Milano Municipality approved approximately 100 schemes with negotiated contributions on an area of 4 million m² and a gross floor area exceeding 2.2 million m². This was mainly earmarked for residential use, encompassing about two-thirds for private units for sale, about one-third for affordable housing units, and a mere 1.4% for public housing for rent (Pogliani, 2014). Land transferred to public property amounts to half of the total, but about one-third of this land consists of parking lots for the shopping malls; the green areas are fragmented and scarcely accessible to pedestrians. The planned services are not designed to suit the real needs expressed by the residents, as they are driven by commercial purposes and very few facilities are additional to the mandatory N-NDOs.

On a countrywide basis, there is no systematic appraisal of the real outcomes of negotiations, but much criticism focuses on the unsustainable outcomes, mainly as regards public interest and control. Developed locally and on a case-by-case basis, in the absence of national guidelines and monitoring, these NDOs generally ignore planning procedures and result in an unsatisfactory balance of public costs and private advantages (Camagni, 2011; Palermo & Ponzini, 2010). The main shortcomings of these NDOs are the lack of transparency in the process, unsatisfactory governance, inadequate technical skills in directing and assessing private proposals, and finally, limited ability to plan public strategic priorities. The economic feasibility studies presented by private developers are usually very poor, because they are limited to assess the scale of private costs and profits for company balance sheets. They are of limited value for local governments, whose skills and training are often inadequate to evaluate them and appraise their fiscal impact on municipal budget in the long run (indirect costs, i.e. transportation, maintenance, pollution) (Curti, 2006).

2.3 Attempts to use DOs based on direct rationales

The Municipality of Roma introduced a *Contributo straordinario per la plusvalenza* (an extra contribution for value increase) in the Roma General

Plan (approved in 2008). A national law came into force (L.133/2014) that formalised and generalised this practice, and the Constitutional Court confirmed its legitimacy. It concerns a minimum 50% of the private profit (thus, it is based on a direct rationale) that local governments can request as an additional contribution to supply public infrastructure, facilities and social housing (Camagni, 2016). Although theoretically non-negotiable, the fact that there is not always agreement about how to appraise the private profit leaves some room for negotiation. Being too recent, discretionary and levied based on scarce regional regulations, it is still difficult to assess its effectiveness, though the two case studies somehow hint at it.

3. Two case studies in the Milano metropolitan area

Both cases are at an early stage, as they have only recently been approved. The negotiations between municipality and private developers are of paramount relevance for understanding the duality between planning and negotiations about value capture in Italy. Besides, they allow some appreciations about the transparency and accountability of negotiations.

Generally, negotiations are non-public and are discussed only at some limited political and administrative levels. When signed and approved, the agreement is public and accessible, although generally the enquiry may ask time and many bureaucratic obstacles. In both Milano developments, however, the guidelines for the agreements have been broadly debated in the city councils and in plenty of public meetings, and the full agreements are now available online.[1]

The first case is in the city of Sesto San Giovanni, just to the north of Milano (Arcidiacono et al., 2016). This city (90,000 inhabitants) grew as a high-density urban centre linked to three major private corporations of heavy industry: Breda, Marelli and Falck. The negotiated plan rezoned the former industrial Falck site (1.3 million m^2) to create new residential, production, retail, shopping and leisure activities (640,000 m^2 of gross floor area) and to provide new infrastructure, services and a wide park, along with a hospital and health research centre of national interest (Figure 9.1). The base of the agreement was set in 1997, and final approval arrived in 2015; meanwhile, market conditions changed, a variety of successive developers and investors appeared and a long political debate in the city council took place. This debate strongly influenced the negotiation process to obtain additional NDOs so that the final agreement includes local public benefit totalling EUR 128 million of N-NDOs and EUR 120 million of NDOs (including some contributions as public land value capture, anticipating the next introduction in law of the *Contributo straordinario per la plusvalenza*).

---

1 See, for example, the agreement in Milan's case: www.comune.milano.it/wps/portal/ist/it/ servizi/territorio/pianificazione_urbanistica_attuativa/progetti_in_istruttoria/scali_ferroviari

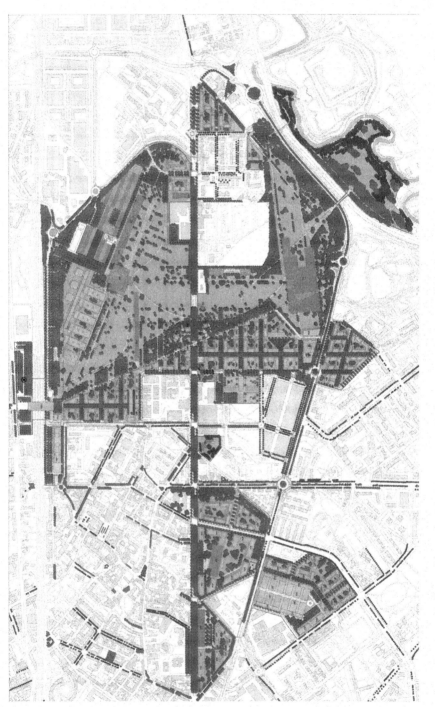

Figure 9.1 Masterplan Falck site

Source: RPBW (Renzo Piano Building Workshop) project 2014 and Variante 2016.

The developers will provide almost half of the total area for green and public services, redesign the railway station and restore old heritage industrial buildings. In accordance with national law, private developers are generally obliged to pay the soil remediation costs as N-NDOs. Since the site falls in a short list of national highly polluted industrial areas, a contribution still came from national and regional funds but the developers are charged to pay most of the total costs of decontamination (EUR 280 million). The total expected profit for the developers from selling the buildings amounts to EUR 4.2 billion; the net revenue, excluding land acquisition cost and all development costs (included all the contributions), is estimated worth EUR 223 million. The fact that this figure is much lower than all DOs together addresses the problem of disposing of reliable studies to appraise development profits in a more accurate way.

The second case refers to the transformation of seven disused railyards in Milano (Figure 9.2). This plan is crucial for the future of the city of Milano and its metropolitan area (respectively, 1.3 million and about 4 million inhabitants) as it realises an improvement both in the public transportation system, including a redesign of sustainable mobility solutions, and in urban liveability (new inclusive neighbourhoods). At the same time, it also illustrates the use of obligations based on direct rationales (Pogliani, 2017). A large political and extremely controversial debate in the city council arose regarding the nature and the public strategies involved in the rehabilitation of these yards that were previously state owned but have recently been privatised (under special bylaws, FS State Railways, owner of the land, acts as a private company and is allowed to sell the land and building rights). This public debate influenced the negotiations with the developer. Finally, the Municipality of Milano, the Region Lombardia, FS State Railways and few private landowners signed a special Program Agreement in July 2017. This agreement acknowledges the value recapture scope and proposes a mix of N-NDOs and NDOs. The total development area covers 1.1 million m^2 in several locations, with a building capacity of 674,000 m^2 for mixed uses. The developers will build one-third of the total residential gross floor area as social and affordable housing for sale and rent, deliver more than half of the total area for parks and public facilities, pay EUR 327 million as N-NDOs (133 million for *oneri*, to pay urbanisation costs, and 194 million for soil remediation), EUR 81 million as NDOs, meant for the improvement of the transport system and the betterment of urban connections, and EUR 50 million as public land value capture (this last contribution was agreed in the draft agreement, which was sealed before the introduction in law of the *Contributo straordinario per la plusvalenza*).

There is, however, criticism about the unknown duration of the project, the variability of market conditions and the controversial use of different methods to appraise the economic feasibility studies. The current demand for greater transparency and public evaluation is of paramount importance, *a fortiori* in this case, because of the most peculiar former public nature of FS State Railways company.

Figure 9.2 Seven Milano railyards

Source: DAStU Politecnico di Milano, 2014.

4. Concluding remarks

Developer obligations are one of the tools for capturing land value and support the realisation of infrastructure and facilities at the local level. An insight into the rich Italian mix of regulations and negotiations raises some relevant questions about their appropriateness and feasibility.

The dedication of land for public facilities (*standard urbanistici*) is a long-standing mandatory provision in municipal plans based mainly on the expropriation mechanism. Despite its partial and fragmented implementation, it has undoubtedly improved housing quality conditions and urban liveability, but they no longer provide enough public infrastructure. The introduction of the *perequazione* tool offers a different perspective, because it proposes to distribute among all urban landowners the building rights and the obligations. Though not embedded in national legislation yet, it is successfully applied in local practice. Likewise, the mandatory fees (*oneri di urbanizzazione* and *contributo sul costo di costruzione*) are crucial to improve public services.

Nevertheless, these N-NDOs do not provide enough results, so municipalities have introduced discretionary and additional contributions (NDOs) in major transformations, as the cases in Sesto San Giovani and Milano show. These NDOs (included the new *Contributo per la plusvalenza*) should be regulated to support social policies (such as affordable housing on-site), to enforce sustainable and energy-saving architecture and to promote time reduction in carrying out urban projects of public interest. A combination of increased N-NDOs and NDOs may act as an anti-cyclic strategy, obtaining higher contributions in times of higher profits.

The success of public-driven strategies in negotiation procedures requires an improvement of political and technical capability (especially more reliable studies on urbanisation and infrastructure costs that allow calculating the feasible size of obligations) to guide and govern development, to avoid risks of corruption and inequality among actors, and to lead to a transparent public discussion.

The two major projects in the Milano metropolitan area presented in this chapter reflect a successful negotiation, because finally a notable share of negotiated obligations related to public priorities has been added to the mere dedication of land and fees that are mandatory by law. They also suggest that greater transparency and accountability through a wide public debate with local stakeholders regarding the goals of such obligations and their link to the development plan are highly recommended.

References

Arcidiacono, A., Bruzzese, A., Gaeta, L. & Pogliani, L. (2016), *Governare i territori della dismissione in Lombardia. Caratteri Contesti Prospettive.* Sant'Arcangelo di Romagna: Maggioli.

Arcidiacono, A. & Pogliani, L. (2013), *Negotiation and Planning in Milano*. Paper in 7th PLPR Conference, Portland, US, March.

Astengo, G. (1967), 'Primo passo', Urbanistica, No.50-51, pp.3-4.

Camagni, R. (2011), 'Risorse per l'azione urbanistica', in Arcidiacono, A. & Pogliani, L. (eds.), *Milano al futuro. Riforma o Crisi del governo urbano*. Milano: Edizioni, pp. 105–124.

—— (2016), 'Urban Development and Control on Urban Land Rents', *The Annals of Regional Science*, Vol. 56, No. 3, pp. 597–615.

Campos Venuti, G. & Oliva, F. (2010), *Città senza cultura*. Bari: Laterza.

Crook, T., Henneberry, J. & Whitehead, C. (2016), *Planning Gain. Providing Infrastructure and Affordable Housing*. Chichester: Wiley Blackwell.

Curti, F. (ed.). (2006), *Lo scambio leale*. Roma: Officina edizioni.

Falco, E. (2016), 'History of Land Value Recapture in Italy: A Review of Planning and Fiscal Measures Since 1865', *Journal of Planning History*, Vol. 15, No. 3, pp. 230–245.

Healey, P. (2007), 'The Struggle for Strategic Flexibility in Urban Planning in Milan', in Healey, P. (ed.), *Urban Complexity and Spatial Strategies*. New York: Routledge, pp. 77–118.

Ingram, G. K. & Hong, Y-H. (2012), *Value Capture and Land Policies*. Cambridge, MA: Lincoln Institute of Land Policy.

Istituto Nazionale di Urbanistica. (2016), *Rapporto dal Territorio*. Roma: InuEdizioni.

Mazza, L. (1997), *Trasformazioni del piano*. Milano: Franco Angeli.

Micelli, E. (2002), 'Development Rights Markets to Manage Urban Plans in Italy', *Urban Studies*, Vol. 39, No. 1, pp. 141–154.

Palermo, P. & Ponzini, D. (2010), *Spatial Planning and Urban Development: A Critical Perspective*. New York: Springer.

Pasqui, G. (ed.). (2017), *Le agende urbane della città italiane*. Bologna: Il Mulino.

Pogliani, L. (2006), 'Pianificare per accordi in Lombardia', in Curti, F. (ed.), *Lo scambio leale*. Roma: Officina edizioni, pp. 100–129.

—— (2014), 'Expanding Inclusionary Housing in Italy', *Journal of Housing and the Built Environment*, Vol. 29, pp. 473–488.

—— (2017), *Infrastructure and Value Capture in Italy and the Challenge of Milano Railyards Agreement*. Paper in 11th PLPR Conference, Hong Kong, China, February.

Scattoni, P. & Falco, E. (2011), 'Equalization and Compensation in Italy: Empirical Evidence for a New National Planning Act', *Planning Practice and Research*, Vol. 26, pp. 59–69.

Urbani, P. (2000), *Urbanistica consensuale*. Torino: Bollati Boringhieri.

10 Spain

Developer obligations and land readjustment

Demetrio Muñoz Gielen

1. Introduction

Public bodies in Spain deploy different public value capture (PVC) tools. The tax upon transfer of property title (*Impuesto sobre Transmisiones y Actos Jurídicos documentados*) and the capital gains tax on land or real property (*Impuesto sobre el Patrimonio*), both collected by regional governments, are very volatile. They depend very much on construction rates, and provided a total of €8,381 million in 2016. Municipalities collect construction fees (*impuesto sobre construcciones y obras* and *licencias urbanísticas*), which are very volatile, too, and also very dependent on construction rates. These fees provided €900 million in 2016. Municipalities collect also a land value tax (*Impuesto sobre el Incremento de Valor de los Terrenos de Naturaleza Urbana* or *impuesto de plusvalías*), a pure land value capture (LVC) tool based on direct rationales that suffered also during the last economic crisis and collected €2,577 million in 2016. It is charged at the moment of transfer of title, and is nowadays severely under pressure because it is not based on real land value increases but on oversimplified appraisals. The most important PVC tool, besides DOs, is the Property tax (*Impuesto de Bienes Inmuebles*), which charges the value of land and buildings and collected €13,454 million in 2016, about 25% of all municipal incomes. This is the only PVC tool which during the crisis increased its revenues (Poveda & Sánchez, 2002: 3; Pedraja & Suárez, 2011: 24; Ré & Portillo, 2011: 15; Voz Pópuli, 2014; El País, 2016, ABC, 2016).

Besides these instruments, public bodies (mostly municipalities, sometimes also regional governments) also use developer obligations (DO), which are most of the time implemented through land readjustment (LR). DOs in Spain consist mostly of N-NDOs, and additionally of some less regulated NDOs.

2. Non-negotiable developer obligations (N-NDOs)

Spain disposes of an extended set of N-NDOs. They are obligatory when development happens through LR (*Reparcelación*), which is often the case, and are prescribed in four different legal sources:

- On-site public infrastructure

    Regional legislation, based on a previous common body of national legislation,[1] prescribes a set of urban standards (*estándares urbanísticos*) about dimensions and quality of on-site public infrastructure (roads, public space, parking places, parks, serviced plots meant for social facilities – the land, not the social facilities themselves) (López Rodríguez, 2007). The amount of land prescribed for public purposes depends on the building density (more infrastructure in compact urban areas than in suburban areas)[2]. The local legally binding land-use regulations (the General Land Use Plan – *Plan General de Ordenación Urbana* – and the Detailed Plan – *Plan Parcial*) prescribe the location, dimensions of the infrastructure, etc. Developers must both cede the land necessary for this infrastructure (*cesiones*) and to construct the infrastructure on it (*cargas de urbanización*).

- Large public infrastructure

    In addition to the urban standards, municipalities can also prescribe in the General Plan that owners of developable land must cede, for free, land meant for large infrastructure serving a much wider area than the development area (*cesiones*). Sometimes this large infrastructure is located inside (on-site) and sometimes outside (off-site) the development area (i.e. to cede land located on-site meant for a large park, or off-site meant for a highway). If located off-site, the owners of the land needed for the large infrastructure become part of the readjustment pool in the development area, sharing the development profits with the landowners of the development area (i.e. they all share together the final serviced building plots in the development area).

- Inclusionary zoning of affordable housing

    Since 1992, municipalities can prescribe in General and Detailed plans a minimum percentage of affordable housing (*reservas de suelo*). Also,

---

1 Spain is a decentralized state, with a system of constitutional parliamentary monarchy. From the 1980s onwards, 17 Autonomous Communities (*Comunidades Autónomas*, from now on 'regions') came into being, each of them with its own parliament and executive power. The decentralization of competences to the regions is such that Spain became de facto a federal state.
2 For example, the 1998 Regulation of the region of Valencia prescribed that with a floor area ratio of 1 m^2 floor space per m^2 land, at least 63% of the plan area must be used for public space (15% for green areas, 20% for public facilities and 28% for roads).

they can specify on which parcels that housing to be built. In Spain, the Basque Country was the first region that introduced in legislation minimum percentages of affordable housing, and also the region that has prescribed so far the highest percentages (75% in developable land and 40% in consolidated urban areas) (Burón Cuadrado, 2006; Muñoz Gielen et al., 2017). The serviced building plots zoned for affordable housing are inscribed as such in the Property Register, so the owner can only develop affordable housing on it. The price of land for affordable housing is regulated and much lower than for free-market housing. All landowners share this burden.[3]

- Public share in betterment

National planning law prescribes that municipalities must capture part of land value increases, on top of all other obligations mentioned previously. This follows the Spanish constitutional principle that 'the community shall have a share in the benefits from the town-planning policies of public bodies' (Section 47, 1978 Constitution). In developable areas, municipalities had until 2007 the right to 10% of the building rights, and from 2007 onwards between 5% and 15%. Landowners are obliged to cede without any charge to the municipality the serviced building parcels that are needed to build this percentage (*cesiones*). Note that they are ceding land, but not building rights, because following planning law, these building rights are not considered to be owned by the landowners, but by the community. Municipalities should earmark these plots to be used only for affordable housing.

The first three sorts of N-NDOs are based on indirect rationales: the internalization of development impacts. The last one is based on a direct rationale: the community must have a share in land value increase. The first one (on-site infrastructure) must be directly connected to the development that contributes; the other three not. All of them need to fulfil a public purpose and are earmarked (though the public share in betterment is not always effectively spent on affordable housing, as it should be), and all of them are distributed proportionally to all landowners, through LR (see Section 4). The first one (on-site infrastructure) is allocated proportionally among all landowners in the development area. The other three are allocated proportionally among all landowners within all development areas within the municipal boundaries.

---

3 Landowners who receive building plots for affordable housing receive more plots than those who receive plots for free-market housing, proportional to the difference in market value.

3. Negotiable developer obligations (NDOs)

Additionally to the previously mentioned N-NDOs, Spanish public bodies can also negotiate contributions:

- Developers can negotiate with municipalities complementary commitments (*compromisos complementarios*). Initially, regional legislation almost did not regulate these NDOs, and some municipalities did so through local, non-legally binding policy. NDOs can include similar obligations as N-NDOs, and in addition, also obligations that cannot be prescribed through N-NDOs (for example, the building of social facilities, not only ceding the land for free, but also the constructions; or payment of pecuniary contributions to the municipal budget). It seems that lately, some regions are tending to regulate negotiations (e.g. region of Valencia).

- If after approval of the General and Detailed plans and the subsequent signing of the Development Agreement, it turns out that the infrastructure provision costs are higher, there is some room to negotiate who is going to pay for them. For example, in the region of Valencia, if infrastructure provision costs exceed 20% of the budget, following planning law, the developer could not charge the additional costs (*costes adicionales*) on the landowners, and he was not obliged to pay them either. However, in practice, developers and municipalities often did negotiate who assumes these additional costs. It seems that municipalities used their statutory powers to approve the Land Readjustment Plan (*Proyecto de Reparcelación*) as a leverage in these negotiations. The Land Readjustment Plan follows the approval of the General and Detailed land-use plans, and is necessary to develop the land. Since 2014, in this region new legislation has made more difficult to negotiate such contributions.

There is not a clear direct or indirect rationale after these NDOs, at least not in legislation and policy. Hypothetically, the first one is keener to follow a direct rationale, and the second one an indirect one. Both NDOs should fulfil a public purpose and are earmarked, but they are not always necessarily connected to the development area, especially the first sort. The second sort is sometimes allocated proportionally to all landowners within the development area, and sometimes paid only by the developer (in some regions, the developer – *agente urbanizador* – and the landowners are not necessarily the same; there developers usually own only part of the land, and other landowners must cooperate with them through compulsory LR).

4. Embedment of developer obligations into land readjustment

Almost all urban development in Spain (especially greenfield and urban extension, but also urban renewal and densification) is implemented through

LR (Muñoz Gielen & Korthals, 2007: 69; Muñoz Gielen, 2010: 125–128). Only some plans are implemented through public land banking and development.[4] Regarding private land development, only urban densification in plots already provided with infrastructure that do not require property readjustment and/or the construction of new public infrastructure is exempted of LR.

N-NDOs are most of the times part of the LR procedures, and their effectiveness depends on the availability of two coercive instruments: compulsory land readjustment and expropriation. In general, despite public bodies having since the 1970s statutory powers to apply compulsory readjustment, only in the 1990s did they begin to apply it more assertively, leading to more effective N-NDOs. Some regions have introduced the possibility of selecting a third party as implementer of LR (*agente urbanizador*), who doesn't need to own land. Here public bodies apply compulsory readjustment with this implementer as beneficiary. This has weakened the position of landowners, who cannot anymore delay LR, and has clearly improved the effectiveness of N-NDOs (Muñoz Gielen & Korthals, 2007). The possibility of negotiating NDOs with different parties wanting to become *agente urbanizador* (municipalities select him in a public tender, after considering different proposals of different developers) seems to have increased the amount of NDOs, too. Other regions have improved the effectiveness of LR and, therefore, of DOs, through the use of expropriation (threatening non-cooperating landowners with expropriation). Expropriation compensations most of the time include the future value of the land, including any subsequent development value, which makes it relatively expensive for municipalities. However, it seems that before the start of the economic crisis in 2007, rocketing housing prices gave landowners more incentive to participate in LR instead of being expropriated, because market prices rose so fast that calculations of compensation sums in expropriation were soon outdated (Muñoz Gielen et al., 2017: 128–133).

Overall, the effectiveness of DOs through LR increases when landowners or the developer (the *agente urbanizador* in some regions) commit in a Development Agreement (a private law contract) to the implementation and payment of DOs. Public bodies have the statutory powers to condition the definitive approval of the detailed land-use plan to the developer signing such an agreement. This was first a choice of municipalities, and thus did not always happen. Since the 1990s, this has been legally prescribed, so landowners and developers must always back both N-NDOs and NDOs in a development agreement. This has improved the amount of obligations (Muñoz Gielen, 2010: 284).

---

4 Strategic developments, e.g. large industrial sites, some public facilities, social housing and other individual cases; large infrastructure, e.g. highways, railways, airports, seaports, etc.; and some urban renewal projects with strategic importance, mostly in the oldest or more distinctive urban historic areas.

5. Evolution of and dynamics between N-NDOs and NDOs

The central Spanish government introduced in 1975 and 1976 the urban standards (on-site infrastructure), the first sort of N-NDO mentioned in Section 2. They were intended to remediate the dramatic lack of public infrastructure in urban development in the 1960s. During the 1980s and 1990s, the other three sorts N-NDOs were introduced (large infrastructure, inclusionary housing zoning and additional land value capture). In the 1980s the use of poorly regulated NDOs increased because N-NDOs did not provide enough resources. NDOs provided additional contributions to the existing N-NDOs (thus not jeopardizing them) and improved, through the development agreement, the commitment of developers to the effective implementation (construction or payment) of the contributions. Since the mid-1990s, the use of NDOs has increased because of booming real estate markets and because a modification of the LR regulation in some regions (of which Valencia was the first) introduced more competitiveness among landowners and developers that strengthened the negotiation position of municipalities. With time, NDOs have been criticized because of a lack of transparency and this seems to lead to regularization into new, additional N-NDOs.

6. Transparency negotiations and effects of transparency on effectiveness of DOs

Negotiations in Spain take place in a highly regulated context. First, planning law prescribes that all future development possibilities must be prescribed in the legally binding, local General Land Use Plan, which must cover the entire municipal territory. Spain deviates here from many other countries, where, before the negotiations, future building possibilities, if prescribed, are not prescribed in detailed, legally binding zoning plans as is the case in Spain, but in more vague, non-legally binding policy documents (Muñoz Gielen, 2010: 88–91; Janin Ravolin, 2017: 9–12). Thanks to this, possible additional use and building possibilities that result from negotiations are easy to identify.

Second, there is a high certainty beforehand about the N-NDOs, which are prescribed in regional legislation and later on in the local, legally binding land-use plans. This is often before developers buy the land. Only the mentioned NDOs are not always known beforehand and can be negotiated. Because N-NDOs have a legal status, and are most of the time approved beforehand, developers in general accept them without discussion (Muñoz Gielen & Tasan-Kok, 2010). In theory, prescribing obligations before or at least together with the land-use regulations lowers land prices, which could explain why developers accept these obligations without controversy, but there is no empirical evidence of this. Sometimes, NDOs are prescribed beforehand in local, non-legally binding policies, thus before land-use regulation decisions. However, they might also be prescribed after the land-use plans are approved. Finally, there is overall a high formal transparency about the results of negotiations because development agreements (the full document) are public and available online.

7. Empirical evidence of actually obtained obligations

In general, Spanish municipalities obtain for free the legal urban standards of local, on-site public infrastructure: between 30% and 60% of the surface of development areas in peri-urban sites with low urban density, and 60%–80% in urban areas with higher density. Also, municipalities obtain the serviced building plots needed to build the legal percentage of building rights that belong to the community (10% until 2007, between 5% and 15% since then).[5] This also seems logical, as these standards and percentages are prescribed in regional and national legislation and municipalities are not allowed to diverge from them. There are no discussions or controversy regarding their obligatory character, and all developers internalize them from the start in their designs and financial calculations.

Those N-NDOs of which achievement depends on the municipality being willing to operationalize them (large public infrastructure and inclusionary housing zoning) show different results, however. Regarding the possibility of prescribing to developable land the free cession of the land needed for large public infrastructure, the results are different. Large municipalities seem to have quickly taken advantage of this statutory power, while the experience in small, rural municipalities shows a more nuanced picture. Here municipalities did initially not use this statutory power and as a consequence, municipalities have not obtained much. However, they are increasingly using these statutory powers. Regarding inclusionary housing zoning, a miscellaneous picture arises. The degree to which public bodies zone land for affordable housing as N-NDOs or NDOs is unclear, because the available data does not allow to draw generalizable conclusions. There are many examples of public bodies using inclusionary zoning and obtaining good results in practice, as the case of Vitoria/Gasteiz in Basque Country shows (Gozalvo Zamorano & Muñoz Gielen, 2017).

8. Illustrative case: improving effectiveness LR with an active public approach

The city of Vitoria-Gasteiz (244,000 inhabitants) in Basque Country shows the best results of combining LR with an active public governance approach (Muñoz Gielen et al., 2017). In the 1990s, Vitoria-Gasteiz developed ambitious plans for two large urban expansions on its greenfield surroundings: 'Salburua' (359 ha) and 'Zabalgana' (284 ha). More than 400 private parties

---

5 These building plots must be used for social/affordable housing, but often municipalities do not do such, but sell these plots and use the revenues for other policy goals.

owned around two-thirds of the land, and public bodies owned the rest. The plans included high standards of N-NDOs (much public infrastructure of high quality), regulated both in regional legislation and, complementarily, in the 2001 General Land Use Plan. This General Plan also included the obligation to bear the costs of constructing not only the urban standards but also some additional off-site, large public infrastructure (€64 million). This additional contribution went beyond the minimal legal requirements, and was thus negotiable.[6] In addition to the infrastructure, in 1994, the regional Basque government introduced legal minimum percentages of social and affordable housing, which initially amounted to 65% of the number of housing units in greenfield developments; this figure rose to 75% in 2006 onwards. To meet these percentages, landowners must cede some serviced building plots for free to the Municipality (*cesiones*) and offer additional plots for a regulated maximum price to any developer or housing association wanting to construct social/affordable (*reservas de suelo*). In Salburua and Zabalgana, the 2001 General Land Use Plan prescribed in total 21,742 housing units, of which 70% should be social/affordable units, more than the regional legal percentage of 65% at that time. Thus, this additional 5% needed to be negotiated.

Anticipating that landowners would not easily implement the plans with such high standards (especially the obligations additional to the legal minimal requirements), the municipality prescribed the compulsory expropriation of all those landowners not willing to agree, which resulted thus in an active governance approach. At that time, expropriation was expensive for the municipality, because legislation on expropriation compensated landowners for the future value of their land, including any subsequent development value minus the minimum legal requirements, but not minus the additional negotiated obligations. However, in this specific case, landowners profited more participating in LR than with expropriation.[7] In 2000, after some years of negotiation, most landowners signed a development agreement with the municipality in which they accepted the prescribed

---

6 The urban standards prescribe the free cession of the necessary land for off-site infrastructure, but not bearing the costs of construction.

7 Compensation sums in expropriation at that time were based both on the future development value and the legal urban standards of infrastructure (thus, future development value minus the costs of this infrastructure, excluding the costs of constructing off-site infrastructure) and on the legal requirement of 65% social/affordable housing (but not 70%). However, compensation sums in this case were lower than were the profits of participating in LR for three reasons. First, voluntary participation in land readjustment included the possibility of profiting from later modifications of the land-use plan to allow more possibilities for building, as happened in 2004, 2011 and 2012. Second, voluntary participation avoids the risks inherent in expropriation (the amount and the moment of compensation). Third, escalating housing prices from 1997–2007 gave landowners more incentive to participate, because market prices rose so fast that calculations of compensation sums were outdated. This stimulated the participation of landowners in LR and, thus, diminished the financial risks of the semi-public governance approach (public bodies did not need to expropriate much land).

non-negotiable obligations and the additional contributions. The result was abundant public infrastructure of high quality and the free cession to the municipality of serviced building plots for affordable/social housing. Moreover, landowners assumed the obligation of offering serviced building plots with a low regulated price that were also intended for affordable/social housing. On these plots, together with the plots that belonged to public bodies (initially one-third of the land was in public hands), 15,193 affordable/social units (70% of the total number of housing units) were planned for construction. In 2004, the municipality increased the building possibilities on its land to build 2,831 extra social/affordable housing units (increasing the total to 74%). In 2011 and 2012, new modifications were introduced to the land-use plan to make it possible to increase again the building possibilities; however, little has been built since then because of the economic crisis. Approximately 80% of the total units have been built thus far.

The municipality and the regional government built affordable/social units on their plots, and private parties have done the same on the private plots zoned for social/affordable housing. This combination of LR and an active governance approach (threatening with expropriation and building part of the affordable/social units) resulted in a large amount of social/affordable housing; in the period 2002–2005, approximately 70% of all new housing production in Vitoria-Gasteiz was social/affordable, while the equivalent figures in the whole Basque Country and in Spain were 30% and 8%, respectively (Burón Cuadrado, 2006: 13–14).

9. Illustrative case: improving effectiveness LR with the urbanizing agent

The region of Valencia was the first one to give municipalities the statutory power to select a third party (not necessarily owning land, although most of the times owning at least some) as implementer of LR (the 'urbanizing agent'), and to apply compulsory LR with this third party as beneficiary. This urbanizing agent is thus responsible for the property readjustment and the infrastructure provision. Case *Camino Hondo del Grao*, an old industrial site covering 5.7 ha in the City of Valencia, illustrates the working of this 'Valencian model'.

The 1988 General Land Use Plan foresaw here only some new public roads and a school, but in 2003 a developer proposed to add more public infrastructure and facilities and to rezone the industries into 465 free-market apartments and some offices. The owners of 81% of the land (the former industries) decided then to join together in an association and submit an alternative proposal, which in July 2004 became selected by the local council (see Figures 10.1 and 10.2). That is, these landowners became the urbanizing agent. In the following years, several developers bought the land and took over the role of urbanizing agent. The existing buildings, except three historic industrial buildings, were demolished in 2007.

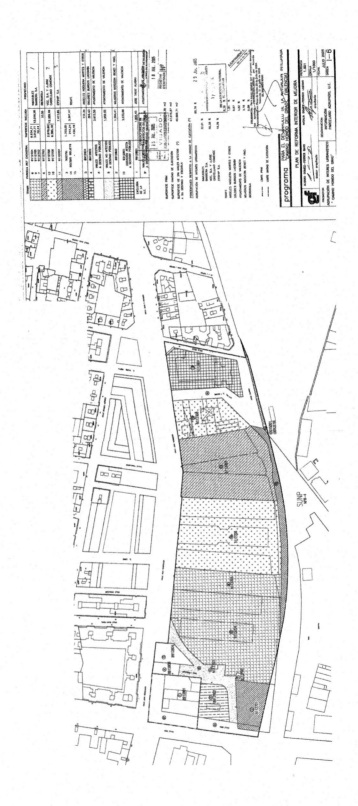

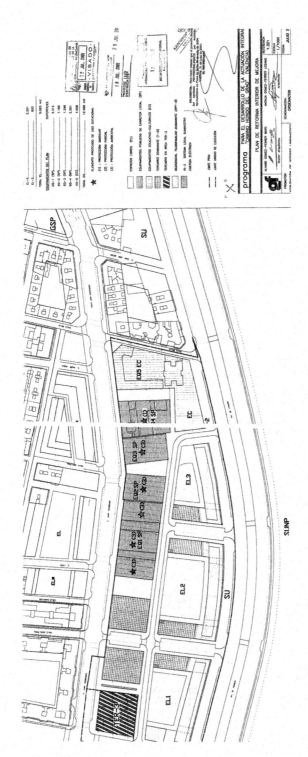

Figures 10.1 and 10.2 Camino Hondo del Grao, former situation and new zoning

Source: PAI 2004.

In addition to the N-NDOs (60% public infrastructure and green spaces, and infrastructure provision), the municipality demanded (based on local, non-legally-binding policy) the free cession and refurbishing of the three historic industrial buildings (refurbishing costs, approx. €4 million), plus a payment of another €4 million. The landowners transferred the historic buildings to the municipality, but, once the economic crisis started, the developer who bought the land went bankrupt without fulfilling the rest of negotiated obligations. Finally, in 2016, the new urbanizing agent (a bank who inherited the land after the developer went bankrupt) agreed with the municipality a payment of both obligations (€8 million, €4 million + €4 million) in kind, in serviced building plots (approximately 10% of the total floor space), which the municipality will use for affordable housing.

References

ABC (2016), *Cuánto ha subido el IBI mi ayuntamiento durante la crisis?* Consulted on-line on 30 October 2017, 12 June.

Burón Cuadrado, J. (2006), 'Land Reserves for Subsidized Housing: Lessons Learned from Vitoria-Gasteiz', in *Architecture, City and Environment*, Vol. 1, No. 2, Universitat Politécnica de Catalunya.

El País (2016), *El impuesto a la propiedad de las viviendas sostiene las arcas municipales.* Consulted on-line on 30 October 2017, 10 January 2016.

Gozalvo Zamorano, M. J. & Muñoz Gielen, D. (2017), 'Non-Negotiable Developer Obligations in the Spanish Land Readjustment: An Effective Passive Governance Approach that "de facto" Taxes Development Value?', in *Planning Practice & Research*, Vol. 32, No. 3, pp. 274–296.

Janin Ravolin, U. (2017), 'Global Crisis and the Systems of Spatial Governance and Planning: A European Comparison', *European Planning Studies*, Vol. 25, No. 6. http://dx.doi.org/10.1080/09654313.2017.1296110.

López Rodríguez, B. (2007), 'Influencia de los estándares urbanísticos en los nuevos desarrollos residenciales', in *Boletín DF+S*, 52/53, pp. 109–178.

Muñoz Gielen, D. (2010), *Capturing Value Increase in Urban Redevelopment.* Leiden: Sidestone Press, 478 pages.

Muñoz Gielen, D. & Korthals Altes, W. (2007), 'Lessons from Valencia: Separating Infrastructure Provision from Landownership', *Town Planning Review*, Vol. 78, No. 1, pp. 61–79.

Muñoz Gielen, D., Maguregui Salas, I. & Burón Cuadrado, J. (2017), 'International Comparison of the Changing Dynamics of Governance Approaches to Land Development and Their Results for Public Value Capture', *Cities*, Vol. 71, pp. 123–134.

Muñoz Gielen, D. & Tasan-Kok, T. (2010, article, first author), 'Flexibility in Planning and the Consequences for Public Value Capturing in UK, Spain and the Netherlands', *European Planning Studies*, Vol. 18, No. 7, pp. 1097–1131.

Pedraja Chaparro, F. & Suárez Pandiello, J. (2011), 'Financiación municipal: equilibrios, especialización e incentivos', in *Revista Española de Control Externo*, Vol. XIII, Mayo, No. 38, pp. 15–41.

Poveda Blanco, F. & Sánchez Sánchez, A. (2002), 'La financiación impositiva municipal. Propuestas para su reforma', *Papeles de economía Española*, No. 92, pp. 101–119.

Ré Soriano, D. & Portillo Navarro, M. J. (2011), *La participación en los tributos del Estado de las entidades locales en el marco de la financiación local*, Documento de Trabaja nr. 1, Serie Hacienda Territorial, Cátedra de la Hacienda Territorial y del Observatorio de la Hacienda Territorial, Servicio de Publicaciones, Universidad de Murcia, España, p. 66.

Voz Pópuli. (2014), *Otra subida del IBI? La recaudación por el Impuesto de Bienes Inmuebles aumenta un 47% en lo que va de crisis*. Consulted on-line on 30 October 2017, 18 March.

11 Developers' obligations in Portugal

The imperfect equation for value capture

Ana Morais de Sá and
Paulo Vasconcelos Dias Correia

1. Overview of public value capturing tools and developer obligations

1.1 Taxes as public value capture tools

1.1.1 Capture of betterments and unearned gains

The effects of industrialisation only reached Portugal's main urban centres in the second half of the twentieth century. Facing urgent needs of urban land for residential uses and social purposes, the promotion of urban development by the private sector became legal for the first time in 1965, through land subdivision schemes (*Operações de Loteamento*). Until then, the dominance of a rural society and economy, a dictatorial regime and a residual entrepreneurial bourgeoisie led public authorities to assume the monopoly of urban planning and development. In this context, the need for public value capture tools was not significant, as land value increase occurred mostly in public land.

Nevertheless, even before 1965, three different attempts to create effective public value capture tools are worth mentioning, all regarding land value increase in rural properties, resulting from governmental actions or decisions. The first, in 1948 (*Encargo de Mais-Valia*) defined a capture of 50% of the increased economic value caused by public investment in infrastructure. Later, in 1958, a new tool was created with the specific propose of capturing land value increase which resulted from a major public work (the first bridge connecting the city of Lisbon to the south bank of the Tagus River). In 1961, the scope of the *Encargo de Mais-Valia* was widened in order to also charge land value increase resulting from the approval of land-use plans. The rationale behind all these tools was that the increased value resulting from governmental actions or decisions belongs to the community, although the *direct rationale* was not explicitly formalised through law. Charged as *wealth redistribution taxes*, the *Encargo de Mais-Valia* can be classified as a *betterment contribution* when charged in exchange for a public investment in infrastructure, or as a *developer obligation* if charged in exchange for land-use regulation decisions at the moment of issuing the permits leading to the new urban uses or new building possibilities. As the *Encargo de Mais-Valia* was regulated in national legislation, not much room for interpretation was left for the municipalities, which justifies its classification as *non-negotiable* value capture tool.

With the new 1965 law (which boosted the dominance of private-led urban development) and due to a weak system of value capture tools, betterments and unearned increments on land value were now retained in private land and were not transferred to society.

The first Land Act came into force in 1970, together with urban land scarcity, land speculation, lack of affordable housing and the need for more effective public-led initiatives. Shortly after the democratic revolution in 1974, a new law addressed the main concerns of the previous one. However, it was not further developed into effective land policy tools, and in the following decades, private developers continued to lead urban development through ad hoc land subdivision schemes (most not framed by any land-use plan or assembling mechanisms), while the public administration mainly focused on development control. After joining the European Community in 1986, Portugal's economy opened up and progressed considerably, boosting an even higher demand for private-led urban development.

In 1988, a new legal framework treated betterments as standard capital gains and taxed them through the income tax. Although this law increased tax revenues, it did not prevent land hoarding and speculation. The moment of collection of the income tax does not correspond to the moment when betterments are more significant (typically, at the moment of land-use change or after public investment in infrastructures). This fact, quite often, causes fiscal inefficiencies and inequities: those who pay for these economical gains are not necessarily those who benefit the most. Additionally, when betterments are taxed as capital gains, it is not easy to distinguish between the value increase caused by public actions or decisions, from one generated by private developers or by the economic growth. In other words, it is not easy to efficiently redistribute fiscal responsibilities between all taxpayers along the urban life cycle (land and property owners, developers, citizens in general).

Unlike France, Spain and some Latin American countries (Smolka, 2013), in Portugal, law does not explicitly include direct rationales, nor mentions the *social function* of land and, therefore, the limits of property rights are not clearly defined and assigned. Does the right to build constitute a private faculty, inherent to the right of private land ownership? Or does it correspond to a public subjective right attributed by public authorities through plans, planning approvals and/or building permits? Under these vague legal norms, local governments' ability to tax betterments under a direct rationale and mitigate land speculation, regulate the real estate market and implement land-use planning was (and still is) quite limited.

1.1.2 Land and property tax and tax upon transfer title

For quite some time, the property tax and the tax upon transfer of owner-ship title have been the main sources of municipal revenues, mainly in the municipalities with rising real estate markets. Both these instruments have a long tradition in Portugal as *wealth redistribution taxes*. However, since the 1980s (when real estate property was no longer a clear demonstration of wealth), the nature and the legitimacy of these fiscal tools have widened. With the growing activity of the real estate market, the tax upon transfers of ownership title (*Imposto Municipal sobre as Transmissões Onerosas de Imóveis* – IMT) was also justified as way to capture some of the betterments and the unearned increments on land and property, although the *direct rationale* was not explicitly formalised through law.

While IMT clearly had a positive impact on public revenues, the effects on the medium long terms were controversial. Since 2009, as local govern-ments began to feel the impact of the financial and economic crisis through a declining real estate market, it became evident that municipal financing could no longer be dependent on this tax.

When the new municipal property tax (*Imposto Municipal sobre Imóveis* – IMI) came into force in 2003, significant changes to the previous law were introduced to improve its efficiency and effectiveness as a value capture tool. Once more, the *social function* of the property is not clearly assumed in the law, but the *indirect rationale* is, as the *benefit principle* was assumed as the main foundation of the new tax. However, in practice, the tax base value comprises five basic site components (floor area, type of usage, situation, age and quality of construction), and only the one regard-ing *situation* potentially contributes to improve the correspondence between the benefits created on private property by public decisions or actions and tax burden, i.e. follows a direct rationale. Despite some problems, IMI can play a relevant role as a value capture tool and on municipal fiscal health, as a stable, ongoing revenue source that enables the long-term provision of public infrastructure.

1.2 Developer obligations as public value capture tools

1.2.1 Few negotiable developer obligations

With the 1965 law for private land subdivision schemes, new forms of value capture took place, defining new obligations for private developers. Private developers had to provide and finance for local infrastructures according to the layout expressed on the zoning plan in force (at the time, named as *Plano Geral de Urbanização*), in order to get the development permits. The law specifically referred to local road networks, open and green spaces, car parking, sport facilities and commercial and industrial areas. However, the scarcity of zoning plans opened up space for more informal negotiations, changing these originally *non-negotiable developer obligations* to a *kind of* negotiable developer's contributions to local infrastructures.

In the absence of binding land-use plans, the lack of a national legal framework to regulate minimal standards for public infrastructure, combined with a passive public administration approach to urban development and development control, very often resulted in local government's low levels of demands towards developers' obligations and allowed for some arbitrariness in the negotiations.

1.2.2 Non-negotiable developer obligations – TMU and TRIU

It was in a context of intense urban growth and lack of urban infrastructure that a new legal framework for private land subdivision schemes came into force in 1984, redefining private developers' obligations. In order to reinforce local government's autonomy, promote fiscal decentralisation and strengthen municipal financial feasibility, new municipal revenues were created.

For the first time, private developers had to pay a one-time charge applied to new developments, the so-called *Taxa Municipal de Urbanização* (TMU), to co-finance major off-site public infrastructures and facilities. Through the payment of this charge, private developers would get the required development permit.

According to the *benefit principle*, the prevailing rationale of TMU was that public expenditure, directly or indirectly related with the new off-site infrastructures, needed to support the new developed areas, should be at least partially covered by the economic and financial benefits generated in private land. Landowners and developers should internalise the costs of mitigating the impacts of their urban development on the existing urban infrastructure and facilities. Just like the *Taxe d'Aménagement* in France, the *community infrastructure levy* in England, or impact fees in US, TMU fits in the classification of a non-negotiable developer obligation (N-NDO) (Muñoz Gielen & Lenferink, 2018).

Legally charged by local governments as a fee, the nexus between public expenditure and the value charged had to be clear. However, the absence of a consistent national legal framework that would guide or establish the criteria for collecting this municipal fee often led to lack of reasoning regarding the values charged by each municipality. In most cases, TMU values were fixed in municipal rules and charged by unit of permitted floor area, without any evidences of connection with the needed public investment values for financing the infrastructures and facilities included in municipal planning instruments and investment plans.

Different studies have concluded that the values charged in most municipalities were clearly insufficient to cover the real municipal expenditure with public infrastructures and facilities. However, in the absence of a concerted supra-municipal strategy, this option was also a way of increasing competitiveness among local governments in attracting more private investment for urban development.

In the 1980s, the initial purpose of TMU was to finance the provision of the lacking new major off-site infrastructures. Later, in the 1990s, the law evolved to also include the estimated expenditures for maintenance, repair, or renewal in the medium and long terms. Additionally, the payment of this fee started to be required also for urban regeneration and all developments with a significant impact on the urban system (even those without land subdivision). With a substantial enlargement of the scope regarding these fiscal contributions, a new name for this value capture tool was adopted: *Taxa pela Realização, Manutenção e Reforço das Infraestruturas Urbanísticas* – TRIU.[1]

Although its scope was significantly amplified, its revenues still focus on physical infrastructures. The financing of the so-called *soft* infrastructures (e.g. social housing, housing affordability, carbon-free infrastructures) is generally supported through other value capture tools and revenues sources.

Very often, the nature of TRIU as a fee was challenged by the absence of a clear nexus between public expenditure in off-site infrastructures and the value charged to private developers. According to a new law introduced in 2006, *the indirect rationale* supporting TRIU has now to be clearly demonstrated and justified (economically and financially), namely by taking into account the municipal investment plans corresponding to the options defined in municipal binding land-use plans regarding the main public infrastructure systems. Moreover, under the *benefit principle*, different TRIU values can now be charged in distinctive areas of the municipality. Spatial tax differentiation can also be justified to promote efficiency in the implementation of specific urban policies, namely through the introduction of tax relief measures.

TRIU is also recognised as a potentially efficient tool for capturing betterments. The absence of other effective and efficient betterments taxes legitimises TRIU as not only being an indirect value capture tool, which allows cost recovery, but also as a direct value increase capture tool, by returning to the community part of the economic gains created in private land through public investment in the infrastructure systems.

Despite the debate about lack of reasoning, connection and proportionality between the *obligation* and the expected *development* has diminished, TRIU revenues are not earmarked (constitutional law in Portugal does not allow this). In a context of scarce municipal revenues, this fact determines that, very often, TRIU revenues are spent for purposes different from those that justified its collection.

---

1   A direct translation to English would be *Fee for the Provision, Maintenance and Renewal of Urban Infrastructures*.

1.2.3 N-NDO – Cedências

With the 1984 law for private land subdivision schemes, other N-NDO based on indirect rationales were reinforced. Since then, along with TMU (later TRIU), private developers have to meet other development obligations, namely: guaranteeing the building of on-site local infrastructures at their full expenses and providing land to the municipality for this local infrastructure (e.g. local road network) and also for other social purposes (e.g. open and green spaces and public facilities). Both these contributions are charged when development permits are to be issued.

The provision of land for free to the municipality with public purposes (*Cedências*) was first regulated in 1973 by a national law, based on the *indirect rationale* that private developers should mitigate the impacts of their development operations. At the time, most municipalities were not significant landowners (they still aren't), and the access to urban land through the real estate market faced significant constraints as a result of land speculation.

In 1984 the scope of the public purpose of these land contributions was clarified: *Cedências* only refer to the land for major open and green spaces and for public facilities. Although these land contributions should be defined by taking into account the needs as estimated in binding land-use plans, very often municipalities adopt the standards values prescribed in the national law, which are stated as a proportion of the allowed floor area (e.g. for a residential area of multifamily buildings, around 60 m² of land for each 120 m² of floor area). Land contributions for building local public infrastructures result from legally binding land-use plans. In the absence of a local detailed plan, where the urban layout is defined, the zoning plan or the municipal master plan (MMP) establishes maximum urban standards that will guide the layout definition for public space and private plots.[2]

During the following decades, some adjustments to the law were made in order to enlarge the scope of the public purpose of *Cedências*. However, as with TRIU, its scope does not include *soft* infrastructures in its broadest sense, such as social housing, housing affordability and carbon-free infrastructures.

Private developers can also pay this obligation in monetary units, or the land to be given may be located outside the urban development limits. Taking into account the existent level of supply of public infrastructure and the

---

2 As in many countries in Europe, the planning system in Portugal includes three municipal plans: the MMP (*Plano Director Municipal*), a structure plan, which defines for the whole municipality the strategic spatial planning policies; the zoning plan (*Plano de Urbanização*), with more accurate proposals regarding land-use zoning; and the local detailed plan (*Plano de Pormenor*). All the three types of plans are legally binding for both the public and private sectors; therefore, permits for development proposals can only be issued if they are in conformity with plans in force. Because only the MMP is mandatory, this plan has been (and still is) the bedrock of the planning system and of development control.

existent and future needs in the surrounding areas, municipalities can decide for the most convenient option. In theory, this flexibility brings advantages to the accomplishment of the public interest. In practice, as monetary compensations are not earmarked, in many cases municipalities opt for this alternative as a way of increasing financial municipal revenues in the short term, undermining the practice of a systematic municipal land acquisition policy.

1.2.4 *Public and private land assembly* – Perequação

In 1990, in another attempt to reinforce the role of public administration in spatial and urban planning, a new legal framework for municipal land-use plans came into force and the so-called *first generation* of MMP (structure land-use plan covering the whole municipality) was extensively implemented in Portugal.

These plans defined large new urban areas, without any demonstration of their economic and financial sustainability. Allegedly to avoid land value speculation, MMPs prescribed over-sized urban areas and ended thus up encouraging speculation, since public administration had no effective tools or powers to control land hoarding and encourage private landowners to commit with the plan or to force a timely development and financing (e.g. value capture tools or expropriation). Once more, as in the previous decades, public administration was ill equipped to control private-led urban development.

In the late 1990s, the previous municipal three-tier planning system was strengthened with a new legal framework. One of its main concerns was to promote a shift from the prevailing urban development practice founded on ad hoc land subdivision projects to a more systematic approach to urban development implemented with assembly mechanisms, such as land readjustment (LR).

LR (*Perequação*, from the Latin *per aequere*)[3] came into force with four main objectives: *(i)* to redistribute the economic gains assigned by the plan between landowners and between them and public administration; *(ii)* to provide land for the location of infrastructures, public facilities and other urban spaces of collective use; *(iii)* to avoid speculative behaviours like land hoarding; and *(iv)* to increase municipal financial resources to implement, maintain and repair public infrastructure.

Although LR is not often mentioned as a value capture tool in the literature, these objectives stated in the law demonstrate it can serve as such. Not only is the *indirect rationale* present, but also the *direct rationale*, under which at least part of the economic gains assigned by public actions and decisions should be recovered by the community. In short, the rationale for LR is not only a question of making private landowners/developers pay for

---

3 Meaning to make an equal distribution between different parts.

the infrastructures needed to support their projects or for the impacts these projects will have in the off-site infrastructures; it is also a matter of recouping the public share to be applied in public good. However, the possibility of applying compulsory LR to pursue the public interest faces significant constraints, as it in practice requires the support of all landowners.

As in land subdivision schemes, private developers included in LR projects have to meet some N-NDOs, namely to build and pay for local infrastructures according to the binding land-use plans in force and co-finance off-site infrastructures through the payment of TRIU. In order to promote flexibility in compensations and adjustments to landowners, another N-NDO similar to the transferable development rights (often named as *Créditos de Construção*) is embedded into LR regulation. Landowners, who have not received their full share in readjusted plots, can sell their unused development rights. Although this market-based tool is described with some enthusiasm in Portugal, it has not had a significant impact.

2. Conclusions

The decrease of the traditional growth-dependent municipal revenues and the shift from urban sprawl towards urban regeneration reinforces the need for new tools for financing public infrastructure. Through public value capture, local governments can recover part of the economic value created by public actions or decisions and return it back to the community.

In Portugal, legislation neither explicity includes *direct rationales*, nor refers to the *social function* of land. Under this vague conceptual framework, in which property and development rights are not clearly assigned, taxes on betterments and unearned increments on land value have been ineffective and inefficient. Under this framework, value capture has been mainly supported by N-NDOs based on *indirect rationales*, as TRIU and *Cedências*. Even in the case of the property tax, *a wealth redistributions tax*, it is the *indirect rationale* that prevails.

There are no formal NDOs in Portugal, and so far, there is no relevant experience with informal ones. In practice, in the course of urban development, there is some margin for negotiation regarding minor specific issues, but mostly within the constraints imposed by legally binding land-use plans or related national rules. The exception would be some informal negotiations that take place when the impact of the new developments over the existent public infrastructure is considered to be extraordinary. In these cases, in addition to paying TRIU, private developers might have to assume other costs related to the provision of some needed off-site infrastructures. Although N-NDOs are less flexible to changing market dynamics or different policy contexts, in a country where the planning culture is relatively recent and the practice of *win-win* negotiations between the public and private sectors is still scarce, they tend to assure more transparency and accountability to the urban development process.

Despite of what was mentioned, a shift from a laissez-faire approach by public authorities to urban development to more collaborative planning processes, whereby NDOs can play an important role for achieving consensus, also makes part of the Portuguese political agenda. In this sense, LR seems to be the appropriate environment for the development of these more informal approaches to DOs.

As it was discussed, public value capture relevance goes beyond the municipal fiscal health issue. When urban development is mainly controlled by the private sector, as it is the case in Portugal, value capture also relates to the effectiveness and efficiency of land policies. Only within an environment of coordination between value capture, land policies and municipal financing will local governments eventually be able to prevent some market failures, while promoting a more equitable and sustainable redistribution of the benefits and costs of the urban development process.

References

Ingram, G. K. & Hong, Y-H. (2012), *Municipal Revenues and Land Policies*. Cambridge, MA: Lincoln Institute of Land Policy.

Muñoz Gielen, D. & Lenferink, S. (2018), 'The Role of Negotiated Developer Obligations in Financing Large Public Infrastructure After the Economic Crisis in the Netherlands', *European Planning Studies*, pp. 768–791.

Smolka, M. O. (2013), *Implementing Value Capture in Latin America: Policies and Tools for Urban Development*. Cambridge, MA: Lincoln Institute of Land Policy.

12 Use of Negotiable Developer Obligations (NDOs) in urban planning and land development systems in Turkey

Sevkiye Sence Turk and Fatma Belgin Gumru

1. Introduction

Turkish Reconstruction Law (No. 3194), as a field under public law, allows three basic means to produce urban plots. These means are: 'voluntary method' (private land development), 'land readjustment' and 'compulsory purchase' (public land assembly and development). Through land readjustment (LR) municipalities are not able to obtain from landowners more than 40% of the land for social and technical infrastructure. In most cases, the contribution was not enough to meet the social and technical infrastructure envisioned in the local spatial plans. Besides, landowners only provide the land for the on-site services, but not for off-site services, and also, they don't pay for the construction of the on-site services. To obtain the land still needed, municipalities must acquire it through compulsory purchase. However, municipalities cannot proceed this way, due to their financial constraints. Although there is no established contribution percentage in the voluntary method, the contribution percentage in LR (40%) is accepted in practice as a threshold (Turk, 2004). The amount of social and technical infrastructure envisioned in the local spatial plans is often more than 40%, but usually landowners do not want to cede more than this percentage. Therefore, municipalities sought alternative solutions to the methods described in the Reconstruction Law (No. 3194) (Ulkü, 1997). The alternative solutions have been produced in connection with the local spatial plans (*imar planı*) and through plan notes (*plan notu*). While local spatial plans should include the detailed land-use regulations, in time it became more common for such details not to be given. Instead of this, the specification of basic decisions included in the local plans was being left to the discretion of the administration staff, which included the detailed land-use regulations in plan notes. In a legal sense, although plan notes are supplementary to local spatial plans, they supersede the decisions of local spatial plans. In practice, plan notes can be used for different purposes. One of them is that they can set up the rules related to extra development rights in return for extra contributions for social and technical infrastructure. Through the use of plan notes, some large-scale projects in metropolitan areas in Turkey introduced

NDOs (Turk, 2018). They are usually referred to as '(planning) protocols' (*Protokol*) (Hasol, 2008). However, they are not regulated in public law.

Formally, a regulatory (plan-led) planning system is currently in place in Turkey. In this system, urban development is guided by land-use plans, and changes in the land-use plans are subject to certain procedures. But NDOs, which lie within the realm of private law, do not always fit into the planning system. In practice, negotiations can lead to plan amendments that do not comply with the land-use plans. Therefore, they function as a 'workaround' that enables a certain level of flexibility in the planning system. They are also capitalised on as a tool to legitimise and execute development projects that would not be otherwise acceptable pursuant to the current planning legislation (Hasol, 2008). In the literature, the use of NDOs has not been discussed sufficiently from the perspective of a developing country. The aim of this chapter is to examine the use of NDOs in urban planning and land development systems in Turkey.

In this chapter, an extreme case study approach (Flyvbjerg, 2006) is used. The studied case is selected to maximise the provision of information related to NDOs. In Turkey, NDOs have been used in large-scale projects since the early 2000s, and large-scale projects are mostly concentrated in Istanbul. Although there are some examples of NDOs in other metropolitan areas (Erkan & Arslan Avar, 2017; Kilinç Urkmez et al., 2012), compared to Istanbul, their number is limited. In Turkey, NDOs have been used in two different ways so far. One is related to the provision of on-site infrastructure and direct off-site infrastructure in close proximity to the project. The other is for legalising or resolving legal problems related to large-scale projects. In this study, the selected case study in Istanbul includes these two different uses of NDOs. The findings and conclusions of this study can be generalised for Turkey.

Following the introduction, the second section of this chapter briefly gives the context of Turkey. The third section examines a case study in Istanbul as an attempt to reveal the use of NDOs in urban planning and land development, and the fourth section provides an overall evaluation and concluding remarks.

2. The context of Turkey

In theory, a regulatory (plan-led) planning system has been implemented in Turkey. In practice, since the beginning of the 1990s, the Turkish planning system has evolved into a discretionary planning (project-led) system (Ozkan & Turk, 2016). The degree of flexibility has a tendency to increase in practice, and this has happened in two ways. The first one relates to the delegation of planning authority. This policy has been implemented both by delegating planning powers from the central government to local governments, and by transferring powers to departments of the central government who may create their own plans (Ozkan & Turk, 2016). The second one is related to a deregulation policy (Balaban, 2012). Due to both policies, municipalities began to make their own plans and to change them more often (Unlü, 2005), and also to produce their own local solutions (Ulkü,1997). Plan notes, both in the formation of flexibility in Turkish planning practice and in production of local solutions, have been important tools (Ozkan & Turk, 2016).

In Turkey, large-scale projects have emerged since the beginning of the 2000s, and these projects urged a new organisational structure and functioning of the planning system. Most of them have evolved as public and private partnerships with TOKI (Affordable Housing Authority) and developed with revenue sharing model under specific affordable housing legislation independently from the planning system. The use of the NDOs on large-scale projects has become widespread and even normalised in metropolitan areas, especially in Istanbul (Taşan-Kok, 2004). The framework of NDOs has been extended further during the period from the early 2000s until today. While in the early 2000s, NDOs included the provision of on-site infrastructure areas and off-site infrastructure or financial payments related to the construction of social and technical infrastructure, today, in addition to this, they can be also used for legalising or resolving legal problems related to large-scale projects.

3. Case study

3.1 Methodology

This section provides the details of the practice related to NDOs in the Marmara Forum in Istanbul. Since NDOs are not regulated in planning legislation and lie within the realm of private law, the agreements are realised between administrative units (senior officers or the major) in municipalities and developer firms (investors). Because NDOs are not formalised in the public planning processes and the agreements are not public, there is no transparency. Therefore, collecting reliable data and information is quite difficult. In this chapter, the authors have used different sources. Data are provided from the materials in the media and interviews with some key actors (city council members who represent different political parties, a municipal bureaucrat, an officer in a developer firm, representatives from NGOs related to the subject). In addition, secondary data (various reports, valuation reports, court decisions, municipal official reports etc.) were also used as sources.

3.2 Marmara Forum

With 15 million inhabitants, Istanbul is the most populated city in Turkey (Turkstat, 2017) and one of 30 metropolitan areas in the country (Union of Municipalities in Turkey, 2016). The Istanbul metropolitan area, which is governed by the Istanbul Metropolitan Municipality (IMM), is made up of 39 districts, each governed by its own district municipality (Istanbul Metropolitan Municipality Council, 2016a). This study focuses on the case of the Marmara Forum complex located in the Bakirkoy district.

The Marmara Forum complex consists of a shopping mall, an indoor amusement centre and offices (Figure 12.1) (Multi Turkey, 2016). The total surface of the development area is 106,211.53 m². The floor area ratio (FAR), according to the decisions of the detailed local plan, is 2. However, the total floor area (323,179 m²) is beyond the FAR because part of the floor space (car park area) is not included into the FAR due to plan notes.

Formerly, the Marmara Forum was located within the Çırpıcı meadow that was 520,000 m². It belonged to the Treasury before ownership passed into private hands in 1954. After that, the area was used as a stone quarry by a private-sector firm until 1995. In 1995, in the upper land-use plan, its function was changed to an administrative centre, education and cultural facility areas, and indoor and outdoor sports areas. Then, some parts of the area were sold to CarrefourSA (a Turkish and French partnership) in 1996. After this sale, the land-use function was changed into a business centre and trade area. Especially, the fact that the investor was foreign facilitated this change. According to the plan decisions, the Marmara Forum complex was first to be developed by CarrefourSA, but during the construction, on January 25, 2008, it was sold to the Multi Development (a Dutch company). After this, the complex was developed by Multi Turkey Real Estate Development & Investment Corp. (Multi Turkey, 2016). The architecture project was prepared by Tabanlioglu Architects (Kirecci, 2011), one of the most prestigious architecture firms in Turkey.

Figure 12.1 The Marmara Forum complex

In Turkish metropolitan areas, local level plans are approved on two different levels. While local land-use plans are approved by the metropolitan municipality, the detailed local plans are approved by the district municipality. In metropolitan areas, responsibility for building permission and control belongs to the district municipalities, but the metropolitan municipality, in some cases, can fulfill this responsibility, too. In this example, the local land-use plan related to Marmara Forum was approved on April 4, 2003 by the Istanbul Metropolitan Municipality (IMM). The detailed local plan was approved on March 8, 2004 by the Bakirkoy District Municipality. Because of the size of the complex, the developer had the obligation to submit a preliminary project. A preliminary project includes urban design and architectural solutions. In order to get a construction permit, the preliminary project had to be approved by the IMM. In the Marmara Forum case, before the approval of the preliminary project, in 2004, an agreement was made between CarrefourSA (first investor and developer of the complex) and the IMM. According to this agreement, the developer had to cede land and build the roads (highways), junctions and overpasses in the close vicinity of the project. Additionally, the developer had to supply some infrastructures such as canalization, water, rainfall retaining walls and greening and afforestation in the project area. In the agreement, the developer was given a certain time to perform these tasks. After the agreement, the preliminary project was approved by the IMM. After the approval of the preliminary project, a construction permit was issued by the Bakirköy District Municipality on August 17, 2004, and the construction of the complex started. In the phase of the construction, a plan change was made on July 17, 2006, and with the plan change, a junction and road connections surrounding the Marmara Forum were added and the road area was expanded. Because of this, the construction permit was rearranged by the Bakirköy District Municipality on December 22, 2006. After this plan change, the additional road area was also ceded by the developer (Multi Turkey) by using the voluntary method. All the cessions together were under the contribution percentage in LR (40%), which is accepted in practice as a threshold. After the cessions, because of faulty construction in the highway, the setback distances of the Marmara Forum decreased and a non-compatibility to the detailed local plan occurred. Therefore, the construction of part of the complex was stopped to comply with the setback distances in the detailed local plan (Insaat Trendy, 2009). Then, the construction began again, going at full speed, and the complex was opened on March 31, 2011 (Multi Turkey, 2016).

However, the IMM in 2011 requested the cancellation of the construction permits from the Bakirköy District Municipality, which did not fulfill this request. These two municipal bodies were governed by two different political parties. However, the IMM has responsibility for control related to the implementation of the detailed local plans. When there are deficiencies and irregularities, these had to be removed. If these are not removed, the IMM has the authority to remove deficiencies and irregularities. In this case, the IMM cancelled the construction permit of Marmara Forum, on November 19, 2011 by using this authority. Then, the Metropolitan Municipal Council decided to demolish the complex on January 11, 2012. The IMM also cancelled the occupancy permit on May 28, 2012. There were two justifications to demolish the complex. The first was that the detailed local plan defined the cession for public use of a car park. However, this car park was not ceded when the Marmara Forum was constructed (Emlak Kulisi, 2016). The second was that while the floor area ratio specified in the detailed local plan needed to be calculated after the public areas (car park) have been excluded, it was calculated over the entire parcel. Multi Turkey sued over the cancellation of the demolition order. The court rendered its verdict against Multi Turkey, so the complex had become illegal. In September 2015, the developer approached the IMM, offering additional contributions in return to the amendment of the land-use plan to conform the illegal structures into it (Tulumbacı, 2015). The developer requested that the Metropolitan Municipal Council grant the Metropolitan Mayor the authorisation to enter into a planning agreement with the developer (Istanbul Metropolitan Municipality Council, 2015). The Metropolitan Municipal Council unanimously voted for the re-evaluation of the offer (Istanbul Metropolitan Municipality Council, 2015) because some council members opposed such an agreement that would legalise an illegal structure (January, 2015). However, finally, the Metropolitan Municipal Council, with the opposition party voting against, granted the Metropolitan Mayor the authorisation to enter into a planning agreement (Istanbul Metropolitan Municipality Council, 2015).

In May 2016, the parties settled on the developer's obligation, and the Istanbul Metropolitan Municipality Council approved the 'agreement on conditional donation' (Istanbul Metropolitan Municipality Council, 2016b) and amended the land-use plan so as to legalise Marmara Forum (Istanbul Times News Agency, 2016). In this agreement, the developer gave additional contributions to the previous ones. The developer donated to IMM the Garden Office Block with 33,136 m² of office space as well as a plot of 16,000 m² adjacent to the Bakirkoy subway station (Istanbul Times News Agency, 2016). In addition, the developer ceded parking space for 100 vehicles, space that was designated for the exclusive use of the IMM (Aksu, 2016). There are also some reactions from the district and metropolitan council members in response to the approval of the agreement. Some of them believe that the Metropolitan Municipal Council should not be a part of legalising the illegal. It is also considered that such an approach can pave the way to legalise all illegal buildings in Istanbul (Aksu, 2016; T24 Online Newspaper, 2016). Also, they consider that the decision of the Council can be taken to judicial appeal (Aksu, 2016; T24 Online Newspaper, 2016), and they defined the additional contributions as an institutional bribe (Saritac, 2017). Other council members, however, consider that this is a conditional donation and does not offer any advantage to any of the parties (Istanbul Times News Agency, 2016). After the agreement, the local spatial plan for Marmara Forum was approved on October 18, 2016. In November 2016, the amended local spatial plan was put on public display (Emlak Kulis, 2016). The Bakirköy District Municipality filed a lawsuit against the plans, but the case has not concluded yet. See, for a total overview of the planning process in the Marmara Forum, Figure 12.2.

	The site was under treasury ownership	
1954	🏠	Passing of the site to private ownership
1996	Partial sale to CarrefourSA	
	Land use change to business centre and trade	
2003	Approval of the local land use plan (IMM)	
2004	Approval of the detailed local plan (BDM)	
	🤝	Agreement between CarrefourSA and the IMM
	Approval of the preliminary project and the construction permit	
2006	Amendment of the plan and the construction permit	
2008	🏠	Sale of the complex to Multi Development (while under construction)
2011	Grand opening of the Marmara Forum	
	Cancellation of the construction permit issued for Marmara Forum (IMM)	
2012	Approval of the demolition of the complex (IMM Council)	
	Cancellation of the occupancy permit (IMM)	
	⚖️	Multi Turkey filed a lawsuit for the cancellation of the destruction order (the case concluded with a verdict against Multi Turkey)
2015	Multi Turkey approached the IMM with a draft agreement	
2016	🤝	Settlement of parties on the developer's obligation
	Approval of the amended local spatial plan for Marmara Forum (IMM)	
2017	⚖️	BDM filed a lawsuit against the plans

Figure 12.2 The process of NDO in The Marmara Forum complex

4. General evalution and conlusions

Based on the Marmara Forum case, the findings of this study can be listed under the following four headings:

1 *Roles of the actors involved:* As seen in the Marmara Forum case, together with the approval of plans by the municipal council, NDOs are also negotiated between the senior officers (or metropolitan major) at the metropolitan municipality, the metropolitan municipal council members, and the private-sector actors. The metropolitan municipality mayor has to receive authorisation from Metropolitan Municipal Council to enter into a planning agreement. To grant the authorisation depends closely on the political structure of the council. That is, if the ruling party in the municipal council is dominant, such protocols are likely to be made.

2 *The nature and content of NDOs:* In the case of Marmara Forum, there were two agreements. A first agreement was used for the purpose of the mitigation of negative impacts. Therefore, a study was made to these negative impacts. However, no such study was carried out for the second agreement. The main motivation behind the second agreement was the legitimisation of an illegal development project. The other motivation was to make the development acceptable through extra contributions.

3 *The dichotomy between the planning legislation and practice in Turkey:* With the construction boom in the 2000s (Balaban, 2012), authorities in Turkey have been striving to overcome the rigidity of the current planning system by introducing certain elements of flexibility in order to create a favourable environment for developers and to meet the demands of the market. Municipal councils' decisions in favour of making planning agreements, particularly for large-scale development projects, are one of these elements of flexibility. In addition, the state has become even further dependent on the private sector during the same period due to the global financial trends. The planning system in Turkey is obliged to operate under neoliberal conditions. Therefore, this can lead to an increase in use of NDOs, and the existing dichotomy between the planning legislation and practice can be sharpened.

4 *The impact on land development practice:* Different from other land development tools, NDOs have an important degree of flexibility. They include the cession of both land and buildings for public use. Therefore, they can be attractive for both municipalities and developers. For municipalities, NDOs mean to provide an increase in the contributions, which were lower in the 'formal', public law N-NDOs. For developers, NDOs mean to provide contributions in different forms; for example, in form of money, land or building area.

However, since there is no threshold for the size of a project for which an agreement will be made, there are no criteria by which to define under which conditions and on what basis an agreement can be made. The negotiations and the agreements are not transparent and auditable, no criteria are defined to clarify where the developer contributions will be used and finally, the procedure in the event of an issue in the execution of the agreement is vague. Another risk is the increasing commodification of the grant of development rights by local authorities.

References

Aksu, F. (2016), 'Marmara Forum bağış karşılığı yasallaşıyor' (Marmara Forum to Be Legalised in Return of Donation), *Hurriyet Daily Newspaper*. www.hurriyet. com.tr/marmara-forum-bagis-karsiligi-yasallasiyor-40102622, 11May 2016. (in Turkish).

Balaban, O. (2012), 'The Negative Effects of Construction Boom on the Urban Planning and Environment in Turkey: Unraveling the Role of the Public Sector', *Habitat International*, Vol. 36, pp. 26–35.

Emlak Kulisi. (2016), *Marmara Forum AVM imar planı değişikliği askıda! (The Plan Amendment for Marmara Forum Mall Is on Display!).* http://emlakkulisi.com/ marmara-forum-avm-imar-plani-degisikligi-askida/502614, 29 November 2016. (in Turkish).

Erkan, G. H. & Arslan Avar, A. (2017), 'Clash of Public Law and Private Law as Results of Protocol-Governed Planning: The Izmir Basmane World Trade Center Case', *Planlama*, Vol. 27, No. 2, pp. 152–168. (in Turkish).

Flyvbjerg, B. (2006), 'Five Misunderstandings About Case-Study Research', *Qualitative Inquiry*, Vol. 12, No. 2, pp. 219–245.

Hasol, D. (2008), *Yolsuzluk odağı imar planı değişiklikleri (Corruption-Oriented Plan Changes).* www.doganhasol.net/yolsuzluk-odagi-plan-degisiklikleri-2.html, 17 September 2017. (in Turkish).

Insaat Trendy. (2009), *Istanbul'a 620 Milyon Euro'luk Yeni Yatırım Marmara Forum'un Temeli Atıldı (The 620-Million Euro New Investment Marmara Forum Breaks Ground).* www.insaattrendy.com/istanbula_620_milyon_euroluk_yeni_ yatirim_marmara_forum_un_temeli_atildi_.html. 17 April 2017. (in Turkish).

Istanbul Metropolitan Municipality Council. (2015), *Resolution no.1459.* www. ibb.gov.tr/tr-TR/Pages/MeclisKarari.aspx?KararID=32005, 10 April 2017. (in Turkish).

―――― (2016a), *Yetki Alanı (Jurisdiction).* www.ibb.istanbul/SitePage/Index/82, 5 May 2017. (in Turkish).

―――― (2016b), *Resolution no.705.* www.ibb.gov.tr/tr-TR/Pages/MeclisKarari. aspx?KararID=33362, 10 April 2017. (in Turkish).

Istanbul Times News Agency. (2016), *IBB 40 bin m2'lik yer İçin kaçağa göz yumdu (IMM to Tolerate Illegal Buildings in Return for 40 Thousand Square Metre Plot).* www.istanbultimes.com.tr/bakirkoy/ibb-40-bin-m2-lik-yer-icin-kacaga-goz-yumdu-h35346.html, 11 May 2017. (in Turkish).

Kilinç Urkmez, G., Ozgür, H. & Genc, F. N. (2012), 'The Possible Sources of Ethical Issues in Urban Physical Planning in Turkey', *Turkish Studies*, Vol. 13, No. 1, pp. 45–65.

Kirecci, T. (2011), '375 dönüm AVM'ye 350 marka getirdi (375 Decares of Shopping Mall Attracts 350 Brands)', *Milliyet Daily Newspaper*. www.milliyet.com.

152   *Sevkiye Sence Turk and Fatma Belgin Gumru*

tr/375-donum-avm-ye-350-marka-getirdi-ekonomi-1369280/, 26 March 2017. (in Turkish).
Multi Turkey. (2016), *Marmara Forum*. www.forumturkey360.com/marmara-forum, 10 March 2017. (in Turkish).
Ozkan, H. A. & Turk, S. S. (2016), 'Emergence, Formation and Outcomes of Flexibility in Turkish Planning Practice', *International Development Planning Review*, Vol. 38, No. 1, pp. 25–53.
Saritac, S. (2016), *Marmara Forum AVM'ye İBB'den büyük kıyak! (IMM Does Great Favor for Marmara Forum Mall!)*. www.habertempo.net/istanbul/marmara-forum-avmye-ibbden-buyuk-kiyak-h11888.html 24 March 2017. (in Turkish).
T24 Online Newspaper. (2016), 'Kaçak AVM, belediyeye bağış karşılığında yasallaştı! (Illegal Mall to Be Legalised in Return for Donation!)', *T24 Daily Newspaper*. http://t24.com.tr/haber/7-yildir-kacak-faaliyet-gosteren-marmara-forum-bagis-karsiliginda-yasallasti, 12 May 2017. (in Turkish).
Taşan-Kok, T. (2004), *Budapest, Istanbul, and Warsaw: Institutional and Spatial Change*. Delft: Eburon.
Tulumbacı, R. (2015), *Marmara Forum'dan IBB'ye cazip teklif (Appealing Offer from Marmara Forum for the IMM)*. www.emlaktasondakika.com/haber/avm/marmara-forumdan-ibbye-cazip-teklif/108851, 22 March 2017. (in Turkish).
Turk, S. S. (2004), 'The Applicability of Urban Land Acquisition Methods for the Provision of Serviced Residential Land in the Turkish Case', *International Development Planning Review*, Vol. 26, No. 2, pp. 141–166.
—— (2018), 'Comparison of the Impacts of Non-Negotiable and Negotiable Developer Obligations in Turkey', *Habitat International*, Vol. 75, pp. 122–130.
Turkstat. (2017), *Adrese Dayalı Nüfus Kayıt Sistemi Sonuçları (Results of Address Based Population Registration System)*. https://biruni.tuik.gov.tr/, 02 March 2018. (in Turkish).
Ulkü, H. (1997), *Belediyelerin toprak rantlarını kente ve kamuya kazandırma çalışmaları (Studies for Value Capture of Municipalities)*, TMMOB Harita ve Kadastro Mühendisleri Odası, 6. Harita Kurultayı, Hilton-Sa Oteli, Ankara, 3–7 March, pp. 179–201. (in Turkish).
Union of Municipalities in Turkey. (2016), *General Statistics*. www.tbb.gov.tr/belediyelerimiz/istatistikler/genel-istatistikler/. 10 March 2017. (in Turkish).
Unlü, T. (2005), *Plan Modifications Within the Contexts of Planning Control Mechanisms: Mersin Case*, Unpublished PhD Thesis, Ankara: METU.

Interviews

Adem Sakarya (Old IMM Officer), 20 April 2018.
Erhan Demirdizen (Urban Planner, Mediator), 10 February 2018.
Nuray Çolak (Urban Planner, Representative from Chamber of Urban Planner), 15 February 2018.
Not given name (Officer in developer firm), 22 April 2018.
Osman Gökçebaş (Councilor, IMM Legal Commissioner), 11 Mayıs 2016 (Istanbul Times News Agency, 2016).
Serdal Kılavuz (Councilor, IMM Commissioner), 24 Mart 2016 (Saritac, 2016).

13 Infrastructure contributions and negotiable developer obligations in China

Zhi Liu and Xinman Zeng

1. Introduction

China has experienced rapid urbanization for the last four decades. According to the National Bureau of Statistics of China (2018), between 1980 and 2017, urban population increased from 191 million to 790 million at an average rate of 3.9 percent per year, and the share of urban population over total population increased from 19.4 percent to 58.5 percent. As a result, cities have expanded outwards rapidly, and a large amount of rural land has been converted for urban development. The value of land has also increased significantly due to the conversion. This provides an opportunity for a practice of land value capture known as land concession fees, which are paid by developers to secure the land-use rights for real estate development. Municipal governments use the land concession revenues to finance land conversion and urban infrastructure facilities. In addition, municipal governments require developers, without negotiations, to make additional public infrastructure contributions as part of the land transfer (or concession) contract. The practice of negotiable developer obligations also exists in limited cases. All these can be understood in the context of China's land management system and urban planning system.

2. Land management system

China's land management system is unique. By the constitution, all urban land is state-owned, and rural land is collectively owned by the villages (except the rural land owned by the state by law). There is no private ownership of land. The Land Management Law stipulates that the conversion of rural land to urban land requires the transfer of land ownership from the village collectives to the state, and the state may, in the public interest, lawfully expropriate rural land and compensate the villages accordingly. Except for the land that is appropriated for specific (mainly public) use by the state, the state leases the state-owned land to developers for real estate development. At the city level, the state is represented by the municipal governments.

In practice, a municipal government would first expropriate rural land for urban spatial expansion according to urban master plan (*cheng shi zong ti gui hua*), and service the land with basic infrastructure facilities, which include roads, water, electricity, gas, telecommunications, drainage, flood protection, and site leveling. Then the municipal government would sell the use rights of the serviced land to a land user (either public or private entity, or a developer) for pre-specified land use. The land-use regulations, including some additional infrastructure facilities, are determined by the urban regulatory detailed plan (*kong zhi xing xiang xi gui hua*) and specified in the land concession contract to the developer.

The requirement for additional infrastructure contributions often arises from the large scale of residential development. For many years until recently, Chinese cities tended to favor the concession of large parcels of land for new residential development. The parcels could be large enough to accommodate a number of high-rise residential apartment buildings, with the number of homes ranging from a few hundred to even thousands. The basic infrastructure facilities mentioned earlier are not sufficient to serve such a large neighborhood. Additional public economic and social infrastructure facilities – such as roads within the neighborhood, library, kindergarten, primary school, and public space – are needed.

The land-use regulations usually include a number of parameters. For example, the type of land use, the years of lease (40 years for commercial land use, 50 years for industrial land use, and 70 years for residential land use), floor area ratio (FAR), inclusionary housing, and additional infrastructure contributions. A developer who secures the use rights for the land is supposed to strictly follow the land-use regulations and deliver the required infrastructure contributions (Zhu, 2004).

The land concession fee is determined either by negotiated agreement between the municipal government and developer, or (predominantly) by competitive tendering. It is an important source of fiscal revenues of municipal governments. By regulation, the compensation to villages for the agricultural land taken is set at the agricultural production value, and the value of the converted land for urban use is determined by the urban land market. As the value of land for urban use could be multiple times higher than its original value for rural use, the municipal governments are able to collect a large amount of revenue from land concessions. The revenue is mainly used to fund capital investment for urban development and infrastructure. As a monopoly supplier of urban land, municipal governments further use land as collateral to borrow from commercial banks. For many years until recently, China's Budget Law did not permit municipal governments to borrow. However, municipal governments found a way to bypass the law; they created government-owned local finance vehicles and provided them with land assets so that they were able to use land as collateral to borrow for public infrastructure investment projects.

Land concession revenues, together with borrowing with land as collateral, constitute what is known as land-based finance in China. It has contributed significantly to urban development over the last two decades. But it is not sustainable, as land supply is increasingly limited in many localities and constrained by the national farmland preservation policy. Moreover, compensation paid to the villages/farmers has been increasing, significantly reducing the net concession revenues to the municipal governments. Facing continuing urbanization, municipal governments are under enormous fiscal pressure to provide public infrastructure services. Under this situation, they tend to rely increasingly on the additional infrastructure contributions through the land concession process.

3. Urban planning and implementation

The urban planning system in China consists of an urban master plan (*cheng shi zong ti gui hua*) for the whole city and regulatory detailed plans (*kong zhi xing xiang xi gui hua*) for specific segments of the city, especially in the new development areas. Figure 13.1 illustrates the scale and scope of a typical regulatory detailed plan. It is formulated on the basis of an approved urban master plan, and is carried out by the municipal planning authority. At this planning stage, there is little room for the developers to participate, as they do not know before tendering if they would secure the land for real estate development. Table 13.1 gives a list of mandatory and suggestive control parameters that are determined by planners through the regulatory detailed planning process.

The regulatory detailed plan is implemented through a planning permit system, which constitutes a construction land-use planning permit (*jian she yong di gui hua xu ke zheng*), a construction project planning permit (*jian she gong cheng gui hua xu ke zheng*), and a planning opinion note on project site selection (*jian she xiang mu xuan zhi yi jian shu*). A developer who secures the use rights of a particular land parcel through successful tendering is required to submit a real estate development project design to the municipal planning authority for review and approval. Once the design is approved, the developer will obtain the two planning permits and the siting opinion note, which are required before civil works start. The specifics of the regulatory detailed plan are the basis for the planning authority to issue the permits and the siting opinion document.

4. Developer obligations

Infrastructure contributions specified in the land concession contract in China are not the same as the developer obligations elsewhere. The former ones are a result of the municipal government conditioning the land concession contract before tendering in the context of state ownership of land. The latter ones are the result of the government conditioning the land-use regulations in the context of private ownership of land (Muñoz Gielen, 2010).

The common practice of infrastructure contributions in China is rigid. The role of the planning authority is predominant. The specific contributions

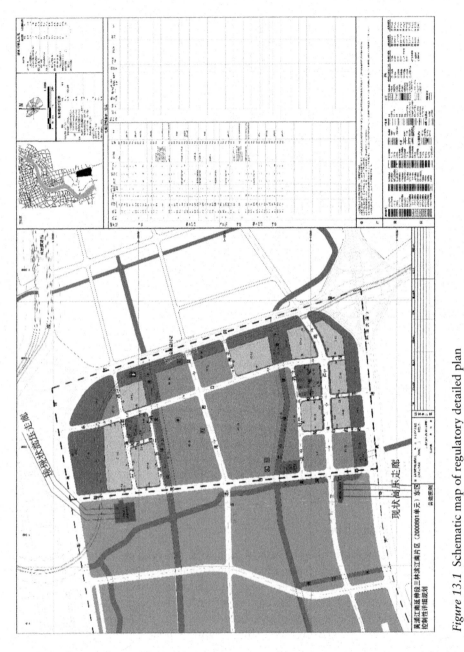

Figure 13.1 Schematic map of regulatory detailed plan

Source: Shanghai Municipal Administration of Planning and Land Resources www.shgtj.gov.cn/ghsp/ghsp/index.html

Table 13.1 Control parameters determined by the regulatory detailed plan

Land Use	Land Use Control	Land boundaries
		Land use area
		Type of land usage
		Compatibility of land use
	Environmental Capacity Control	Floor area ratio
		Building density
		Density of residential population
		Ratio of green space
		Ratio of open space
Building Construction	Building Construction Control	Building height
		Building setback
		Building interval
	Urban Design Guidance	Building volume
		Architectural color
		Architectural form
		Other environmental requirements
		Combination of architectural spaces
		Design for landscaping furniture
Public Infrastructure Facilities	Municipal Infrastructure Facilities	Water supply
		Drainage
		Power supply
		Transport
		Others
	Social Infrastructure Facilities	Educational
		Medical and health
		Commercial service
		Administrative office
		Cultural and sports
		Ancillary
		Others
Behavior Activities	Traffic Activity Control	Traffic organization
		Direction and number of entrances and exits
		Loading and unloading site regulations
	Environmental Protection Regulations	Noise, vibration, and other allowable standards
		Allowable discharge of waste water
		Allowable emissions of exhaust gas
		Solid waste control
		Others

Source: China Academy of Urban Planning and Design. *A Collection of Urban Planning Information (Fourth Volume): Regulatory Detailed Plan*, Beijing: China Construction Industry Press, 2002: 18. (in Chinese)

and the FAR are determined at the planning stage of regulatory detailed plan, at which the developers are not involved. To the developers, more contributions mean higher cost or lower profit under the fixed FAR. The only flexibility that they have to cope with the higher cost is the bidding price for the land concession contract. If the required infrastructure contributions are more extensive, the developers would tend to bid lower prices for the contract.

The FAR determined by planners may not be optimal from the market perspective. Developers often know the real estate markets better than the planners. Driven by the interest of improving profit margin, developers have strong incentives to ask for a higher FAR after securing the concession contract. Under this circumstance, negotiable developer obligations emerged in some cities in the past. When the municipal government agrees with a developer that a higher FAR could be accommodated, it is then concerned with the increased needs for public infrastructure facilities generated by the additional FAR. In order to get the developers to provide more public infrastructure facilities, some municipal governments negotiate with the developers in the form of a land-use regulation decision. For example, they allow the developers to go for a higher FAR, in exchange for a lump sum payment to the government or more public infrastructure facility contributions. In some cases, municipal governments adopted ad hoc procedures for the negotiations, such as creating a committee chaired by the mayor or a deputy mayor to discuss and vote for or against the submitted proposals. In other cases, corruption happened through informal, under-the-table negotiations.

We carried out interviews with municipal government officials and real estate developers to learn the past experience of negotiated FAR adjustments. We found that the FAR adjustments could be easily implemented through a review and voting process by the government planning committee. After reaching an agreement with the government, the developer is required to pay a large sum of predetermined land compensation payment to the city's land bureau for the additional floor areas above the originally planned limit. Sometimes, when the developer promised to provide extra public infrastructure services such as paving a public road, part or all of the compensation payment was waived. The Ministry of Housing and Urban-Rural Development (MOHURD) organized a spot check on projects permitted for construction in the second quarter of 2010. It was found that 2,150 projects out of a total of 98,577 reviewed (2.2 percent) involved adjustments to the plans and FAR, and the adjustments were more common in the secondary cities than in the major metropolises such as Beijing and Shanghai (Cai et al., 2017).

A major concern for the practice is the lack of transparency and monitoring, which lends opportunities for bribery and corruption. In 2012, MOHURD issued a Guideline on the Management of FAR on Construction Land, which includes a directive for the adjustments of regulatory FARs. It states that without a due process, FARs shall not be adjusted after the land transfer to the developer; if deemed to be necessary, the adjustment shall be conducted in accordance with the measures specified in the Guideline, instead of the ad hoc government review and voting meetings to decide the case. Under the Guideline, the FAR adjustments are permitted only in the following cases: (i) changes in the development conditions of the plots, due to the revisions of urban and rural plans; (ii) changes in public service facilities, public safety facilities, the size of the land leased or allocated, and the relevant construction conditions, due to the construction needs of urban and rural infrastructure; (iii) changes in the relevant policies; or (vi) other conditions stipulated by laws and regulations.

The Guideline elaborates a rigorous procedure for the FAR adjustments, which turns out to be rather complicated and time-consuming in practice. It is not uncommon that it takes more than a year to complete the procedure. This imposes a significant cost on the developers seeking the FAR adjustments. Moreover, many municipal governments do not have the institutional capacity to follow the procedure. As a result, they are not willing to consider and process the FAS adjustments.

5. Application of developer obligations in Shenzhen

Located north of Hong Kong, the city of Shenzhen became China's first Special Economic Zone in 1980. Since then, it has grown from a small town to a world metropolis with a population of 12 million. It has also been in the forefront of policy reform. Its innovative application of negotiable developer obligations leads the rest of the country.

Infrastructure contributions in Shenzhen can be seen in both new development and redevelopment (especially urban village redevelopment). Just like in other cities, infrastructure contributions are mainly used for new development in Shenzhen. Compared to other cities, Shenzhen manages infrastructure contributions in a more professional and transparent way. Land tendering is held by the Shenzhen Land Property Trading Center, with details of all transactions posted to the public on the center's website. In comparison, much less details could be found about land transactions in other cities. The land concession announcements in Shenzhen spell out the detailed conditions specifically stipulated for infrastructure contributions (Table 13.2). These conditions are mainly stipulated for commercial and residential land rather than industrial land.

The practice of negotiable developer obligations in Shenzhen emerged mainly for urban redevelopment, especially urban village redevelopment. Shenzhen's spatial expansion is heavily constrained by the geographic extent of the municipality. The city has almost run out of developable land outside the existing built-up areas and protected areas. Further urban development has to be accommodated through urban redevelopment. Since 2012, the redevelopment that took place on developed land in Shenzhen has exceeded the incremental area of new land development. In 2016, Shenzhen Municipal Government announced a five-year plan for urban renewal, which included about 200 industrial park and urban village renewal projects, covering a total land area of 30 square kilometers (Shenzhen Municipal Planning and Land Resource Commission, 2016).

Table 13.2 Public infrastructure contributions in Shenzhen's land concession announcements

Forms of Infrastructure Contributions	Specific description
Municipal Infrastructure Facilities	Bus terminal station, public green space, public square, parking lot, charging station, garbage station, public toilet, etc.
Social Service Facilities	Primary school, kindergarten, neighborhood committee office, post office, community service center, etc.
Inclusionary Housing	Housing for research and development firms, public rental apartments for young talents, dormitories, canteens, etc.
Other Public Facilities	Industry and commerce institute, sub-terrainian business, conference and exhibition center, theater, integrated corridor monitoring center, etc.

Source: Shenzhen Land Property Trading Center www.sz68.com/

Urban villages are a spatial phenomenon in many Chinese cities (see Figure 13.2). A few decades ago, these cities were typically surrounded by rural villages and farmland. With urban expansion, the municipal governments first expropriated the farmland, as it did not involve significant payment for the resettlements of villages. However, after years of urban expansion, these villages are now surrounded by urban development and their locations become more and more premium and valuable. They become a prime target for urban redevelopment when cities run out of land at the urban fringe areas.

However, redeveloping urban villages is very costly, as population density is high and the public facilities (such as schools, parks, and public spaces) are seriously deficient due to its rural land-use pattern. The building density of some urban villages in Shenzhen reached more than 70 percent or even 90 percent of the land coverage. The "handshake buildings," which refer to those privately constructed residential buildings so closely located that the residents of two neighboring buildings could shake hands from their respective windows, are very common. If the usual urban land-use planning parameters are used, a sizable portion of land area (often up to 30 percent) would have to be devoted for public facilities; this limits the size of land area for profitable residential and commercial development. Therefore, the urban village redevelopment project would not generate sufficient profits to attract the developers if the regulatory FAR is used. Under this situation, the government has to take initiatives, such as negotiable developer obligations, to enable developers to do the project with a higher FAR.

At present, urban renewal in many cities is led by the government. But Shenzhen carries out urban renewal differently (see Figure 13.3). Shenzhen's urban renewal follows the principle of "market operation under government guidance." The government acts as a "referee" and mainly plays a

Figure 13.2a Bai Shi Zhou, the largest urban village in Shenzhen before renewal

Figure 13.2b Bai Shi Zhou Village Renewal

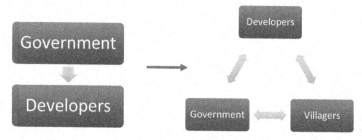

Figure 13.3 Implementation models of urban renewal: traditional model (left) and new model in Shenzhen (right)

role of setting the rules, providing guidance, and facilitating the market. The design and implementation of the renewal project would rely on the market agents (developers, financiers, and village committees) to negotiate and cooperate with the original owners of the village properties.

Procedurally, Shenzhen municipal government allows the village property owners and the developer to form a business partnership, and encourages them to come up with a feasible renewal project and declare to be the market agents for the project. The formulation of the renewal plan is not dominated by the government, but is carried out by a design firm entrusted by the project declaring parties. After the approval by the municipal planning authority, the renewal plan can be implemented to transform the urban village. If relocation of the village property owners is needed, the developer could negotiate with them to reach an agreement of relocation compensation, property acquisition, and development benefit sharing. If they can't reach an agreement, then the project will be aborted or turned over to other developers.

The government will safeguard the public interests and intervene to ensure that the public facilities and public services meet the urban land-use planning standards. As mentioned earlier, when a significant portion of the urban village land is devoted to meet the standards of public infrastructure facilities, the project with the FAR typically specified in the regulatory detailed plans may not be profitable. To enable the project, the government negotiates with the developer on a higher FAR until the point when reasonable profit can be reached. After successful negotiations, a deal would be made that the developer provides the required public infrastructure facilities in the renewal area (which generally account for 30 percent of the redevelopment cost), and the government awards the developer a higher FAR for the redevelopment.

6. Conclusion

The practice of infrastructure contributions through the land transfer process is common in China. It is an effective way for developers to deliver additional public infrastructure facilities specified by planners as part of the real estate development projects. But it is not the most efficient in terms of resource allocation. Urban planners may not know the real estate market as well as do the developers, but the developers do not have a role in the regulatory detailed plan which determines the infrastructure contributions. The practice of negotiable developer obligations emerged some years ago, but it was later subjected to a mandatory procedure and was limited to only a few situations allowed by the government guidelines. In recent years, Shenzhen became a pioneer city in using negotiable developer obligations successfully for urban village renewal projects. This demonstrates the value of negotiable developer negotiations in China's urban development.

China is undertaking land policy reform with a clear direction. In the near future, village collectives would be allowed to transfer the use right of their rural construction land to developers for urban real estate development, without going through the state expropriation, as long as the new urban land use conforms to urban planning. This reform would break the monopoly supply of urban land by the municipal governments. If materialized, the village collectives would continue to own the rural land, but they would be able to share the development benefits with the developers; they are also required to pay a share of the land value increase to the government either as a tax or a fee. Under this scenario, municipal governments would have incentives to use developer obligations to ensure that sufficient public infrastructure facilities are provided for the volume of development preferred by the developer and village collective. Therefore, it could be anticipated that the developer obligations will have a wider application in Chinese cities. As of now, it will be important to learn lessons from the Shenzhen experience as well as international experience, and strengthen the mandatory procedure of developer obligations so that it is transparent, effective, simple, and practical.

Acknowledgements

The authors are grateful for the helpful comments from Demetrio Muñoz Gielen and Erwin van der Krabben.

References

Cai, H., Wang, Z. & Zhang, Q. (2017), 'To Build Above the Limit? Implementation of Land Use Regulations in Urban China', *Journal of Urban Economics*, pp. 223–233.

Muñoz Gielen, D. (2010), *Capturing Value Increase in Urban Redevelopment*. Leiden, The Netherlands: Sidestone Press, p. 478.

National Bureau of Statistics of China. (2018), *China Statistical Yearbook*. China Statistics Press. (in Chinese). Beijing, China.

Shenzhen Municipal Planning and Land Resource Commission. (2016), *Shenzhen's Thirteenth Five-Year Plan for Urban Renewal: Text and Atlas*. (in Chinese).

Zhu, J. (2004), 'From Land Use Right to Land Development Right: Institutional Change in China's Urban Development', *Urban Studies*, Shenzhen, China. Vol. 41, No. 7, pp. 1249–1267.

14 A proposed framework of developer obligations to unleash land supply in Hong Kong

Land readjustment

K. W. Chau, Lennon H.T. Choy and
Lawrence W. C. Lai

1. Introduction

The leasehold system is a salient feature of land management in Hong Kong (HK). Land value capture (LVC) can be exercised through premium assessment in the process of lease modifications for changes in land use and/or development intensity. Land premium is well known to have constituted a lion's share of government revenue (22.3% in 2017, C&SD, 2018). Developer obligations (DOs), by contrast, receive less attention than in other countries. As the least affordable city in the world in terms of housing provisions (Demographia, 2018), starting from summer 2017, HK has embarked on a city-wide debate (Task Force on Land Supply, 2018) on certain proposals for increasing land supply of at least 1,200 hectares including major reclamation from the sea. A parallel short-to-medium term proposal is to unleash privately owned land in the New Territories (NT) areas for housing development. Public-private partnership (PPP) appears to be a contentious though sensible model because of allegations of potential collusions between private developers and the government. In response to these concerns, this study revisits the concept of a land readjustment (LR) mechanism in NT in which private developers must contribute substantial portions of their own land parcels, as non-negotiable DOs (N-NDOs), to public housing and infrastructure development. This study starts with an overview of DOs in HK, followed by a discussion of the institutional factors that underlie the underutilization of privately owned farmlands for urban development in the NT. Then an LR framework is proposed, highlighting major considerations in the institutional design, followed by a conclusion.

2. Developer obligations in HK: an overview

HK was under British colonial rule from 1841 to 1997. Basically, HK's land management resembles in some ways the British system. There is no betterment levy on land value gain, nor compensation for non-public purpose curtailment in land value.[1] Both direct and indirect LVC are enabled by the development control system. Direct LVC can be exercised administratively through a premium levy for a change of land use and/or development intensity, change in lot boundaries or a renewal of the Crown (government) lease. Indirect LVC can be in the form of NDOs laid down as conditions in various development permits, including planning conditions for granting statutory planning permissions. These descriptions, nevertheless, are somewhat oversimplified. In reality, LVC mechanisms are way complicated by the peculiar leasehold system in HK, particularly the one in the NT.

Except for a piece of land granted to the Church of England (Sheng Kung Hui), all land in HK has been leased under fixed terms of years of 999, 99, 75 or 50 years, etc. with or without rights of automatic renewal. Vested by the mini-constitution in HK, a.k.a. the Basic Law, which is an outcome of the Sino-British Joint Declaration 1984, to a large extent the colonial land management system has been adopted by the HK Special Administrative Region (HKSAR) government since July 1997. All rights pertaining to land straddling over 1997, including those embedded in the communal farmland in the NT granted during the colonial period, were extended to 2047. As of today, there has been little discussions concerning the HK land management system beyond 2047, though the HKSAR government has granted new leases beyond 2047 since 1997.

In the urban areas, government leases granted in early colonial years were virtually "unrestricted" in terms of use or building form. Cost-benefit analysis governed land use effectively in the old days, before reinforced concrete and elevators became prevalent. Direct LVC for development carried on unrestricted leases was futile because no premium was payable subsequent to land grants. To cater to the development of the city, the colonial government soon started granting land leases with restrictive covenants governing land use, building height and intensity, site coverage and the like. Direct LVC has been effectively exercised whenever changes in land use are requested by the lessees. However, under the Basic Law, all leases upon expiry are automatically renewed until 2047 upon payment of an annual nominal land rent, which curtails the HKSAR government's LVC capacity via lease renewal.

It was not until the aftermath of the *Singway Case* (1974) HKLR 275 in the 1970s that indirect value capture via negotiable DO (NDO) was made possible under the Town Planning Ordinance (TPO) on both unrestrictive and restrictive leases. Landowners may accept NDO in order to obtain planning permissions to renew their premises. Public facilities such as bus

---

1 For curtailing private development rights, compensation is only payable for resumption for "public purposes" under the Lands Resumption Ordinance (Cap. 124). Such purpose has been given a liberal interpretation by the court to include implementation of a profit making urban renewal scheme that does not provide for in situ rehousing of owners of flats or shops.

depots, libraries, clinics, community halls, public parks, elderly and youth centres, etc. have been provided by private landowners to fulfill the conditions laid down in the planning permissions.

The institutional arrangements for land in the NT was far more complicated than those in places outside it because of the communal ownership of much land. As they were recognized by the colonial government as legally inherited from imperial China when it took over the NT from China in 1898 and subjected all land to the common law, the HKSAR government after 1997 continues to honour this. The British colonial administration conducted a cadastral survey to determine owners, lot boundaries and land uses, and record them on maps for various demarcation districts (DD). The DD lots are irregular in shape and many are under communal control. Unlike the Japanese colonization of Taiwan, the British colonial government did not modernize the rural land ownership pattern of the NT except for the land mass to the immediate south of the Kowloon Range, a place called New Kowloon, where urban development under a modern layout was contemplated early. The government purchased the New Kowloon DD lots from villagers, laid out, formed and sold the land as leasehold interests.

For the NT outside New Kowloon and Cheung Chau, a total of 350,000 land parcels were recorded in the 477 DD lots. In 1905, instead of granting a lease for each individual land parcel, the colonial government issued so-called Block Crown Leases (BCL) to owners of DD lots. Generally, there are only two types of land uses in a BCL, namely building and agricultural. For decades, LVC for agricultural land on BCL was not a concern because there were no better alternative uses for the land. Besides, even if there existed any higher value use, direct LVC could be exercised through premium levy as it involved a change of use specified in the BCL. This wishful thinking, however, was challenged by the *Melhado Investment Ltd. Case* (1983) HKLR 327. The court held that the land use recorded in the schedule to a BCL not restrictive but merely descriptive. The judgement of the *Melhado Case* clarified property rights to land use, as open storage needs no lease modifications insofar as no new building was involved. A huge rent gap existed between farming and higher value activities such as open storage. Massive conversion of farmlands into "brownfield" sites has happed as a natural economic consequence of the *Melhado Case*, which also reprieved the capacity of LVC by the government. As a remedy, a new set of planning regulations was applied to the NT in 1990 under an amended TPO. Indirect LVC mechanism via NDO was eventually enabled by way of planning gains when landowners seek planning permissions.

Compared to the previous development of new towns under various PPP models, the planner under the 1990 TPO amendment has failed to transform fallow farmlands and brownfield sites into well planned habitats. Difficulties in site assembly due to fragmented ownership complicated by communal land holdings and missing owners aggravate the problems of land assembly. In each communal unit, as a *Tso* or *Tong*,[2] members collectively own the land. There are about 4,000 *Tsos* and 2,000 *Tongs* in the NT, controlling roughly 6,000 acres of land (Nissim, 2016). Landed interests can only be inherited by male descendants, the identities of whom are registered in the ancestral registrar kept by the manager of the communal unit. A manager is appointed or elected to deal with administrative matters, including buying or selling land. For decades, majority consent from the communal unit members sufficed to authorize him to handle transactions in landed matters. Selling *Tso* or *Tong* land to members outside the communal units such as developers for large scale development projects (e.g. Fairview Park and On Lok Yuen) was not uncommon. Direct and indirect LVC could then be exercised throughout the land-use exchange process. In recent decades, nonetheless, transactions of *Tso* and *Tong* land appeared to be put on hold as legal challenges were raised concerning whether majority or unanimous consent should be obtained to authorize the manager to sell communal land. The Court of Appeal case *Man Ping Nam v Man Tim Lup* (2016) CACV 39/2010 shows that, whether majority or unanimous approval is proper is not a simple legal matter. Abruptly halting sale of *Tso* and *Tong* land has caused a significant hold up for large development projects in the NT, and this is not desirable from a housing point of view.

There were also other forms of land grants in the NT, besides the BCL. From the cadastral survey until 1984, land grants were made subject to the *ad hoc* notifications in government gazettes, which laid down for blanket control of all new leases the common development parameters. Land grants of this type are called Gazette Notification (GN) Lots. After 1984, new land grants (also called the New Grant Lots) in the NT largely followed the practices in the urban areas (i.e. land leases with lot-individualized restrictive covenants). Direct LVC can be exercised through premium levies during lease modifications for change of land use. After the introduction of planning control in the NT in 1991, NDOs can be imposed when landowners seek planning permissions.

For many years in the past, private land exchange was an option for BCL, GN and New Grant Lots owners to convert piecemeal land parcels into sites for comprehensive development. Direct LVC through land premium assessment and indirect LVC through negotiated obligations were possible. Road, utilities plants, schools, parks and other public facilities have been provided by the private developers in the land exchange programmes. Table 14.1 depicts the direct and indirect LVC features in HK by types of land leases and geographical locations.

---

2 According to Nissim (2016), a Tso is a landholding trust for the worship and upkeep of the grave of a named ancestor. There is no hall to accommodate ancestral tablets in a Tso. A Tong is with similar purposes as a Tso but further extends to the provisions of educational and welfare fundings to the beneficiaries, and building halls for ceremonial functions.

Table 14.1 Land value capture features in HK by lease type and location

Location	Lease Type	Land Value Capture Features	
		Direct	*Indirect*
Urban	Unrestrictive lease	X – No premium payable	√ – NDO via planning conditions and land exchange
	Restrictive lease	√ – Change in land use X – Lease expiry	√ – NDO via planning conditions and land exchange
Rural	Block Crown Lease (BCL)	X – As a result of the *Melhado Case*	√ – NDO via planning conditions and land exchange
	General Notification Lots (GN Lots)	√ – Change of land use	√ – NDO via planning conditions and land exchange
	New Grant Lots	√ – Change of land use	√ – NDO via planning conditions and land exchange
	Proposed land readjustment (LR)	√ – N-NDO via compulsory contribution of land for public infrastructure and public housing	√ – NDO via readjustment and land exchange

3. New mechanism for developer obligations – land readjustment

LR has a has been put to practice in many countries for a long time (Hong & Needham, 2007; Van der Krabben & Lenferink, 2018; Gozalvo & Muñoz Gielen, 2017), including Japan, Korea and India. In the nineteenth century, the morphology of land ownership for farmland in China and Japan, like other countries in Asia, was similar. Plots of farmland were irregular in shape, size and level with lots of communal holdings. Meiji Japan soon introduced LR to transform its traditional land pattern to a modern rectilinear one and original landowners obtained redelineated land in proportion to the amount of land they originally held, netting a contribution to the state for public facilities like roads and other uses. Japan soon applied this policy to colonial Taiwan, treating it as an agricultural and mining base in its empire. In Mainland China, soon after 1949, all rural land was collectivized and old cadastral boundaries became history. Interestingly, HK was the only place where the traditional Chinese form of rural land patterns has survived political upheavals and shaped land uses and politics up to now. To alleviate the stifling housing demand in HK, we propose LR as a new approach to transform the rural farmland into urban development.

In HK, this approach is a special way of executing a "transfer of development rights" within the existing land administrative framework. The DD lots under agricultural use in the NT are invariably irregular in shape, size and level, and hence are unfit not only for urban development but also for modern agricultural purposes. In the HK case, for example, they frustrate land conversion from open storage spaces to urban development unless all neighbours cooperate in agreeing to a joint development scheme in the form of a master layout plan (MLP), approval of which is a prerequisite for obtaining planning permissions. Such cooperation is often missing especially when urban land values are expected to rise. The lack of cooperation can be due to missing owners, sentimental attachment to land, or simply holding out. Holding out is now particularly problematic for land held under ancestral ownership by a *Tso* or *Tong*.

One possible proposal to facilitate LR is this: a developer who intends to implement an MLP approved by the Town Planning Board (TPB) planning permissions, but who cannot assemble all DD lots in a planned area, may apply to the government land administration with an LR plan. In such a plan, each owner of hitherto communal land, for which there is no unanimous consent to transfer ownership, is given regularized sites either in situ or in other locations in the MLP already acquired by the developer, with road access provided by the developer. In addition, private land within the MLP area already acquired by the developer is dedicated to government for homeownership scheme or public housing. Upon acceptance by government, the ownership issue of the MLP is deemed settled and the lot boundaries on the LR plan become the *de jure* boundaries of the relevant DD and are registered at the Land Registry.

This broad-brush approach respects private property rights of all landowners without frustrating good projects approved by the TPB. It saves the transaction costs of the compulsory sale of private land, resumption of private land by government, litigation among parties, and surrenders and regrants of land on a piecemeal basis. This LR process helps release a large amount of land for housing and other suitable uses in the interest of parties involved, achieving a win-win-win outcome.

Adopting LR in HK could potentially unlock more than 1,000 hectares[3] of privately owned land in the NT. Referencing a recent successful private land exchange application,[4] LR may contribute 100,000 new housing units in the NT, and hundreds of billions of HK dollars in land premiums to

---

3 Figure estimated by the discussion paper for the Task Force on Land Supply dated December 19, 2017 (see Task Force on Land Supply, 2017).
4 In November 2017, an approval of land exchange was granted to a private landowner, which will convert 49.7 ha of farmland into a 4,730-unit residential cum recreational development complex by 2025 (see SCMP, 2017). Total premium payable in this private land exchange application is HK$15.9b (US$2b).

the government. LR serves as an alternative to conventional land assembly methods such as massive land taking,[5] which may be prone to dispute,[6] severe criticism[7] and opposition. We posit that LR will bring about Kaldor-Hicks efficiency[8] and hence is the preferred model to unleash privately owned farmland for urban development in HK.

Similar to other land exchange applications, when seeking ultimate approvals from the TPB for the LR projects, NDO can be levied in terms of planning gains. The proposed LR mechanism will add a new dimension: N-NDO. We propose all LR projects must contribute a finite portion of land holdings as N-NDO for public infrastructure and public housing purposes. It is similar to, but somewhat different from, "cost equivalent" land levied in LR projects overseas.

4. Major considerations of N-NDO and land readjustment in HK

The LR model to be implemented in HK should operate administratively under the existing land management system. It should avoid any prolonged legislative process and honour both the protection of private property rights under the Basic Law and the sovereignty and authority of the HKSAR government as the *de jure* land manager. A coordination unit can be setup by the public authority.

The minimum thresholds to initiate an LR project can be a point for discussion. The majority landowners and the public authority should assure that the LR plan is attractive to minority landowners, or else the proposal may fall through. To incentivize the minority landowners to take part in LR, all replotted land can be connected to roads such that future development can meet all requirements of the building regulations. Bonus land parcels to minority landowners may even be given for other considerations such as the preservation of heritage and community.

The sizes of the replotted land parcels for the private landowners will depend on the N-NDO levy for public infrastructure and facilities, etc., adopted in the LR model. Two key considerations, however, should be

---

5 Known as resumption or compulsory purchase in HK and the UK; eminent domain in the US; expropriation in Australia. The New Development Areas (NDAs) developments in HK including the North East New Territories NDAs adopt this approach.

6 In the US, although the State Supreme Court in *Kelo vs City of New London* (2005) ruled no violation of federal constitution on private property rights for land taking that entails public purposes, subsequently it led to legislation in 44 states forbidding the use of eminent domain for economic development.

7 On February 22, 2018, Mr. Kenneth Lau Ip Keung, Chairman of Heung Yee Kuk, blamed the government for paying compensation far below market value for resumption of rural land. He argued that the government did not share the fruits of city development with indigenous villagers (see *The Standard*, February 23, 2018).

8 Kaldor-Hicks efficiency suggests that the better-off parties can compensate the worse-off parties until no one will be benefited from further bargainings.

taken into account to determine the N-NDO in HK. First, compared to overseas countries, generally there are fewer surface roads in massive housing development sorts of projects in HK. Second, since the landowners are still subject to premium assessment after readjustment, a lower N-NDO is considered appropriate in HK; otherwise, it will defeat the purpose of LR: redistributing the gains among all stakeholders.

For illustrative purposes, assuming there are 1,000 ha of privately owned agricultural land taking part in LR, if a 50% N-NDO is to be implemented in HK, it means there will be about 500 ha of land available for public housing, recreational and other facilities to benefit the general public. Assuming one-quarter of that land, i.e. 125 ha, is to be used for public rental housing development, it will create about 95,000 additional housing units,[9] which could absorb over 60% of the public housing application queue as it stood in December 2018.

5. Concluding remarks

In our LR proposal, the developer has the social obligation to survey all cadastral boundaries, acquire most of the private lots, identify minority owners and devise a sound master layout plan for a DD with sites for minority owners. In the layout, the developer also has the obligation to specify sites and even build public housing as part of a PPP scheme, as a *quid pro quo* for government provision of road access and other public utilities. A coordination unit can be set up by the public authority to facilitate the LR processes. In cases wherein preservation of tangible or intangible heritage elements are needed, the LR model should enable the stakeholders to raise their concerns. TPB and the public authority should act as the gatekeepers.

The government should enable LR by i) assisting the preparation of the MLP and ii) proclaiming the land exchange as readjustment of land parcels which does not amount to a sale of communal property, merely an adjustment to it. It honors the protection of private property rights under the Basic Law and the sovereignty and authority of the HKSAR Government as the *de jure* land manager in HK. This proposal would be desirable from an efficiency and equity standpoint to facilitate cooperation in bothersome MLP cases by adopting a policy of positively enabling the transfer of property rights based on LR within the same DD. This proposal will be most feasible within the existing government administrative framework. There would thus be neither any need for legislation[10] or major government spending. The policy should be acceptable to the public, as it is development according

---

9 Estimations based on Hung Fuk Estate in Hung Shui Kiu, where 4,900 units are located on a site of 6.4 ha.

10 Under S4(2) of the Town Planning Ordinance (Cap. 131), the town planning board may recommend to the chief executive in council the resumption of any land that interferes the approved MLPs. This section of law may provide the legal basis to deal with the minority's oppositions.

to MLPs approved by the TPB in a statutory planning process in which the public can inspect the proposal, air opinions and raise objections as usual.

It would not involve highly contentious issues of re-entry, compulsory acquisition or resumption of private land by government.[11] No expropriation of land rights in terms of area or value is involved and the minority landowners actually derive benefits from betterment of their land especially due to gaining vehicular access and other infrastructural services. Their right to put a certain amount of land under agriculture is unfettered, and no forced demolition of buildings is involved. The development process can be streamlined, saving developers time (statutory appeals, litigation) and costs (paying those who are holding out their tiny land parcels), and saving public time costs of waiting for new housing supply.

This study proposes the introduction of N-NDO into the land conversion system in Hong Kong because it gives rise a transparent framework that help eliminate concerns like collusion and transfer of interests for projects that entail both public and private parties. The proposed LR model is a low-transaction-cost mechanism to unlock development potentials of private owned farmland, disorganized brownfield sites and underutilized *Tso* and *Tong* land in the NT. While the proposal may be contentious in an increasingly political society like HK, we opine that if LR has been contributing to the urban developments in many countries with diverse social, legal, political and cultural backgrounds, there is no compelling reason why it cannot be implemented in HK.

Acknowledgements

The authors would like to acknowledge Mr. Alwin Chan for his legal advice about the transactions of *Tso* and *Tong* land in the NT. All faults, however, are the authors'.

References

Attorney General vs Melhado Investment Ltd. (1983), HKLR 327.
C&SD. (2018), *Government Revenue (General Revenue Account and Funds)*. www.censtatd.gov.hk/hkstat/sub/sp110.jsp?tableID=193&ID=0&productType=8.
Demographia. (2018), *14th Annual Demographia International Housing Affordability Survey: 2018*. www.demographia.com/dhi.pdf.
Gozalvo Zamorano, M. & Muñoz Gielen, D. (2017), 'Non-Negotiable Developer Obligations in the Spanish Land Readjustment: An Effective Passive Governance Approach that "de facto" Taxes Development Value', in *Planning Practice & Research*, Vol. 32, No. 3, pp. 274–296.
Hong, Y. H. & Needham, B. (2007), *Analyzing Land Readjustment: Economics, Law and Collective Action*. Cambridge, MA: Lincoln Institute of Land Policy.

11 For example, Choi Yuen Tsuen and the Guangzhou-Shenzhen-Hong Kong Express Rail Link (XRL) Project.

Man Ping Nam as the manager of 'Man Sham Chung Wu' registered under S.15 of the New Territories Ordinance vs Man Tim Lup and others. (2016), CACV 39/2010.

Nissim, R. (2016), *Land Administration and Practice in Hong Kong*, 4th edition. Hong Kong: Hong Kong University Press.

Singway Co. Ltd. vs Attorney General. (1974), HKLR 275.

SCMP. (2017), *SHKP Pays Record HK$15.9b Premium to Convert Sai Kung Farmland into Housing Project.* 7 November 2017.

The Standard. (2018), *Ding din as Kuk Hits Court "provocations"*, 23 February.

Task Force on Land Supply. (2017), *Tapping into the Potential of Private Land.* Discussion paper 13/2017. www.devb.gov.hk/filemanager/en/content_1054/Paper_13_2017.pdf.

——— (2018), *Land for Hong Kong: Our Home, Our Say!* Hong Kong. https://landforhongkong.hk/file/booklet/Land_Supply_En_Booklet.pdf.

Van der Krabben, E. & Lenferink, S. (2018), 'The Introduction of Urban Land Readjustment Legislation as an Institutional Innovation in Dutch Land Policy', *Habitat International*, Vol. 75, pp. 114-121.

15 Value capture from development gains towards public utility

The case of Seoul, Republic of Korea[1]

Klaas Kresse, Myounggu Kang, Sang-Il Kim and Erwin van der Krabben

1. Land readjustment (1966–1984)

Land readjustment (*tojiguhoegjeonglisa-eob*) was introduced to Korea by the Japanese in the colonial period, and applied extensively during Japanese occupation and the first decades of modernization. This study focusses on the period of rapid urbanisation and development from the early 1960s on, when land readjustment became almost 100 per cent self-financing with the introduction of cost-equivalent land (Sohn, 2003). This means infrastructure and public goods provision could be financed through voluntary land contributions by the landowners in exchange for the right to capture the entire land value increase over the remaining land (Lee, 2002).

At the time, resource scarcity and a lack of financing were the major bottlenecks for a planned urbanisation in Korea. In the face of these challenges, land readjustment played a crucial role, as it was capable of tackling the three challenges: housing provision, implementation of basic infrastructure, and reorganisation of illegal housing, simultaneously.

1.1 The land readjustment process

Developer obligations are embedded in the self-financing land readjustment scheme as non-negotiable land contributions to the public with an indirect value capture rationale. In this policy, the land within the project boundary is developed first, and then redistributed to the landowners with the reduction of land reserved for public facilities (public facility land) and another part of the land sold on the market in order to finance infrastructure, public facilities and other project costs (cost equivalent land). The project implementers may be either the private landowners, a landowner's association acting as the representative of private landowners or a public developer (Jo, 2015).

---

1 This chapter is a condensed version of a paper entitled 'Value Capture Ideals and Practice – The Evolution of Value Capture Policies in the Case of Seoul, Republic of Korea', which is currently under review. The basis for this paper has been presented as a working paper at the special session on developer obligations at the PLPR conference 2017 in Hong Kong.

In the case of Seoul, the vast majority of projects have been implemented by the planning authority of the Seoul Metropolitan Government (Kim, 2015). Nationwide, about two-thirds of the land readjustment projects have been carried out with the local planning authorities as the implementing body, while about one-third of the projects were driven by private associations of landowners. On the national scale, projects developed by public developers, such as KLHC or KNHC, have not been significant with this policy (Lee, 2002). With land readjustment, the public applies a passive governance approach by designating itself the role of manager and regulator of the land development, without taking any financial risks or responsibilities. This, however, allowed high levels of privatisation of the development gain.

1.2 Causes of land value increments and its capture

Land value increments during the period of rapid urbanisation have been high, due to a combination of socio-economic factors (unearned increment), intangible factors (legislation changes by the public) and tangible developments (betterment). In the Korean case, the macroeconomic factors – specifically, national economic growth and large-scale migration to the capital – have had a considerable impact on the land value increase in Seoul. The costs of development have, however, been covered by the landowners through the sales of cost equivalent land on the market. An illustration of factors creating land value increments and the capture thereof by the public based on the work of Hong & Brubaker (2010) can be seen in Figure 15.1.

The Korean public has not captured development gain on top of the public facility land, even though the macro socio-economic factors and the public's changes to the land-use regulations created the foundation for an argument that supports a higher rate of public value capture with a direct value capture rationale. Instead of arguing with a direct rationale, the amount of developer obligations during land readjustment has been justified from a perspective of cost recovery, therefore applying developer obligations as an indirect value capture tool. At the time, land contributions are calculated such that land development, infrastructure and services investments are self-financing with land values (Lee, 1993; Jung, 1994). The public's passive governance approach of facilitating urban development without the public's financial involvement is, however, achieved in this scheme. Therefore, the developer obligations embedded in the land readjustment scheme can best be described as a profit-sharing arrangement between the public and the private landowners. While the qualities of the self-financing land readjustment scheme are undisputed for a poor developing country, the excessive private value capture of land value increments has led to social tensions. Private wealth tended to accumulate among landowners, and therefore lead to an increasing stratification of society (Lee, 1994; Kim, 1997). As a result, the emerging social tensions led to the abolishment of the land readjustment policy in the early 1980s.

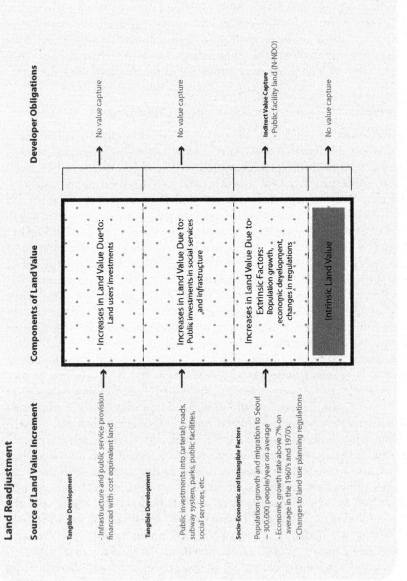

Figure 15.1 Sources of land value increments and developer obligations with land readjustment

2. Joint (hapdong) redevelopment process (1983–1998)

Joint (hapdong) redevelopment emerged in the early 1980s, when the easy-to-develop areas in the city's fringe and greenfield sites became scarce. In this scheme, developer obligations are embedded into the joint redevelopment policy (*jutaegjaegaebal*) as an indirect, non-negotiable value capture instrument. In the joint redevelopment process, the landowners, a construction company and the local public engage in a profit-sharing arrangement that allows the public to maintain a passive governance approach in which no financial commitment from the city is required. Landowners provide the land, while the construction company takes care of all cost for demolition, temporary housing for the residents, and apartment construction. The original landowners choose between compensation in kind or cash according to the land value they contributed in the first place. The construction company makes a profit by selling surplus apartment units on the housing market. In this policy, the public achieves its planning goals of improving infrastructure and providing new and improved public facilities in a trade for a higher density allowance (Kim, 1998). Two conditions are needed for the joint redevelopment scheme to work: first, a supportive housing market; and second, a collaborative local public authority that allows for increased densities in their legislation (Kim, 2004), (Shin, 2009).

While formally, the local administration initiates the project, in practice, the construction companies take the initiative, act as implementing bodies and negotiate with the landowners' association (Lee et al., 2003). The joint redevelopment principle has influenced also other, later redevelopment policies, such as the redevelopment project (*jaegaebal sa-eob*) and the housing site development policy (*taegjigaebal sa-eob*).

2.1 Land value capture and developer obligations in joint (hapdong) redevelopment

The increase in land value in joint redevelopment is not only due to the investments of the implementing body, but also to the high growth rate of the national economy, the continuing migration and under-provision of housing in Seoul (unearned increment); public investments into infrastructure and services off-site (betterment); and intangible factors, such as the changes to density and land use (see Figure 15.2).

The developer obligations in the joint redevelopment policy are indirect value capture instruments that consist of two types of contributions: first, public facility land for streets, parks and other public infrastructure; and second, an additional land contribution for low-income housing. Both the contribution ratio of public facility land and the low-income housing ratio were non-negotiable. Developer obligations in the joint redevelopment policy remain an indirect value capture instrument; however, with the contributions for low-income housing, an externality mitigation rationale is added to the cost recovery rationale.

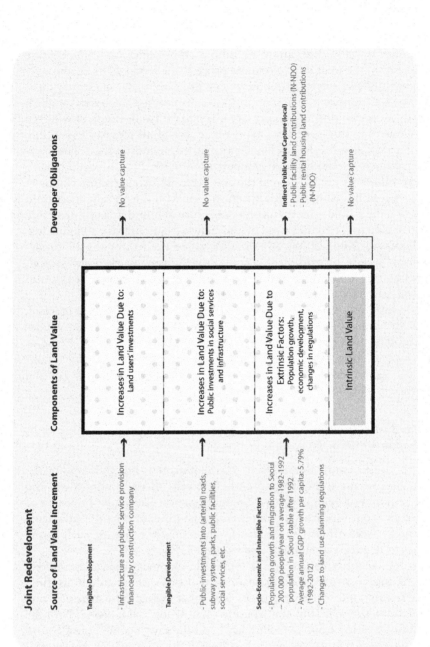

Figure 15.2 Sources of land value increments and developer obligations with joint redevelopment

3. Pre-negotiation system (since 2009)

With increasing prosperity, the macroeconomic environment in Korea changed. In the early 1990s, as a countermeasure to land speculation, sky-rocketing land prices and privatisation of development gains, the Development Gain Recapturing Act emerged. The development charge, a DO based on this law, has been implemented as a non-negotiable, direct value capture instrument of land value increments due to betterment or changes to land-use regulations with the purpose of curbing speculation and redistributing part of the development gains. Whether a site is subject to the development charge depends on its location, size and purpose. Public projects and private projects of national strategic interest are fully or partially exempt from the development charge. The amount of developer contributions is non-negotiable and calculated according to the formula:

$$Development\ Charge = (Development\ gains - Development\ costs) \times 0.25$$

The collected contributions are split equally between the central government's and the local governments' special accounts. The development charge facilitates cross-subsidising of unrelated public projects off-site and intends to promote a balanced regional development. However, in most jurisdictions, the development charge did not make a significant contribution to the fiscal health of either national or local governance, and is therefore relatively ineffective (Lee, 2016a).

Since 2009, however, with the pre-negotiation system in Seoul, an experiment with a new public contribution has emerged. This system has been initiated as an experiment with the intention to capture significant land value increment over privately owned land, while keeping the obstacles for development low. Most of these privately owned sites selected in the experiment are designated as 'public facility sites', which obligates the private landowners to provide certain facilities and services according to the 'public facility plan'. Nevertheless, landowners can freely buy and sell this land without public interference. A small number of the selected sites are, however, publicly owned sites with a public facility obligation. Despite the leverage that the land ownership gives the public in these cases, value capture in the pre-negotiation system is not conducted in exchange for land sales, but based on the changes made to rules and regulations. Therefore, both cases can be considered DOs, regardless of public or private ownership prior to negotiations.

The pre-negotiation system (*sajeonhyeobsangjedo*) is a direct, negotiable value capture instrument, which argues that part of the development gain belongs to the community and should therefore be redistributed to the community as a contribution of some sort.

3.1 The pre-negotiation development process

As with the development charge, the Development Gain Recapturing Act forms the legal basis, which allows public interference with private property rights for the common good. Specifically, the National Territory Act's Enforcements Decree provides the base for collecting contributions for infrastructure costs in exchange for land-use changes or alterations to the building restrictions (Lee, 2016b). These contributions may be financial contributions and donations, such as land or property, but might also appear as maintenance and service activities for roads, rivers and public activities on- or off-site in exchange for the rights to redevelop specific sites. The negotiable development charges are applied for under-utilised industrial or infrastructural land, often outdated former public facility sites larger than 10,000 m². On these sites, formerly public land has been linked with a public facility obligation; for example, to provide public goods such as express bus terminals, bus garages, etc., and then been sold at reduced prices to private corporations in order to minimise the burden of public investment. Since the facility plan is then institutionally linked to the now privately owned land, the land cannot be developed or redeveloped without the public facility function unless the site is cleared of these requirements. In the pre-negotiation system decisions with regard to land use (including the public facility plan), density, social overhead capital investments and development fees are negotiated by the negotiation committee, consisting of the public, the landowner and selected experts, prior to the start of the conventional planning process. In these negotiations the 'facility plan', defining the public facilities to be provided on-site, or the potential revoked designation thereof, together with the changes the public makes to the zoning and density regulations, gives leverage to the city government in the negotiations. Part of the contribution of the developer in this policy is mandatory, and there is hardly any negotiation possible about the amount of the developer obligation. However, the composition of the pre-negotiation developers' contribution, whether in kind, cash or labour, is negotiable. The amount is calculated by the formula (Statutes of the Republic of Korea, 2017):

$$PreN - Public\ Contribution = [(FAR\ after\ change - FAR\ before\ change) \times 0.6] / FAR\ after\ change$$

The pre-negotiation process consists of three parts: site selection, negotiation of the development plan and legalisation of the outcome of the negotiations in the local district unit plan. The PreN–Public Contribution rate in the preceding formula is determined prior to the start of the negotiations. Agreements between the private and public parties are made in the second phase. Here, details of the plans are discussed, values calculated by appraisal and deals about the kind and amount of public contributions by the developer are established. The results of this negotiations lead to the detailed development plan and the public contribution plan, which are then submitted to and approved by the municipal joint committee of architecture and urban planning in order to become legally binding as part of the district unit plan in the third phase (Lee, 2016b). No additional negotiations take place once the plan has been submitted to authorities after the pre-negotiations concluded.

3.2 Land value capture and developer obligations in Seoul's pre-negotiation system

The land value increase during the application of the pre-negotiation system is due to intangible factors, such as the changes to the land-use regulations, public investments (betterment) and investments by the developer. As the pressure of migration and economic growth has calmed, the unearned increment plays a lesser role in land value increase than in earlier development phases (see Figure 15.3). With the pre-negotiation system, the public manages to capture part of the development gain as a recompense for changes to the building regulations through investments in public services and infrastructure on-site, and also accomplishes cross-subsidising for services and infrastructure off-site. Similar to the other land policies discussed, the public employs a passive governance approach. It does not have to deal with the burden of financial investments and therefore benefits from urban development according to the publics' planning agenda at little risk. The private sector in this policy benefits from shaping the regulations and constraints, as far as agreed with the public body, in accordance to the corporations' preferences and capabilities.

4. Conclusions

The case of Seoul shows how the application of developer obligations helped to deal with the challenges of fiscal stress during the three phases of development. The developer obligations have evolved from a non-negotiable, indirect value capture instrument in the early phase of economic development into a direct value capture instrument, in which the composition of the developer obligation (not the amount) is negotiable in the experiments with the pre-negotiation system.

We identify four trends and one stable variable in the evolution of value capture policies in Seoul. First, there is a reciprocal influence between the socio-economic setting and the public value capture policy. While the urbanisation policy during the phase of land readjustment manages to unlock private financing for urban development, this policy at the same time gives large profit incentives to the private landowners, which in turn leads to social division and in the end to the abandonment of the policy. Second, in the transition from early development to mature development, the ratio of privately captured land value increments has decreased. Third, the fiscal

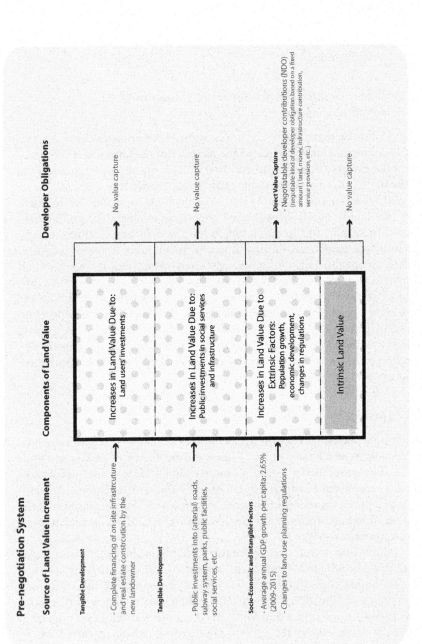

Figure 15.3 Sources of land value increments and developer obligations with pre-negotiation

independence of the local government has been strengthened, allowing the City of Seoul to employ higher levels of cross-subsidising of public initiatives off-site. Fourth, the public planning goal of cost recovery, backed by an economic efficiency rationale, makes way for a value capture policy with increasingly negotiable and – to a certain extent – flexible public planning goals. The stable variable in this analysis is the passive governance style employed in the three selected policies. In the policies discussed here, the public sector avoids financial commitment in the investment in land and infrastructure development, while securing its planning goals through developer obligations in exchange for changes to land-use regulations.

In the phase of land readjustment, the value capture policy has been applied with a cost recovery rationale in the form of non-negotiable land contributions. The joint redevelopment policy is similar in its character as a profit-sharing arrangement between the public, landowners and construction companies. Fundamental to joint redevelopment is the rent gap created by the local public through zoning regulation changes. Here, next to the cost efficiency rationale, a rationale of externality mitigation is introduced. This rationale justifies an additional land contribution for financing low-cost housing.

Recently, the socio-economic setting has dramatically changed. The economy is growing slowly, housing provision in Seoul has reached 100 per cent, and land prices have stabilised. It has become less attractive to invest in land due to reduced profit expectations, and the role of the public has shifted towards initiating development, rather than regulating it. In the pre-negotiation experiment, the governance style remains passive, as public bodies remain reluctant to take financial responsibilities or risks. However, the value capture rationales have changed from indirect, to direct value capture. Different from the policies discussed in the earlier two phases, the pre-negotiation system deals with the redevelopment of privately owned 'public facility' sites, during a period when developable land in Seoul has become scarce. This explains the high ratio of value capture, which can be employed as a redistributional fiscal instrument. This is different from the DOs applied to the development of private sites with the Development Gains Recapturing Act, which are non-negotiable, handle lower value capture ratios (which get split between national and local administrations accounts) and have, in most cases, not captured significant funds to effectively relieve fiscal stress. The pre-negotiation system, on the other hand, promises to capture significant funds and contributes to cross-subsidising public planning goals by adding to the fiscal health of the City of Seoul.

References

Hong, Y-H. & Brubaker, D. (2010), 'Integrating the Proposed Property Tax with the Public Leasehold System', in Man, J. Y. & Hong, Y-H. (eds.), *China's Local Public Finance in Transition*. Cambridge: Lincoln Institute of Land Policy, pp. 165–190.

Jo, J. C. (2015), *Implementing Aspects & Lessons Learned from Korean Land Readjustment.* Anyang-si: Korea Research Institute of Human Settlements – KRIHS, p. 65.

Jung, H. N. (1994), *Land Policies in South Korea: A Political Economy Approach. Land Policy Problems in East Asia: Toward New Choices: A Comparative Study of Japan, Korea and Taiwan.* Honolulu: Korea Research Institute for Human Settlements – KRIHS, pp. 301–327.

Kim, K-J. (2004), 'Inner City Growth Management Problem in Seoul: Residential Rebuilding Boom and Its Planning Issues', in Sorensen, A., Marcotullio, P. & Grant, J. (eds.), *Towards Sustainable Cities: East Asian, North American, and European Perspectives on Managing Urban Regions.* Hampshire, Ashgate, pp. 267–284.

Kim, K. Y. (1998), 'New Form, Classic Problem: Psuedo-Public Residential Redevelopment in Seoul', *Built Environment*, Vol. 24, No. 4, pp. 235–250.

Kim, S-W. (2015), *The Land Readjustment Program. Seoul Solutions for Urban Development (Part 1 – Urban Planning).* Seoul: Seoul Metropolitan Government, pp. 173–192.

Kim, Y. W. (1997), 'Urban Land Development Methods: Urban Land Development and Management in Korea', in Kim,Y. W. (ed.), Korea Research Institute of Human Settlements.

Lee, C-M., et al. (2003), 'A Revenue-Sharing Model of Residential Redevelopment Projects: The Case of the Hapdong Redevelopment Scheme in Seoul, Korea', *Urban Studies*, Vol. 40, No. 11, p. 14.

Lee, H. (2016a), *The Development Gains Recapturing System in Korea: Focussing on Development Charges. Cases of Land Based Financial Instruments in Korea.* Anjang-si: Korea Research Institute of Human Settlements, p. 74.

Lee, S. (2016b), *Pre-Negotiation System for Changing Urban Planning to Share and Vitalize Development Gains. Cases of Land Based Financial Instruments in Korea.* Anjang-si: Korea Research Institute of Human Settlements, p. 74.

Lee, T-I. (1993), 'Recent Urban Land Reforms in Korea: Goals and Limitations. Land Policy Problems in East Asia – Towards New Choices', in Koppel, B. & Kim, Y. D. (eds.), Anyang-si: East West Center and Korea Research Institute for Human Settlements, p. 19.

———— (1994), *Planning the Use of Land in Korea. Land Policy Problems in East Asia: Toward New Choices: A Comparative Study of Japan, Korea and Taiwan.* Honolulu: KRIHS – Korea Research Institute for Human Settlements, pp. 215–234.

———— (2002), *Land Readjustment in Korea. Tools for Land Management and Development: Land Readjustment.* Cambridge, MA, US Lincoln Intitute of Land Policy, p. 29.

Shin, H. B. (2009), 'Property-Based Redevelopment and Gentrification: The Case of Seoul, South Korea', *Geoforum*, Vol. 40, No. 5, pp. 906–917.

Sohn, S-K. (2003), 'Changes in the Residential Features of Seoul. Seoul, 20th Century, Growth & Change of the Last 100 Years', in Kim, K-J. (ed.), Seoul: Seoul Development Institute, pp. 213–304.

Statutes of the Republic of Korea. (2017), *Enforcement Decree of the National Land Planning and Utilization Act.* Presidential Decree No. 27972. K. L. R. INSTITUTE. Sejong-si, Korea Legislation Research Institute.

16 Developer obligations in relation to land value capture in Taiwan

Tzu-Chin Lin and Hsiu-Yin Ding

1. A cursory glance at land value capture

Capture of land value that accrues not from an individual's own effort is a fundamental policy stated in the Constitution of Republic of China, Taiwan (Hu, 2006). Article 143 of the Constitution reads that:

> All land within the territory of the Republic of China shall belong to the whole body of citizens. . . . If the value of a piece of land has increased, not through the exertion of labor or the employment of capital, the State shall levy thereon an increment tax, the proceeds of which shall be enjoyed by the people in common.

A Land value increment tax (*tu di zeng zhi shui*) levied upon transaction of land was therefore introduced in 1954 and continues into the present time.

The rate structure of this tax has always been progressive. The present rates are from 20%–40%. The tax rates were respectively 40%, 50% and 60% during most of the 1990s. The highest rate even reached 100% between the 1950s and 1960s. Despite the high tax rate, the suppressed assessment has kept the effective tax rate down. In the second half of the 2000s, the effective rate was only around 4%–6%. (Hua, 2013). Despite of the under-assessment, land value increment tax accounts for between 20% and 40% of total tax revenue over the course of years 2003 and 2013 for the six major cities (Taipei, New Taipei, Kaohsiung, Taichung, Tainan and Taoyuan) in Taiwan.[1] It is fair to conclude that this tax has supplied a significant tax revenue to local governments, but performs unsatisfactorily as a value capture instrument (Lin & Cheng, 2016).

In addition, a Statue for Collection of Community Development Fee by Construction Project (*gong cheng shou yi fei zheng shou tiao li*) was enacted in 1944 (Chang, 1993: 42). This fee can be levied on lands and improvements that gain direct benefits from specified public infrastructures,

---

1 Ministry of Finance website: www.mof.gov.tw/Eng/Home

including roads, bridges, ditches, harbors, piers, reservoirs, embankments, channel dredging, etc. The amount of fees charged cannot exceed 80% of the total infrastructure costs that largely include construction, land acquisition and mortgage loans. This fee aims to recoup the spillover benefits of certain public infrastructures, and involves no changes of land use. However, this fee stopped its collection during the 1980s, largely because of the political pressure and the lack of consensus on the beneficiaries.

Land use zoning was introduced to Taiwan in the 1980s. Land was divided into urban areas and non-urbanized areas (areas outside of urban areas). Land in the urban areas was zoned in accordance with the urban plans that depict the ideal future development of a city. In contrast, there was a lack of plans in the non-urbanized areas to guide the future land use. As a result, the existing use of land during the 1970s and 1980s was recognized as the legally permissible use (Lin & Ding, 2015). For example, if an area of land in that time period was in farm use, it would be zoned as farmland. This dual system of land-use zoning effectively affects how the land value is captured.

2. Developer obligations in urban areas

In urban areas, Article 27–1 of Urban Planning Law reads that:

> When an interested party formulates or modifies a detailed plan . . . or the original formulating agency modifies an urban plan. . ., the competent authority may request the said interested party to provide or donate from within the area for which the plan modification is made land for public facilities, constructible land, floor areas or a certain amount of money.

In compliance with Article 27–1 of this Act, the Ministry of the Interior has since the mid-1990s published at least seven ordinances (National Development Council, 2014: 37) to specifically handle the expected increase in land value and additional need for public facilities that result from the changes in land uses (see Table 16.1).

Table 16.1 shows that the ordinances were enacted to deal with rezoning of land from or into a certain zone, or between specific zones. The types of land-use zones involved also reflect the popular kinds of land rezoning at various time points in history. In each ordinance, the required contribution from landowners in exchange for rezoning is specified. For example, Ordinance of Rezoning of Industrial Land has set the requirements shown in Table 16.2.

The expert committee of urban planning (*dou shi ji hua wei yuan hui*) consists of 14–22 members. More than half of the committee members need to be appointed from outside of the local governments. External members must include professionals in urban planning, urban design, landscape, architecture or transportation (Code of Organization of Expert Committee of Urban Planning). The required contribution is in principle offered in the

Table 16.1 Ordinances dealing with land use changes in urban areas

Names of Ordinances	Contents	The Year Ordinance Was First Passed
Ordinance of Rezoning of Land Adjacent to Industrial Zone	Rezoning of land parcels that are adjacent to industrial zone into industrial land	June 1994
Ordinance of Rezoning of Industrial Land	For industrial zone to be rezoned into other zones	September 1994
Ordinance of Rezoning of State-owned Enterprise Land	Rezoning of state-owned enterprise land into other land uses	February 1996
Ordinance of Rezoning into Light Industry, Logistics and Retailing Land	For other zones to be rezoned into light industry, logistics and retailing zone	July 1996
Ordinance of Rezoning into Media Industry Land	For other zones to be rezoned into media industry zone	December 1996 (repealed in 2017)
Ordinance of Rezoning of Agricultural Land	For agricultural zone to be rezoned into other zones	February 1997
Ordinance of Rezoning of Agricultural or Conservation Land into Health Care Industry Land	For either agricultural or conservation zone to be rezoned into health care industry zone	August 1997

Table 16.2 Required contribution in ordinance of rezoning of industrial land

Rezoning to Residential Land	Rezoning to Commercial Land	Rezoning to Other Land Uses
The contributed area for public facilities and building sites combined cannot be less than 37% of the total rezoned area	The contributed area for public facilities and building sites combined cannot be less than 40.5% of the total rezoned area	Subject to the decision of expert committee of urban planning at local governments
In all cases, the contributed area for public facilities cannot be less than 30% of the total rezoned area.		

form of land. However, subject to the prior consent of the expert committee, the contribution of building sites can be instead substituted by monetary payment. A formula for the amount of value-equivalent payment (*dai jin*) is set in the ordinance as:

Amount of value-equivalent payment = Appraised value of total area of building sites (after rezone) × area of contributed building sites (after rezone) / total area of building sites (after rezone)

At least three real estate appraisal firms will be commissioned by the local government to value the rezoned area. The highest valuation result among the appraisal firms will be selected to be the appraised value of total area of building sites (after rezone). Moreover, a minimum amount of value-equivalent payment is stipulated as 1.4 times the government-assessed value (*gong gao xian zhi*) of the contributed building sites after rezoning (this government-assessed value serves the calculation of the land value increment tax levied upon transaction of land, and in practice is significantly lower than the market value).

Another example of rezoning of land uses is the Ordinance of Rezoning of Agricultural Land. This Ordinance states that sites of public facilities need to be offered not only to serve the rezoned area, but also neighboring areas. If the developer is not able to offer the public facilities inside the rezoned area, substitute sites should be provided outside. Otherwise, subject to the prior consent of the expert committee of urban planning, value-equivalent payment is an alternative. The determination of the amount of value-equivalent payment is the same as in the Ordinance of Rezoning of Industrial Land (see earlier equation). Moreover, the area of sites for public facilities and substitute sites combined cannot be less than 30% of the rezoned area if the new use is industrial, and the figure cannot be less than 40% if new uses are other than industrial.

By and large, the requirements for developer obligations among various ordinances are similar and only differ in some details. In principle, provision of sites of public facilities is required and a minimum standard (in percentage) is often specified. Value-equivalent monetary payment is often allowed, and its amount is prescribed. Finally, the local expert committee of urban planning oversees the process and enjoys a high degree of discretion in decisions.

3. Developer obligations in non-urbanized areas

Uses of land and its changes outside of the urban areas are regulated by the Regulation of Land Uses in Non-Urbanized Areas. This Regulation is authorized by Regional Plan Act. Article 15–1 of this Act reads: "For the purpose of development and utilization, according to the regional plan, an applicant may submit a development plan enclosed with related documents to the municipal or county (city) government." Furthermore, Article 15–3 reads: "the applicant shall . . . and pay the development impact fees to the municipal or county (city) government for the purpose of improving or increasing public facilities; the foresaid development impact fees may be substituted by buildable land within the development area." In compliance with Article 15–3, an Ordinance of Levy of Development Impact Fee in Non-Urbanized Areas was enacted in August 2001. Article 2 of this ordinance states that "The need for levying development impact fee (*kai fa ying xiang fei*) arises when land development involves changes in the nature of land use and that consequently affects the service level of public facilities and other public interest in the neighbouring areas."

The appended Table 1 of this ordinance specifies the occasions when development impact fees should be applied, and the public facilities that are demanded associated with land development (see Table 16.3).

Table 16.3 Development impact fees in various scenarios of land development

Development Scenarios	Required Provision of Public Facilities	Optional Provision of Public Facilities
Residential use	Connecting roads, schools	Local parks, fire brigade
Industrial use	Connecting roads	Local parks, fire brigade
Commercial use	Connecting roads	Local parks, fire brigade
Recreational use	Connecting roads	Parking lots, fire brigade
Other uses	Connecting roads	Parking lots

Only connecting roads are the mandatory public facilities for all kinds of development, and schools are additionally required for residential developments only. The local governments are given discretion to decide if other public facilities are needed, such as local parks, fire brigades or parking lots. Article 4 of the same ordinance allows the impact fee to be paid by value-equivalent building sites in lieu of monetary payment. The appended Table 2 of this ordinance further formulates the calculation of the development impact fees for connecting roads, schools, local parks, fire brigade and parking lots.

For example, the formula for calculating the development impact fee for connecting roads is shown here (assuming the width of road is 3.5 m):

$$C = NLM \times (3.5 \times 1000) \times (CU + CL)$$

where
C: estimated development impact fee.
NLM: need of additional length (km) of road resulting from the new development.
CU: construction cost of roads per m^2. This figure is subject to the decision of local governments.
CL: land cost of roads per m^2. This figure is subject to the decision of local governments which will take into account both 1.4 times the government-assessed land value and the valuation of real estate appraisers.

Also, the formula for calculating the development impact fee for elementary and junior high schools is shown here:

$$SIF = POP \times Ss \times CL$$

where
SIF: estimated development impact fee.
POP: estimated additional number of students resulting from the new residential development.
Ss: the standard size (m^2) required per student.
CL: land cost of the school per m^2. This figure is subject to the decision of local governments, taking account of both 1.4 times the government-assessed land value and the valuation of real estate appraisers.

Formulations for calculating development impact fees for providing local parks, fire brigades and parking lots are similar to previous equations. The input variables for equations are clearly specified in the ordinances. However, the figures for some variables are at the discretion of local governments to suit the local situations.

Besides the development impact fee, there is a feedback fee (*hui kui jin*). Article 12 of the Agricultural Development Act states that "The change of land use as stated in the first paragraph of Article 10 shall be subject to the payment of a feedback fund based on its business nature of the land in use." In compliance with the Article 12, an Ordinance of Appropriation and Allocation of Feedback Fee Fund for Farmland Conversion was enacted in August of Year 2000. This ordinance specifies the amount of monetary feedback. The land value under the new use is based on the government-assessed value when the rezoning is permitted. In the case of conversion of farmland into land for transportation and logistics-related industry such as driving schools or bus stops, 40% of the estimated land value under the new use is levied as feedback fee. In the case of conversion of farmland into private roads, the levy rate is 20%. In the case of conversion of farmland into historic buildings, the levy rate is 1%. In the case of conversion of farmland into sites for agricultural industry such as agricultural facilities of production, storage, marketing and leisure, the levy rate is 3%. For other farmland conversion not specified in the preceding, the levy rate is 50%. In addition, if the farmland under conversion is classified as prime farmland (*te ding nong ye qu*), or located in areas of farmland consolidation or areas where a significant amount of agricultural resources has been invested, the rate of feedback fee could be raised by another 20%.

Similar to this ordinance is the Ordinance of Appropriation of Feedback Fee Fund for Slope Land. This Ordinance was enacted in November 2000 in compliance with Act 48–1 of the Forestry Act, which states that:

> To encourage long-term reforestation by private individuals and/or organizations, the Government shall establish a reforestation fund. The sources of funding shall be as follows: 1. Allocations from water-rights fees; 2. A reciprocation fund provided by those who undertake development of slope land; 3. Penalty fines for violation of this Act.

The value of slope land after development is based on the government-assessed value under the new uses. The amount of feedback fee depends on the type of development, the levy rate ranges between 6% and 12%. For example, in the cases of mining and golf courts, the fee is 12% of the estimated value of the slope land after development. In contrast, in the case of a driving school, the levy rate is 6%. A discount for the feedback fee is allowed if measures are taken to mitigate the environmental impacts.

Ordinances governing developer obligations in urban areas all originate from Article 27–1 of the Urban Planning Act. In contrast, ordinances governing developer obligations in non-urbanized areas not only originate from the Regional Plan Act, but also from other acts (for example, Agricultural Development Act and Forestry Act) that particularly stipulate the development of agricultural and forestry land. It is also noted that ordinances in non-urbanized areas are not only concerned with land value capture, but also highlight the significance of farmland preservation and environmental protection (Suzuki et al., 2015).

4. Concluding remarks

Specific legislation meant to govern land value capture only started to be enacted during the mid-1990s. Review of the legislation and its enforcement has highlighted a number of features that warrant some attention.

First, Taiwan seems apparently to employ a non-negotiable developer obligations system. Details of developer obligations are almost always prescribed in written ordinances. However, when examined closely, ordinances often specify only the minimum requirements, which leaves room for negotiation. Besides, expert committees are granted a high degree of discretion. In addition, developers are sometimes allowed to choose between monetary payment and contribution of building land, but only if the relevant authorities or expert committee agrees. It is expected that a monetary payment is preferred over land contribution for developers when the land value is on the rise. It is unfortunate that no information is available about the actual negotiation room of developers.

Second, when monetary payment is accepted as a substitute for building land, this amount is often based on a certain percentage of the government-assessed land value (made for the land value increment tax), together with the valuation of real estate appraisers. The government-assessed land value is not tailored made for the purpose of determining developer obligations. In consequence, the assessed land value (even if 40% of the land value is added on) may not be based on real market values. Introduction of the appraisers' valuation indicates the government's intention to reflect the true increase of land value. Given the long-term nature of government-assessed land value, it is best seen as a safety valve to prevent a too-low value estimation.

Finally, the differences in land-use control among urban and non-urbanized areas seem to go together with differences in the rationales behind developer obligations. Determination of developer obligations in urban areas tend to be based on the expected value of land in the new and more valuable use. Obligations of this kind are more in line with the direct rationale that landowners do not deserve the entire increase of land value. In contrast, the development impact fee in non-urbanized areas aligns more with the indirect rationale that landowners are liable to internalization of the negative impacts of the new development. In addition to these two rationales, the more recent introduction of a feedback fee on farmland and slope land seems to have added a new sort of indirect rationale. This fee is earmarked to conserve a better natural environment.

The long discrepancy between urban and non-urbanized areas in land-use control finally led to the enactment of the Spatial Planning Act in 2016. Under the new act, all land in the country is under the same zoning system. Land is divided into four zones: environmental conservation zone, marine resource zone, agricultural development zone and urban development zone. Under the four zones, there are presently 22 sub-zones that specify the permissible land uses. Applications for changes in the permissible land uses will require payment of two different fees: an environmental conservation fee (*guo tu bao yu fei*) and an impact fee (*ying xiang fei*), charged by the central and local governments, respectively. The former is meant for the purpose of environmental conservation, and the latter for improvement of public facilities. How developer obligations will evolve under the new legal regime in practice remains to be seen.

References

Chang, Jing-Sen (1993) *Urban Planning in Taiwan: 1895–1988*, Chang Yung-Fa Foundation for National Policy Research, Taipei: Ye-Jiang Publisher. (in Chinese)

Hu, Chuen-Lei (2006) A Study on Land Policy and Regulation Under the ROC Constitution, *Economic Research*, 6:33–72. (in Chinese)

Hua, Jing-Qun (2013) Issues and Strategies of Property Tax Reform. *Modern Public Finance*, 36: 8–24. (in Chinese)

Lin, Tzu-Chin and Ding, Hsiu-Yin (2015) Farmland Reform, Property Right Reconfiguration and Land Market, *Taiwan: A Radical Quarterly in Social Studies*, 100: 217–228. (in Chinese)

Lin, Tzu-Chin and Cheng, Yun-Ting (2016) The Missing Public Interest in Land: Auctions of Public Land in Taipei City. *Issues & Studies: A Social Science Quarterly on China, Taiwan, and East Asian Affairs*, December 52(4): 1640003-1-1640003-20.

National Development Council (2014) *Evaluation of Obligation and Feedback System of Land Development in Taiwan*. (in Chinese)

Suzuki, H., Murakami, J., Hong, Y-H, and Tamoayose, B. (2015) *Financing Transit-Oriented Development with Land Values: Adapting Land Value Capture in Development Countries*, World Bank Group.

Cited acts

Agricultural Development Act 2016
Code of Organization of Expert Committee of Urban Planning 2004
Forestry Act 2016
Ordinance of Appropriation and Allocation of Feedback Fee Fund for Farmland Conversion 2016
Ordinance of Appropriation of Feedback Fee Fund for Slope Land 2017
Ordinance of Rezoning into Light Industry, Logistics and Retailing Land 2006
Ordinance of Rezoning into Media Industry Land 2017 repealed
Ordinance of Rezoning of Agricultural Land 2018

Ordinance of Rezoning of Agricultural or Conservation Land into Health Care
    Industry Land 2004
Ordinance of Rezoning of Industrial Land 2011
Ordinance of Rezoning of Land Adjacent to Industrial Zone 2018
Ordinance of Rezoning of State-owned Enterprise Land 2018
Regional Plan Act 2000
Regulation of Land Uses in Non-Urbanized Areas 2018
Spatial Planning Act 2016
Statue for Collection of Community Development Fee by Construction Project 2000
Ordinance of Levy of Development Impact Fee in Non-Urbanized Areas 2015
Urban Planning Law 2015

17 Indonesian experience with non-negotiable and negotiable developer obligations
Case study of Surabaya City

Adjie Pamungkas and Ary A. Samsura

1. Introduction

Although the provision of public services and infrastructures traditionally has long been considered as the responsibility of the public sector or government, the involvement and contribution of private investments in that provision have emerged as one of the important approaches in many countries, including Indonesia. Evidently, neither a purely public nor a purely private infrastructure development approach is likely to be sustainable in the long term. Apart from the fact that the public sector has limited traditional sources of financing to fulfil various desires in providing public services, a purely public approach may cause problems such as slow and ineffective decision-making, inefficient organizational and institutional frameworks, and lack of competition and efficiency. A purely private approach, on the other hand, may also cause problems, such as inequalities in the distribution of public services, which can be considered examples of market failure. Moreover, the experience of private involvement in public infrastructure development has not always been without problems. Due to the high risk related to the complexity of the development process and of the size of the investment, public infrastructure development is not always attractive to the private sector. According to the World Bank, private investments in public infrastructure development have increased to more than 600% between 1990 and 1997, but it considerably decreased afterwards in the wake of the East Asian financial crisis with the number of new private infrastructure projects also down by around half (World Bank, 2013). Nevertheless, despite some negative experiences, the Indonesian government – like that of many other countries – continues to view private participation and contribution as one of the key strategies in delivering public services and infrastructure.

The nature and scope of private involvement in public service delivery may vary. One type of these involvements is through developer obligations. In general, developer obligations can be defined as requirements placed by public authorities on private developers to contribute in financing public services as a condition for granting development permits (Alterman, 1990). Developer obligations may come in different forms such as land dedication, payment of a fee, construction of a public facility, or supply of a public service.

In this chapter, the experiences of Indonesia with both non-negotiable and negotiable developer obligations (N-NDOs and NDOs) for public services are discussed. It takes Surabaya City, which is the second largest city in Indonesia and the capital of East Java Province, as a case study. This study particularly analyses developers contributions related to high-rise building developments that are mushrooming in the city due to its fast-growing economic development.

2. Surabaya and high-rise building development

Surabaya City serves as the capital of East Java Province and is located in the northeast of Java island (see Figure 17.1). The city covers a total area of 326.36 km² and is divided into 31 districts. In 2015, the population of the city reached 2.9 million (BPS Kota Surabaya, 2016), but its extended metropolitan area reached up to more than 9 million inhabitants. The city has enjoyed a relatively high level of Human Development Index in comparison with the national average, especially with regard to health, education, and people's purchase ability (BPS Kota Surabaya, 2016).

In terms of economic activities, Surabaya has not only become the hub for the East Java province, but also most of the eastern part of Indonesia. In 2015, the economic growth of the city was more than 7% which is higher than the national average with the main contributions to the city economic activities from commerce, manufacturing industry, hotels and restaurants, and construction (BPS Kota Surabaya, 2016). The high level of economic growth of Surabaya City has contributed to the growth of property prices in the city. Based on the report of UrbanIndo, an Indonesian online real estate

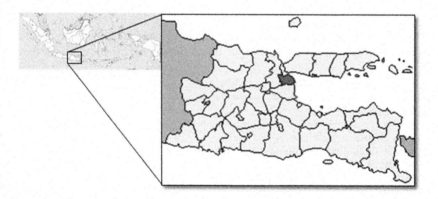

Figure 17.1 Location of Surabaya City in Indonesia
Source: Wikimedia Commons.

database,[1] the increase of property prices in Surabaya is the highest in comparison with other Indonesian big cities since mid-2015. This situation has also further boosted the number of high-rise building developments in Surabaya. At the moment, there are more than 100 high-rise buildings in the city (12 floors or more) and more than 40 are under construction (Table 17.1). Given the fact that almost the same number of permits is being proposed or applied for to construct buildings with more than 20 floors, the number of high-rise buildings in the city would increase significantly in the future. Since, in general, the Surabaya municipality has limited resources to fund the escalating expenditure to provide public services and infrastructure, the increasing number of high-rise buildings in the city can be expected to offer more income to the city through different sorts of contributions.

In Indonesia, permission to develop a property at a certain location is given by the municipal government to a developer through two main stages of the administrative procedure. First, the developer must acquire a letter of reference for the detailed city plan (in Bahasa Indonesia, this plan is called *Rencana Detail Tata Ruang Kota* – RDTRK) from the municipality. The letter is called *Surat Keterangan Rencana Kota* (SKRK), and it contains the information about the characteristics of buildings that can be built on the location of the proposed building based on the RDTRK. The information includes its designated function, maximum height, the number of floors, external perimeter, the building coverage ratio, the floor area ratio, the open green area ratio, the basement ratio, and the municipal utility networks. After the developers acquire this letter, they can apply for the development permit (in Bahasa Indonesia: *Ijin Mendirikan Bangunan* – IMB) from the municipality. The building can be legally constructed only after the IMB is granted to the developer.

Particularly in the period of 2012–2015, the number of development permits issued by the Surabaya municipality for high-rise buildings has increased significantly (see Figure 17.2). It indicates the high interests of developers to invest in high-rise building development in the city.

In 2016, the Municipality of Surabaya commissioned a study to observe potential local revenue as an output of its development, particularly from

Table 17.1 High-rise buildings in Surabaya

Type of Building	*Number of Buildings*
Current High-Rise Buildings (≥ 12 floors)	130
High-Rise Buildings (≥ 12 floors) Currently Under Construction	42
Currently Proposed High-Rise Buildings (> 20 floors)	43

Source: www.skyscrapercity.com

1 www.urbanindo.com

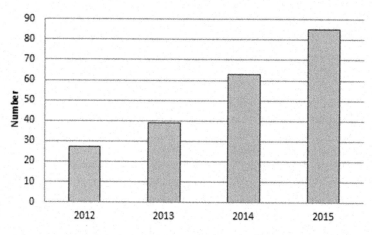

Figure 17.2 Number of development permits issued by Surabaya Municipality for high-rise buildings in 2012–2015

Source: Surabaya Public Works and Planning Agency, 2016.

legalizing high-rise buildings. The study has also predicted two scenarios of the future high-rise building developments in Surabaya City (Badan Perencanaan Pembangunan Kota Surabaya, 2016). The first scenario assumes a declining growth of proposed high-rise buildings. The second scenario follows a more optimistic view of stable continued growth of high-rise building developments. This view is supported by the vice president of Coldwell Banker (commercial advisory group), who indicates that the growth of industrial and housing (especially income) will stay at a high level (Gideon, 2015).

The current detailed plan (RDTRK) of Surabaya which is the main source of building regulations from a spatial planning perspective in proceeding with SKRKs and IMBs, is already more than 15 years old and out of date, and could not accommodate the increasing demand for high-rise buildings in the city. In order to deal with this, the mayor of Surabaya released Mayor Regulation No. 57 in 2015 as a temporary regulation to accommodate the high demand of high-rise building investments until the new RDTRK is legalized.

With regard to the distribution of proposed high-rise buildings, especially based on the development application during 2012–2016, they are spread out all over Surabaya without any specific pattern. The municipality argued that this distribution can be counter-productive for future public services development such as roads, public transport, education facilities, etc., in the city. As a response to this phenomenon, the Surabaya Municipal Public Works and Spatial Planning Agency has proposed six zones for high-rise buildings developments in the city based on different types of zoning patterns.

3. N-NDOs and NDOs as part of value capture in Surabaya high-rise buildings development

Basically, it is allowed in Indonesia to compulsorily charge the developer to contribute to public service and infrastructure development by using several regulations related to taxes and retributions. Those contributions may take place in a different stage of developments. Table 17.2 provides the list of taxes or retributions that can be charged to the developers in each development stage together with their statutory basis especially in Surabaya City.

Using those regulations, it is possible to estimate the revenues that can be captured from property developments in Surabaya City. As mentioned earlier, in 2016 the Municipality of Surabaya commissioned a study to observe and estimate the potential local revenue as an output of its development, particularly from legalizing high-rise buildings until 2021 based on the proposals that are submitted by the developers during 2012–2016. The study also made use of the two scenarios for the future high-rise building developments in Surabaya City, as explained earlier. Based on the decline scenario, the accumulative estimated revenues of Surabaya City from legalizing the high-rise building from 2016–2021 may reach up to Rp. 2.8 trillion (USD 190 million) while the flat scenario may generate up to Rp. 3.3 trillion (USD 230 million).

Among all the mentioned taxes and retributions, the SKRK and IMB retributions can be considered as contributions of developers that are directly

Table 17.2 Surabaya Municipality's revenues related to property development

NO	Stage of Development	Types of revenue source	Government regulation
1.	Pre-Construction	SKRK retribution	Municipal Regulation no.5/2012.
		IMB retribution	Municipal Regulation no.12/2012.
2.	Construction	Advertising tax	Mayoral Regulation no.14/2009.
		Land and building tax	Municipal Regulation no.10/2010.
		Hotel tax	Municipal Regulation no.4/2011.
		Restaurant tax	Municipal Regulation no.4/2011.
3.	Operational	Street lighting tax	Municipal Regulation no.4/2011.
		Acquisition tax (BPHTB)	Law no.20/2000
		Advertising tax	Mayoral Regulation no.14/2009.
		Waste retribution	Municipal Regulation no.10/2012.

Source: Surabaya Municipality.

applied in exchange for land-use regulations decisions through the issuing of development or building permit, i.e. as DOs. For the SKRK, the retribution is basically meant to cover the fee to produce the maps related to the city land-use plan (RDTRK). In early 2018, however, the mayor of Surabaya proposed to revoke the regulation to remove this fee; thus, the SKRK can be obtained without any charge with an intention to ease the procedure to get the building permit and attract people, especially businessmen, to build and develop their activities in the city. With regard to the IMB retribution, the amount depends on the function and the size of the area of the proposed building. The way to calculate the retribution is already specified in the regulation that make it non-negotiable (N-NDO). The amount of revenue that can be expected from granting the IMB itself based on the Municipal Regulation no.12/2012 is not that much. The retribution that has to be paid by a developer to get an IMB can vary from Rp. 200,000–1,000,000 (USD 14–70) per building. However, the legalisation of high-rise building can open up opportunity for revenues from different kinds of other related taxes and retributions (see Table 17.2), the amount which turns up could be much more than estimated based on two scenarios as shown earlier.

Apart from the mentioned SKRK and IMB contributions, any municipality in Indonesia in general can also make an agreement with a developer for an extra contribution by providing a variety of measures related to public services. The contribution can be included as part of agreement to grant the development permit (IMB) to a developer. The value or form of this kind of contribution can be negotiated on a per-application basis, which means that this contribution can be considered NDOs. For Surabaya City, this contribution has been clearly mentioned in the Mayoral Regulation no.75/2012, and it can be used as a condition to granting the IMB, especially when a specific infrastructure or utility that is required in the related SKRK is not yet available. The regulation specifies the contribution as the proportion of the land that is going to be dedicated for public infrastructure based on the type and the size of the proposed development. The regulation identifies three different kinds of development types, which include industrial, commerce, and residential areas. For the industrial area of five hectares up to ten hectares, the developer has to provide infrastructures with a proportion of at least 22% of the total area. Above 10 hectares, the proportion is 30%. For the commerce area, the amount that should be contributed by the developer is 20% of the total area when the size of the proposed development is from 3 to 25 hectares and 40% when the size is more than 25 hectares. For the residential area, the regulation has specified three different proportions: 30% of the total area when the area is less than or equal to 25 hectares, 40% when the area is 25–100 hectares, and 41% when it is more than 100 hectares. Although the regulation stipulates the exact amount of land to be provided with the infrastructures, the specific form of the infrastructure can be a subject to negotiation between the municipality and the developer.

Another form of contribution that can be obtained from developers is through the implementation of corporate social responsibility (CSR). In Indonesia, based on Law no. 40/2007, it is obligatory for any corporation to have a CSR policy, especially those that carry out business activities that do have an impact on the environment. Although this law does not yet have any specific operational guidelines, some municipalities have used it as a tool to ask for contributions from private companies to provide public services, especially to improve the social and physical conditions in its surrounding areas and to minimize the potential social conflict that may emerge after the development. Usually, big area developers that also manage the area implement their CSR policy after the project has been completed and has become proven operational, which is logical because the company can already securitize the revenue streams and contribute to public services. However, some municipalities in Indonesia have already asked for it, since it is obligatory for the company to do it anyway, as a part of negotiation before granting the development permit (SKRK or IMB) to the developers. Then they could be considered NDOs. Since the contribution can be specifically aimed at the improvement of the surrounding areas of the related company and development, the form of contribution can vary and depends on the problems in that particular area. It is, therefore, hard to find the data that show the total amount of contributions through CSR policy in Indonesia. In many cases, the contributions are in-kind contributions to specific activities or developments. Some examples are:

- enhancing access to surrounding areas;
- improvement of environment quality in surrounding areas;
- minimizing the flood risk in surrounding areas;
- mitigating traffic conditions after the building comes into operation;
- developing community buildings for the community in the surrounding areas.

In Surabaya City, several infrastructure developments have been fully funded through CSR. For instance, in 2014, the municipality has made an agreement to develop a new public open space based on CSR (Faizal, 2014). The municipality also negotiated with a private company in 2015 to develop a bridge in Keputran, Tegalsari District and pedestrian paths in Ketabang, Genteng District – both are in Centre Surabaya – as part of the company's CSR policy (Humas Kota Surabaya, 2015).

In terms of legalizing high-rise building in Surabaya, some of the developers have been asked to agree to provide contributions to surroundings which later can be considered as their CSRs in the form of:

1   upgrading the image of the surrounding areas;
2   improving connectivity among land parcels;
3   connecting and supporting the implementation of the public transportation system;

4   providing facilities for the disabled;
5   appling green building principles;
6   providing other solutions related to relevant issues in surrounding areas.

Those contributions are discussed during the process of granting the SKRK, and the agreement letters are signed by the owner of the project and then attached as a supporting document to apply for the IMB. The letter can also later be used by the municipality to ensure that this contribution would be implemented.

Despite its successful examples, CSR has also created a debate among lawyers, practitioners, economists, and civil society in Indonesia. The main contentious issues are mainly related to the means of regulating CSR. The introduction of Law no. 40/2007 has invited strong reactions from various actors. While civil society is primarily concerned with the implementation of such regulation, the business community is more concerned with its impact on corporate costs and resulting competitive disadvantages. Consequently, the government has to ensure that these NDOs will enhance the quality of surrounding areas. This enhancement of surrounding areas will come back to the developers as supporting condition for their good business circumstances. For most of discussion between developers and the local government, these mutual benefits are the strongest factor for finding commitment in the process of negotiating the obligations in exchange for issuing of the SKRK or IMB.

Moreover, poor legal enforcement, corruption, and excessive overlap among different laws have been a common problem to all sectors in Indonesia. Consequently, there is a high risk related to legal uncertainties regarding the contents of the contributions, additional administrative costs, and bureaucracy in the implementation of CSR (Koestoer, 2007). With no specific operational standard for implementing CSR, the risk is therefore even higher. There are various cases of alleged corruption related to CSR in several municipalities and provinces in Indonesia in recent years (CSR.id, 2015). The explanation of this situation might rest in the combined effect of factors such as the ill-designed integrity rules and planning policies, the relevance of informal institutions such as the patronage networks, and the existence of perverse incentives. In this light, a clear and effective regulatory framework is therefore certainly required to support private sector contributions in providing public services through CSR.

4. Concluding remarks

The contribution of developers to public services is not uncommon, and it has some legal basis in Indonesia. The related policies can be found, but still need to be improved. In the case of the high-rise building development in Surabaya City, both N-NDOs (SKRK and IMB retributions) and NDOs (agreements in exchange for IMBs and related to CSR) have real impacts for the Surabaya development processes. Although the N-NDOs do not provide much revenue, they would open up opprotunities in the later stages of the development for more contributions from developers through other PVC tools in the form of taxes and retributions. With the significant increase of proposed high-rise buildings in Surabaya, the estimated local government revenues for the city from all PVC tools together turn out to be very high. These large revenues could accelerate future development for Surabaya. For NDOs, although they evidently have created new opportunities for the city in the provision of public infrastructures and services, a clearer regulatory framework is still needed to make sure that the implementation can be more certain in the future.

References

Alterman, R. (1990), 'Developer Obligations for Public Services in Israel: Law and Social Policy in a Comparative Perspective', *Journal of Land Use & Environmental Law*, Vol. 5, No. 2, pp. 649–684.

Badan Perencanaan Pembangunan Kota Surabaya (Surabaya City Planning Board). (2016), *Kajian Penyusunan Potensi Pendapatan: Prakiraan Potensi Penerimaan PAD dari Bangunan Tinggi Kota Surabaya*. Kota Surabaya.

BPS Kota Surabaya. (2016), *Kota Surabaya dalam Angka. Pemerintah Kota Surabaya*.

CSR.id. (2015), *Kaleidoskop 2015: Heboh Dugaan Korupsi Dana CSR*. http://news.csr.id/2015/12/kaleidoskop-2015-heboh-dugaan-korupsi-dana-csr.

Faizal, A. (2014), *Risma Hanya Terima CSR seperti Taman Kota atau Fasilitas Sosial*, 20 March. http://tekno.kompas.com.

Gideon, A. (2015), *Simak Proyeksi Pertumbuhan Industri Properti di 2016. Liputan 6*. http://properti.liputan6.com/read/2357983/simak-proyeksi-pertumbuhan-industri-properti-di-2016, 30 May 2016.

Humas Kota Surabaya. (2015), *Jembatan Ratna akan Hubungkan Jl. Ratna dan Jl. Bengawan*, 16 October. http://humas.surabaya.go.id.

Koestoer, Y. T. (2007), *Corporate Social Responsibility in Indonesia: Building Internal Corporate Values to Address Challenges in CSR Implementation*. Seminar on Good Corporate and Social Governance in Promoting ASEAN's Regional Integration, Vol. 17, January.

World Bank. (2013), *World Investment and Political Risk*. Washington, DC: MIGA.

18 Developer obligations under the New South Wales, Australia, planning system

Glen Searle, Nicole Gurran and Catherine Gilbert

1. Introduction

This chapter outlines the nature of negotiable and non-negotiable developer obligations (NDOs and N-NDOs, respectively) under the New South Wales (NSW) planning system, which controls development in Sydney, Australia's largest city. The scope of both NDOs and N-NDOs in NSW has significantly expanded over the last 40 years as fiscal pressures on state and local governments have increased, and as community demands for better urban infrastructure have gradually mounted in parallel with rising real housing values. The chapter is structured to address the key issues addressed by the book.

2. Overview of public value capture tools and the place of developer obligations in Australia

With its hybrid Anglo American tradition of planning which combines land-use zoning and merit-based discretionary assessment (Gurran, 2011), approaches to developer obligations in Australia can theoretically include fixed (codified) and negotiated (discretionary) models. In practice, under the nation's federal system of government, the planning systems of the six states and two territories have evolved idiosyncratic approaches. These range from virtually no planning system requirements for developers to contribute towards local roads or other services (with utility provisions managed elsewhere in the development process) through to complex and potentially overlaying mechanisms for local and State governments to collect contributions towards local and regional infrastructure, services, and in some cases, affordable housing. In the states of NSW, Queensland and Victoria, contribution plans articulate codified requirements and the uses to which these contributions can be put. Alternatively, agreements for infrastructure provision may be negotiated between planning authorities and developers.

The planning system constitutes the main mode of governing urban development, which is undertaken mainly by private developers on privately owned land and follows the NSW Environmental Planning and Assessment Act 1979 (EPA Act). All but very low-impact development needs permission from the applicable consent authority (either local or state government depending on the scale and nature of the development). Development of public land by a government authority ("the Crown") also requires this permission under the EPA Act.

The main instruments and approaches used in NSW to collect contributions for local infrastructure are outlined in Part 7 of the EPA Act.[1] A variety of contribution approaches have evolved over time. The original EPA Act 1979 included provision for development charges collected by local councils for infrastructure, but concern about accountability led to the introduction of a contributions planning regime under the former Section 94 (now Section 7.11) of the EPA Act. Contribution plans are N-NDOs which set out a basis for collections towards road networks, parks and community facilities according to a fixed formula and expended in line with capital works plans for servicing development carried out by the local government.

Contributions required under former Section 94 and now under Section 7.11 must have a demonstrable nexus in terms of location and timing with the development itself. Contributions can be made in kind or by a contribution of land, or by payment into a council contributions fund. An alternative, allowed under the EPA Act since 2005, is a capital investment levy that comprises a pre-determined percentage of the total value of the development, which is paid as an alternative N-NDO under Section 7.11.

In parts of central Sydney (Pyrmont/Ultimo and Green Square redevelopment areas) and in the northern Sydney suburb of Willoughby, modest contributions for affordable housing can be levied as N-NDOs under inclusionary zoning schemes. These were initially introduced under local and regional (in the case of Pyrmont/Ultimo) instruments, but since 2001 have depended on explicit endorsement via the EPA Act and State planning policy. In late 2017, the state government foreshadowed extending the policy to enable another five municipalities to collect affordable housing contributions.

Voluntary planning agreements (VPAs), a form of NDO, were also made available under the EPA Act in 2005 to capture additional public benefits where planning rules are varied, i.e. when the proposed development does not fit within the existing land-use regulations and require the municipality to modify them in order to allow it. VPAs provide an opportunity for the community to share in part of the uplift in land value accruing from the modification of the land-use regulations. This was particularly important when there was a need for community facilities that could not be obtained through S94 Contribution Plans because there was an insufficient nexus with the development (Planning Institute of Australia, 2016). VPAs offer the potential to generate flexible benefits without the need for nexus. When VPAs cover local infrastructure and open space provisions, they can provide

---

1 Formerly Section 94, prior to amendments to the EPA Act made in March 2018.

an attractive option for developers who are able to control the timing and quality of facilities within their own project, rather than needing to rely on local government provision (Gurran et al., 2009; Wellman & Spiller, 2012).

The public benefits that can be provided by VPAs may be for any "public purpose" including "public amenities or public services", affordable housing, "transport or other infrastructure relating to land", recurrent costs associated with these items, or "conservation or enhancement of the natural environment" (EPA Act Section 7.3). There is wide discretion for both parties as to what is negotiated. The limits are set by what municipalities desire in terms of extra public facilities (some municipalities have defined these in a VPA policy), and by the requirement that developer proposals must have planning merit. Nevertheless, public benefits produced under VPAs have yielded relatively little by way of affordable housing (Searle et al., 2017).

To avoid the perception that development approvals and plan amendments such as rezonings are able to be "bought", a consent authority cannot refuse to approve a development that fits within the existing land-use regulations on the basis that a developer refuses to enter into a VPA (Gurran, 2011). Only when a developer asks for additional development possibilities that require a modification of those regulations is a VPA is necessary to fulfil the required planning merit. Nor can a planning agreement bind a planning authority to grant a development assent or support a planning proposal. In practice, the perception that VPAs compromise the decision-making process persists both amongst members of the public and within the development sector, despite requirements that draft agreements must be publicly exhibited for at least 28 days. Planning agreements run with the title of the land, and so are binding on future owners.

A special N-NDO is able to be levied by the state government under the EPA Act on subdivision (i.e. land) development in declared areas. For instance, in the Western Sydney Growth Centre greenfield precincts, a special N-NDO is levied at a fixed rate per hectare to pay 50 per cent of the costs of regional infrastructure including roads, open space and land required for social infrastructure such as health and education services. This represents an extension of developer obligations from contributions for local infrastructure to contributions for state government infrastructure (with health, education and main roads being state government responsibilities in Australia) as the state treasury seeks to pass on an increasing share of state costs to the private sector and the community under now-dominant neo-liberal precepts. Contributions for such regional infrastructure are mandated as a condition of development consent under the EPA Act.

3. Evolution and dynamics of NDOs and N-NDOs in New South Wales

Since before the 1979 EPA Act, developers have been levied for the cost of local reticulation of hydraulic services for over half a century under the

Sydney Water Act 1994 and prior legislation (Neutze, 1978). They have been required to also contribute towards hydraulic headworks infrastructure in recent decades under the same legislation. These are N-NDOs that are in addition to the Section 94/7.11 contributions introduced in the 1979 EPA Act. The latter contributions have had several stages of evolution after their introduction in 1979. The first was the requirement for local councils to prepare contribution plans for development, which specified the types of infrastructure for which contributions would be levied, and the per unit amounts payable. This was to reduce perceptions that some Section 94 contributions were being used for infrastructure not directly required by levied developments. The next phase emerged to give developers and local councils more flexibility and more opportunity to use contributions to generate extra public benefits. Thus, the EPA Act was amended in 2005 to allow contributions to comprise a fixed percentage of development costs, and to allow voluntary planning agreements (VPAs) as an NDO.

However, in the context of concerns about the escalating unaffordability of housing in Sydney and the potential role of expanded developer contributions in further increasing land and house prices, or in discouraging development, the state government set limits on local contributions from housing development, via special ministerial direction.[2] In 2010, per dwelling maximum contribution values were set at $20,000 (established urban areas) or $30,000 (greenfield areas). But with Sydney housing prices now levelling off, and a different and more fiscally conservative state government in power, these maximum limits are now being lifted, and will be totally removed by 2020.

Levies for affordable housing were introduced in a PPP area in inner Sydney in the 1990s under the provisions of the Growth Centres Act 1974, and subsequently extended to another inner Sydney PPP area and select municipalities. The introduction of VPAs in 2005 gave all municipalities an opportunity to seek affordable housing contributions from developers through NDOs, but relatively few VPAs have included affordable housing (Searle et al., 2017). In the face of rapid Sydney dwelling price increases, declining affordability and lobbying by some municipalities, an amendment to a state environmental planning policy under the EPA Act was proposed in 2017 which would allow government-nominated councils beyond the City of Sydney and Willoughby to require affordable housing development levies as N-NDOs. At the time of writing, this proposed amendment had not yet been implemented.

Contributions for state regional roads as N-NDOs were first made by a state government per hectare levy on greenfield development in Sydney's new North West Sector around 1990, using powers of development consent under the EPA Act. Since the designation of greenfield "growth

2 Made under the former S94E of the EPA Act.

centre" areas in north and south Western Sydney in the 2004 metropolitan strategy, similar state levies on subdivision developers have been payable as a special infrastructure contribution per hectare for regional infrastructure in those areas. This was a reflection of higher per dwelling state infrastructure costs for greenfield, rather than brownfield, development. It also reflected the intention to provide a market signal that reinforced the metropolitan strategy goal of providing most new dwellings in infill/ brownfield areas. However, the nexus between state contributions and the infrastructure funded by contributions is opaque, and it lacks the nexus accountability required in the application of contributions collected under local plans.

Furthermore, there have been claims that such contributions have been passed on to households purchasing new dwellings, exacerbating affordability pressures. In reality, developers will seek the highest price that the market will bear (Gurran et al., 2009). However, delay, inconsistency and uncertainty in setting contribution levies in the growth centres meant that developers were unable to properly factor them into the price of land.

4. Transparency and accountability about negotiations

Standard contributions under Section 7.11 must be levied according to a fixed formula applied to items of infrastructure or public works that are published in contribution plans. Further, as noted, local councils are also required to publish details of VPAs that are negotiated, including the public benefits generated. There is a lack of transparency, however, about the extent to which spending of regional special infrastructure contributions is connected to a particular subdivision or area. PPPs also involve a lack of transparency under "commercial in confidence" provisions employed by the state government, especially where developers are required to pay for infrastructure as under the Barangaroo Delivery Authority Act 2009.

5. Conditioning development to agreement about obligations

There is no scope for developers to negotiate changes to N-NDOs when these are set by a contributions plan, and municipalities condition the development consent to the developer fulfilling these N-NDOs. Of course, these N-NDOs can be appealed by the developer in court. When the development fits within the current land-use regulations, development consent can however not be conditioned on developers agreeing NDOs in VPAs. Only if the developer asks for a modification of the current land-use regulations (for example, rezoning or larger floor space index), can the municipality formally be required to agree to additional NDOs in a VPA in order to achieve sufficient planning merit.

6. Developer obligations in relation to future use and building possibilities: the economic "incidence" of developer obligations

The extent to which developer obligations may discourage new development, or distort land and housing prices, is a subject of considerable debate in Australia. In theory, when obligations are known in advance, they should be passed back to landowners as lower prices (since land values are set by potential profit at the highest use, minus costs). However, if contributions are uncertain, or set too high, they may discourage development, which could in turn reduce new housing supply, with implications for prices across the market (Gurran et al., 2009).

Nevertheless, VPAs are a bit different because they are typically entered into when planning rules are being changed to increase the development potential of a particular site. By definition, their voluntary nature and the fact that they coincide with a planning decision which increases development potential implies that VPAs are neutral or supportive of development. When local authorities define a framework for entering into VPAs, they are more akin to a fixed contribution.

7. Economic appraisal of feasibility of obligations

N-NDO Section 7.11 contribution plans are subject to economic appraisal by the state Independent Pricing and Regulatory Tribunal of New South Wales (IPART) if they propose a developer contribution level above the relevant maximum. The appraisal is based on a range of criteria, including that the proposed development contribution is based on a reasonable estimate of the costs of the proposed public amenities and public services.

For NDOs in the form of VPAs, municipalities employ licensed valuers to calculate the degree of uplift in land values created by excepting developer proposals relative to current planning controls. The uplift estimates are then used to assess the value of offset public benefits that might be required in return by the local government. Nevertheless, the government has provided no guidance about possible methodologies that could be used to measure value uplift and public benefits. This lack of clear guidance has created a number of uncertainties in the system. The relevant section of the EPA Act and accompanying regulations does not specify how much of the value uplift should be captured by municipalities. However, IPART has recommended a rate of 50 per cent of the total value uplift as a starting point for negotiations (IPART of New South Wales, 2016). In practice, public benefits equal to 50 per cent of site value uplift are commonly sought.

8. Empirical evidence of actually obtained obligations

The actual value of contributions under Section 7.11 is in the public domain. These are typically set at either $20,000 (established urban areas) or \$30,000 (greenfield areas) per dwelling allotment, or at 1 per cent of project value or equivalent. Similarly, levies can be extrapolated as a fixed proportion of development capital investment value. The public benefits secured under VPAs are published by the state government and/or the local government concerned. Nevertheless, there is no centrally maintained data on the cumulative value of contributions levied across these different mechanisms. However, the limited sources of local government funding in NSW (federal/state grant; local property taxes – "rates" – and development contributions), means that the latter are a primary source of funding for local infrastructure and facilities.

9. Conclusion

The use of developer obligations, both N-NDOs and NDOs, has expanded considerably in New South Wales over the last half-century. This has been in response to continuing fiscal pressures at state and local government levels, the increasing dominance of a neo-liberal government ideology and rising community standards. Developer concerns over impacts on their profitability have been addressed at various points, including the introduction of municipal contribution plans setting out the exact infrastructure to be funded under Section 94 (later Section 7.11) contributions, and the subsequent capping of such contributions. This has also limited the impact of contributions on dwelling affordability, since developers generally pass on the cost of such contributions to dwelling purchasers rather than reduce prices paid for development sites (given rapid population and demand increases in Sydney and a geographically constrained peri-urban fringe available for development). If contributions had not been capped and if underlying demand had not been increasing as rapidly, developer obligations could have had more serious negative impacts on dwelling affordability.

But the potential for developer contributions to reduce state government outlays on regional infrastructure and on grants to municipalities has caused the government to steadily expand the scope of N-NDOs (and to some extent NDOs in the form of VPAs). Section 7.11 contribution limits are being removed, and the state has significantly expanded N-NDOs for state-provided regional infrastructure.

The state government has been reluctant to borrow by itself for the infrastructure funded by developer contributions, in the form of benefit assessment area bonds or similar instruments, since it perceives increased state debt as a negative signal to investment from interstate and overseas (Searle, 2018). This means that development contributions will continue to play a major role in funding the infrastructure needed for future urban growth. Over the past decade, developers have been able to absorb rising contributions in rising prices for residential land, during a sustained housing boom. However, rather than a certain and consistent framework for levying contributions which can be easily factored into development costs at the time of land acquisition, the NSW framework has become a bewildering patchwork of state and local charging regimes. Further, the reluctance to embed an N-NDO value capture mechanism requiring all landowners or developers to contribute a share of value uplift when major plan changes or infrastructure investment benefit them, but rather to rely on ad hoc NDO voluntary "agreements", may discredit the integrity of the planning process. Thus, overall, developer contributions in NSW – and particularly in Sydney – have generated policy contradictions that will require a change in political direction to resolve.

References

Gurran, N. (2011), *Australian Urban Land Use Planning; Principles, Systems and Practice*. Sydney: Sydney University Press.

Gurran, N., Ruming, K. & Randolph, B. (2009), *Counting the Costs: Planning Requirements, Infrastructure Costs and Residential Development in Australia*, Australian Housing and Urban Research Institute Final Report Series. Melbourne, AHURI.

Independent Pricing and Regulatory Tribunal of New South Wales. (2016), *Submission to the Draft Voluntary Planning Agreement Policy*, December. Sydney, IPART.

Neutze, M. (1978), *Australian Urban Policy*. Hornsby, NSW: George Allen & Unwin.

Planning Institute of Australia. (2016), *Voluntary Planning Agreements (VPAs)*. PIA Policy Paper. Canberra, PIA.

Searle, G. (2018), 'Funding Large Scale Brownfield Regeneration Projects', in Ruming, K. (ed.), *Urban Regeneration and Australian Cities*. Abingdon, OX: Routledge, pp. 74–93.

Searle, G., Gurran, N. & Gilbert, C. (2017), *Do Negotiated Government-Developer Agreements Bring Adequate Public Benefit? Sydney's Voluntary Planning Agreements*. Paper presented at the 11th International Conference on Planning Law and Property Rights, Hong Kong, 22–24 February.

Wellman, K. & Spiller, M. (2012), *Urban Infrastructure: Finance and Management*. London: Wiley Blackwell.

Conclusions

Demetrio Muñoz Gielen and
Erwin van der Krabben

Chapter Introduction defined the problem that this book addresses (filling the knowledge gap about developer obligations' (DOs) practices) and provided the theoretical framework and nomenclature that allow for a cross-country comparative analysis. Chapters 1–18 presented the evidence for each country. This chapter Conclusion goes further by focusing on those debates and evidence that might be relevant for the effectiveness of DOs in achieving better urban infrastructure and, ultimately, sustainable and inclusive cities. This chapter Conclusion does not consist of a summary of the country chapters, but instead introduces those experiences in each country that are relevant for the analyzed debates.[1] In the last section, we provide a general reflection on the potential role of developer obligations for achieving sustainable and inclusive cities.

1. Basic legislative attitude towards property rights vs. development rights

As suggested in the Introduction (Section 1.3.2), introducing DOs based on direct rationales (the land value increase should be captured because it belongs to the community, and not to the landowner) indeed led in some of the studied countries to social and political controversy, because direct rationales address fundamental discussions about property rights over land and real estate. Contrarily, in other countries, this controversy is absent, because there is apparently large support for direct rationales. Throughout the book, we find examples of both. We see also how direct rationales, together with indirect rationales (developers should internalize the negative externalities of development), are sometimes used in combination, and how DO practices evolve with time from the use of one rationale to the other.

In countries where legislation assigns development rights to landowners, i.e. in countries with no direct rationales rooted in legislation, introducing DOs that rely on such direct rationales is complex and will most likely require major legal modifications and political/social support. This is for

---

1 All presented evidence can be found in the respective country chapter or, if not, in the sources made explicit.

sure the case in the Netherlands, New South Wales in Australia and in the US. There are also countries with no direct rationales rooted in legislation that lately however have witnessed an increase of direct rationales in public debate; for example, in Chile, Portugal and the US. Here, after years of absolute predominance of indirect rationales, there has been recently an increase of direct rationales in political discourse and local practices. Time will show whether they end up crystalizing in legislation or not.

But introducing direct rationales in legislation alone does not automatically lead to their effective implementation. We found evidence of countries that have direct rationales in their legislation but often use more productive indirect DOs. For example, the Colombian city of Medellín obtains as much financial contributions through N-NDOs based on indirect rationales as Bogotá with DOs based on direct rationales (*Participación en Plusvalías*), while Bogotá's real estate activity is 4–5 times larger than Medellín's (Pinilla, 2017a: 14–16). In Canada, DOs are most of the time based on indirect rationales, with 'direct' DOs only present in some fast-growing municipalities. See also Chapter 6 on Poland and Chapter 15 on Korea for other examples of countries in which indirect DOs are more successful, despite the fact that direct rationales and tools are present in their legislation. England, with its famous 1942 Uthwatt report and nationalization of development rights in the 1947 Town and Country Planning Act, illustrates this the best. From that time onwards, taxing development gains has been short-lived due to lack of political consensus. Nowadays a betterment levy is absent in the UK, while DOs based on indirect rationales are successful.

These experiences are, however, not conclusive about the opportunity and feasibility of introducing direct DOs. Together with Spain, almost all Latin American countries possess legislation that includes direct rationales, often 'disguised' behind the concept of 'social function' of property or after the principle that no citizen should accumulate wealth that does not result from his own efforts (*enriquecimiento sin justa causa*). Often, these direct rationales are also included in the constitutions of these countries (e.g. Brazil, Spain, Venezuela, Mexico; Smolka, 2013: 8, 14–17, 34). These countries are thus fertile lands for deploying direct DOs. Different countries show the (potential) effectiveness of direct DOs. For example, in Bogotá, Colombia, the use of direct instruments offers interesting results (Pinilla, 2017a: 14–16). Spain, where legislation requires landowners to transfer a certain percentage of their land to the public, and Taiwan, where owners of urban land must transfer land or an equivalent payment in money, provide both successful examples too. The Milano railyards case (see Chapter 9 on Italy) also illustrates how a direct DO is used to capture land value additional to indirect DOs. In Korea, direct DOs in the pre-negotiation system since 2009 are also becoming successful. Finally, in many countries, direct rationales – whether included in legislation and/or jurisprudence (e.g. Spain, Colombia) or in policies and public discourses alone (e.g. lately in Chile, Portugal and the US) – reinforce the effectiveness of indirect DOs by providing additional arguments in their favor. Maybe the same could be said about England, where the 1947 nationalization of development rights, even though not operationalized as a betterment levy since long ago, might have 'ideologically' supported the extensive use of indirect DOs (Zaborowski, 2017).

Finally, there are some countries that have introduced direct DOs with more success than indirect ones. The clearest example of this is the experience in São Paulo with the CEPACs ('communalization' and selling of development rights in the stock markets; see Introduction, Section 1.4.3).

Based on these debates, we formulate the following conclusions.

Conclusions

Evidence from a number of countries shows the potential of using DOs based on direct rationales. However, copying this practice to other countries can be difficult if national, regional or local legislation and policies do not advocate direct rationales (i.e. development rights are not assigned to the community).

Countries with national, regional or local legislation and policies allowing direct DOs might still encounter difficulties in the implementation due to a lack of political and social support. Here, often DOs based on indirect rationales do in practice capture more value than DOs based on direct rationales. Direct rationales might, however, have a positive influence on the effectiveness of indirect DOs, even if those direct rationales are introduced only in policy and public debate, and not in legislation.

In conclusion, we believe that direct DOs are potentially useful but should not blind people to the potential of indirect DOs, because the latter do not address fundamental property rights discussions and in practice can provide significant sources for public infrastructure. We tend to say that introducing them can offer a more pragmatic solution. Both sorts of DOs (based on direct and indirect rationales) are often applied simultaneously, complementing each other.

2. Dynamics and interactions between negotiated and non-negotiable DOs

Many countries covered by this book show a rather pragmatic attitude towards the use of both negotiatied DOs (NDOs) and non-negotiable DOs (N-NDOs) in their land policies. During recent decades, most countries have – often for different reasons – adjusted their DO strategies. This involved change sometimes in NDO practices and sometimes in N-NDO practices – and often in both.

2.1 Debates and evidence

Contradictory trends are visible in all studied countries: sometimes NDOs grow while sometimes N-NDOs do. A specific trend might prevail during a specific period of time, after which the opposite trend takes over. Most of the countries offer an example of both.

Hereunder follows a brief summary per country.[2]

United States of America

DOs in the US (generally named exactions) are based on indirect rationales (internalization of development impact), as can be expected in a country with a long tradition of strong private property protections. The impetus for shifting the costs of development to developers can be ascribed to a variety of factors that came together in the late 1960s and early 1970s, including reduced governmental transfers, increasing demands for higher quality public facilities and infrastructure, closer judicial scrutiny and 'taxpayer revolts' in some states. The applications of DOs vary widely, as localities often have large legislative powers to regulate them (within, however, the state legislative framework and federal jurisprudence). The use of N-NDOs (development impact fees, commercial linkage fees and inclusionary zoning) augmented since the 1970s, and in the 1980s a trend is said to have developed towards NDOs because of uncertainties created by frequent regulatory changes and judicial scrutiny around these fees, and because of buoyant property markets and the opportunity for public local bodies to utilize additional financial sources in a context of diminishing local fiscal revenues. Nowadays, most developments in the US include N-NDOs (in 2002, 25% of city governments in the US used impact fees), while larger developments are more likely to use NDOs, especially in the form of state regulated development agreements. These NDOs, however, while providing both the locality and the developer security and certainty, can be cumbersome, time consuming and expensive. The City of Santa Monica in California, for example, had added NDOs to its existing N-NDO system when granting additional densities, but is now regulating them. Lately, the state of California is limiting NDOs in order to speed housing development. In fast-growing cities on both coasts of the US, where costs of land and housing are suffering from unprecedented skyrocketing increases,

---

2 The country chapters have interpreted the hybrid cases (DOs that could both be categorized as N-NDOs and as NDOs) differently. Hybrid cases are sometimes presented as N-NDOs, and sometimes as NDOs. For example, the Polish contract between the traffic road authority (*zarządca drogi*) and the developer to provide road infrastructure is regulated in legislation and the land-use plan must prescribe the needed roads. However, there is in practice room for negotiations, especially when there is no land-use plan and the development is included in an ad hoc planning permit (DWZ), which does not say much about the needed roads. For that reason, it is presented as NDO. Other example of hybrids are the N-NDOs introduced in the 1990s in the metropolitan area of Santiago de Chile, which were in fact negotiable because of vague regulation; and the Taiwanese development impact fees (in theory, highly regulated free cession of land for public infrastructure), of which legislation however prescribes only minimum percentages and whose equivalent cash payments are calculated based on discretionary premises.

the use of NDOs is starting to support on direct rationales, although in 'disguised' forms such as 'public benefit zoning' (Bailey, 1990: 436; Delafons, 1990: 2, 99–103, 116; Calavita & Wolfe, 2014; Calavita, 2015; Callies & Grant, 1991: 239–241; Peddle & Lewis, 1996: 131–132; Lawhon, 2003; Burge, 2010; Monk & Crook, 2016: 253, 261).

England

In England, NDOs (initially called planning gain, and then planning obligation) increased in popularity since the 1970s because they seemed to obtain larger contributions than the statutory N-NDOs (planning condition) and because of the public policies in the 1980s towards public-private partnership in urban development. This increased use of NDOs led in the 1980s and 1990s to intense debate about their lack of transparency, the risk of abuse and corporate bribery, and the costs, uncertainties and slowness of negotiations. This debate led since the 1980s to regularization of NDOs through policy guidance and local policies, and ultimately in 2010 to the introduction of a N-NDO, the Community infrastructure levy, which nowadays coexists with the older – but now much more regulated – practice of negotiated planning gains/obligations (Jacobsen & McHenry, 1978: 354–357; Loughlin, 1981: 96–97; Bailey, 1990: 431; Delafons, 1990: 116; Healey et al., 1996: 154; Crow, 1998: 366, 369–370; Barker, 2004: 66; Corkindale, 2004: 13–14; Campbell & Henneberry, 2005: 41–42; Department for Communities and Local Government, 2006: 6; Muñoz Gielen, 2010: 177–180; Crook et al., 2016a: 12; Crook, 2016: 68, 71–72, 84–93, 93–97).

Poland

In Poland, there are almost no formal possibilities to require DOs, and the few obligations required in practice, formally speaking, cannot be conditioned to the land-use plan (MPZP), but only, sometimes, to the building permit. It is thus formally impossible both to demand or to negotiate contributions in exchange for the land-use plan. This makes DOs ineffective, because public bodies cannot easily threaten to refuse development. Developers are quite certain about their development rights. Of the few actual formal DOs, the only one somehow effective in practice is the powers of traffic road authorities to charge developers a basic package of roads through a contract (in theory, an N-NDO). Some negotiations appear around the application of this contract, which thus in practice often becomes an NDO, to a certain extent. Also, around the approval of the legally binding land-use plan, some municipalities try unofficial negotiations that end up in civil law agreements (thus, not regulated NDOs). The introduction of the 2015 Act on Revitalisation enlarges the scope of contributions further than a basic package of access roads, but the chances are large that this new provision remains un-used.

Colombia

In 1934, Bogotá, the capital city of Colombia, regulated in local policy DOs, although it is not clear whether they were negotiable or not. Similar practices were common at that time in other Colombian cities like Cucuta or Cali. The 1989 Act (*Ley de Reforma Urbana*) backed this local practice and left it to the municipalities to regularize DOs. Initially, DOs supported on an indirect rationale: contributions focused thus on the infrastructure needed for the development. During the 1990s, jurisprudence declared DOs legitimate with the argument that they consisted of a compensation for the increased land value that was the result of public land-use regulation decisions, i.e. implicitly, jurisprudence considered that at least part of the land value increase was public, internalizing thus a direct rationale. This has contributed to the enlargement of the scope of obligations. With time, obligations became more regulated and less negotiable, but nowadays N-NDOs still coexist with NDOs. In Bogotá, from 2000–2016, N-NDOs have provided for public uses an average of 35% of the surface of urban extension areas, although the construction of public infrastructure on this land delays. In urban renewal sites, more flexible NDOs provide a wider variety of contributions than N-NDOs in urban extension. However, most of urban development in Bogotá consists of replacement of old buildings that do not contribute at all. Medellín extended the use of N-NDOs to all building sites in the city, no matter their size, and has thus significantly enlarged the obtained contributions. Other cities in Colombia followed Medellín's example, e.g. Manizales y Bucaramanga (Pinilla, 2017a, 2017b, 2017c, 2018).

Australia

In the Australian state of New South Wales (NSW) local N-NDOs (Section 94 contribution plans and inclusionary housing zoning) were initially seen as unsatisfactory by developers (because the infrastructure is not necessarily constructed at the time and/or in the location of the development) and local municipalities (because they can charge only local infrastructure, not much social/affordable housing and no additional windfall gain). Alongside these N-NDOs, NDOs were also used, but they were not very effective. In 2005, the state government amended the state's planning legislation to allow for voluntary planning agreements (VPAs), a new type of NDO that allowed for larger contributions than could be sought through N-NDOs and gave more flexibility in the negotiations, while at the same time improved the transparency of NDOs. The use of VPAs has, however, been contested, so the state government has encouraged local regularization and standardization of VPAs that somewhat reduce the room for negotiation. Also, the state government has regulated an enlargement of the local N-NDOs and introduced a state N-NDO meant to pay for regional infrastructure. At the time of writing, the poor results of VPAs to provide affordable housing have led to a proposal for an affordable housing development levy as N-NDO (Searle et al., 2017).

Italy

The 1960s and 1970s saw the introduction in Italy of a set of N-NDOs: *standard urbanistici* (minimum percentages for the whole country), *oneri di urbanizzazione* and *contributo per il costo di costruzione*. The *standard urbanistici* have particularly successfully improved the urban infrastructure in urban expansion, but were also criticized of being inflexible and of leading to an unequal treatment of landowners. In the 1990s, another N-NDO was introduced to help redistribute the *standard urbanistici* among all landowners: the *perequazione*, a sort of transfer of development rights. By the beginning of the 1990s, together with the shift from plan-led towards development-led planning, regional legislation gave municipalities statutory powers to negotiate additional NDOs above the existing N-NDOs, especially affordable housing. They are said to undermine plan-led strategies, lack transparency and not capture much value in practice, but there are also examples with good results. Finally, in 2014, national legislation formalized and generalized to the whole country a sort of N-NDO based on direct rationales that was first introduced in Rome, the *Contributo straordinario per la plusvalenza*, which consists of contributions up to 50% of the development profit and in practice leaves room for negotiations (Pogliani, 2017, 2018). See the cases in Chapter 9 on Italy for a prediction of it's results in practice.

Spain

The central Spanish government introduced in 1975 and 1976 a set of minimum standards of public infrastructure (*estándares urbanísticos*), equal for all the country and non-negotiable, thus a sort of N-NDO, very similar to the Italian *standard urbanistici*. During the 1980s and 1990s, another two N-NDOs were introduced, the one to obtain large, off-site infrastructure and the other to zone affordable housing (inclusionary housing zoning, *reservas de suelo*). Additionally, a fourth N-NDO was introduced that supports on direct rationales: between 5% and 15% (10% until 2007) of the development rights were declared public good (*cesiones*). In the 1980s, the use of poorly regulated NDOs increased because N-NDOs at that time did not provide enough resources. Since the mid-1990s, those N-NDOs (except inclusionary housing zoning) greatly improved their performance (Gozalvo Zamorano & Muñoz Gielen, 2017), and at the same time, the use of NDOs increased because of booming real estate markets and because a modification of the land readjustment regulation in some regions introduced more competitiveness among landowners and developers that strengthened the negotiation position of municipalities. With time, NDOs have been criticized because of their lack of transparency, and this is leading to regularization into new, additional N-NDOs.

Switzerland

In 1980, the federal Swiss government introduced the tax on added land value (*taxe sur la plus-value foncière, Mehrwertabgabe, compensazione del plusvalore*), an N-NDO based on direct rationales that charges the value increase due to land-use regulation decisions. However, its implementation was left to the cantons, which almost did not put it into practice because it was heavily contested by real estate and federalist milieus. Since 2014, this N-NDO is obligatory for all cantons in urban extension. In urban regeneration, 15 cantons out of 26 explicitly allow in their legislation the negotiation of the rate, sometimes leading to a full exemption (see case *Europallee* in Chapter 8 on Switzerland), which makes of it a sort of NDO. Instead of this unpopular N-NDO and supporting old corporative and cooperative traditions, for several decades municipalities and developers have often negotiated infrastructure contributions in exchange for land-use regulation decisions (i.e. NDOs supporting on an indirect rationale). These contributions are mostly limited to basic, directly related infrastructure. From the 1980s onwards, certain communes in Canton Vaud (especially the city of Nyon) started negotiating larger contributions, however without a clear mandate in legislation. In 2007, judicial scrutiny ended this practice, and subsequently, in 2011, Vaud introduced the extended land service tax (*taxe sur les équipements communautaires*) to allow these larger contributions. This new obligation was intended to turn the previous practice of negotiated obligations into N-NDOs, but in practice, they are negotiated (see case *Malley* in Chapter 8 on Switzerland). Some communes (municipalities) in Vaud use now this extended land service tax to fund infrastructure serving the whole commune, so going much further than the tax on added land value and the ad hoc negotiations around infrastructure directly linked to the development (negotiations that are still predominant in the rest of the country) (Viallon, 2017a, 2017b; Lambelet & Viallon, 2018).

Canada

Developer obligations have a long history in Canada. Formal DOs have been used in all provinces for at least 50 years, and informal DOs even longer. They have provided significant revenues for local government, especially in the provinces of Ontario and British Columbia.

In Ontario, subdivision agreements (a sort of NDO meant for on-site, 'hard' infrastructure) appeared before the 1960s without a clear legislative base. Successive legislative modifications formalized this practice, however without regulating them in detail, thus remaining negotiable. As municipalities increasingly enlarged the scope of contributions, this led to tensions and judicial scrutiny. In 1989 and 1997, the Ontario provincial government regularized these NDOs into N-NDOs (named development charges). In the following years, municipalities developed new methods to enlarge the scope of contributions, which led to judicial scrutiny again. Also, municipalities started to negotiate additional 'voluntary' contributions, a practice that the legislative ended in 2015. Besides these development charges, another two sorts of obligations have been applied in Ontario. The first of these are statutory, previously prescribed park land dedications (a sort of N-NDO), to be paid in land or its equivalent in money. Because legislation left some room for municipalities to calculate the equivalents in money, municipalities gradually enlarged the contributions, a practice that since 2015 became more regulated in provincial legislation. Second, in the early 2000s, first Toronto and later other Ontario municipalities introduced density bonuses (a sort of NDO), contributions in exchange for a modification of the zoning bylaws that allow extra building rights. This sort of NDO has provided large revenues, and judicial review has somehow delimited their scope without, however, eliminating their negotiable and discretional nature. Finally, since 2016, new legislation entitles Ontario municipalities to prescribe affordable housing, i.e. inclusionary housing zoning, a sort of N-NDO (Amborski, 2017).

In the province of Alberta, most contributions are obtained through N-NDOs: land dedication for environmental protection, up to 40% of the developable land for public infrastructure and facilities and contributions for off-site infrastructure (the equivalent of development charges). These N-NDOs coexist with negotiations that lead to extra land and a broader set of 'soft' contributions (NDOs). These have been criticized for their lack of consistency and transparency and might soon become regulated in local policy. In the province of Nova Scotia, non-negotiable development charges were introduced for the first time in 2000 in the Regional Municipality of Halifax.

Brazil

In Brazil, the sale of development rights (a DO based on direct rationales) were introduced in the 1970s and 1980s, supporting only on local legislation, and later became generalized in other large cities and consolidated in federal legislation. At the beginning, they were mostly negotiable, but their poor results and lack of transparency led in time to their regularization and generalization, making N-NDOs of them. Their implementation is, however, very diverse, being very successful in cities with active real estate markets. Nowadays, in some cities they provide a relevant share of the municipal budget, e.g. more than 14% of the property tax revenues (1.9% of the municipal budget) in the period between 2005 and 2015 in São Paulo. Other cities obtain lower revenue (e.g. 0.5% of the municipal budget between 2011 and 2016 in Curitiba).

The Netherlands

In the Netherlands, the increased financial risks of public active land policies since the 1990s have fuelled an increase of poorly regulated NDOs, a process that seems to have been reinforced by the effects of the last economic crisis. In 2008, a new planning law introduced a system of highly regulated N-NDOs (development contributions plans, *Exploitatieplan*) for those cases that developers and municipalities do not freely agree NDOs. But as these N-NDOs have many limitations, are inflexible and force municipalities to assume some risks, most municipalities just refuse development if developers are not willing to negotiate the contributions, which in theory are strictly voluntary and should not be a condition for development. Most municipalities use NDOs to charge local, on-site infrastructure and one-fourth of them also to charge off-site, not directly related infrastructure (Muñoz Gielen & Lenferink, 2018).

Portugal

In 1973, a N-NDO (*Cedências*) was introduced to charge on greenfield developments the land needed for on-site infrastructure and social services. In the 1980s, another N-NDO (*Taxa Municipal de Urbanizaçao*, TMU) was introduced to charge on greenfield developments the cost of the provision of major off-site infrastructure. In the 1990s, this TMU (now named *Taxa pela Realização, Manutenção e Reforço das Infraestruturas Urbanísticas*, TRIU) expanded its scope also to urban regeneration and to the costs of maintenance and renewal of this infrastructure, but until 2006, the values charged in most municipalities were on average insufficient to cover the real municipal expenditure in public infrastructures and facilities (lesser than 20 Euro/m^2 of floor area). However, in the 1990s, in rapidly expanding municipalities, the revenues of TRIU had the same relevance (or sometimes ever higher) than the property tax (Morais de Sá & Dias Correia, 2018). The revenues of both *Cedências and* TMU/TRIU were often obtained *in pecunia* instead of in kind, and ended sometimes financing other public expenditures instead of urban infrastructure. There are no formal NDOs in Portugal, and so far, only in exceptional situations (projects with major impact) is there some experience with informal ones.

Chile

In 1976, national legislation introduced the possibility of charging obligations in urban expansion. These obligations were formally N-NDOs. Since the 1990s, these N-NDOs were introduced in greenfield developments in the metropolitan region of Santiago de Chile. Although they were formally N-NDOs, their vague prescriptions made them negotiable in practice. In general, they delivered contributions for off-site road infrastructure, but not enough on-site 'soft' infrastructure and social/affordable housing, and the coordination with public investments has been poor. In urban densification, municipalities have introduced relatively successful NDOs without legal base, which has limited their possibilities. In 2016, a new law of the central government improved the legal framework of DOs by enlarging their scope and clarifying their methodologies and limits, but still excluding the possibility of negotiating obligations.

Turkey

In Turkey, a long-standing practice of N-NDOs did not provide enough public infrastructure because landowners did not contribute more than 40% of their land, and construction costs of the infrastructure had to be paid by the municipality. Since the 1990s, along with a flexibilization of the planning system and an increase of large-scale urban development projects, Turkish municipalities are increasingly introducing NDOs in order to obtain larger percentages and to enlarge the scope of contributions towards off-site infrastructure and monetary contributions for social and technical infrastructure. This increase of NDOs, however, is raising concerns about their transparency and lack of regulation.

China

The basic form of LVC in China are contributions linked to China's unique land management system (all urban land is state-owned, and although rural land is collectively owned by the village, its transformation into urban uses require that land must first be transferred to the state, which is represented by the municipalities, which then transfer the land-use rights to developers). Land leasehold transferring fees have become a major income source for Chinese cities. As part of the land transferring contracts, and additionally to the land transferring fees, the developers are made responsible for designing and providing the necessary on-site infrastructure. These infrastructure requirements are prescribed in the land-use regulations but are not DO because they are provided in exchange for the lease of land, and not in exchange for land-use regulation decisions. So far, DOs (i.e. contributions made not in exchange for land leasehold transfer, but in exchange for land-use regulation decisions) have been only used in urban regeneration when developers, after having acquired land-use rights from the government, negotiate additional building possibilities (higher FAR) in exchange for more public facilities. However, in 2012, the central government regularized these NDOs, which in practice is reducing the possibility for local governments to enter into this kind of negotiations. If in the future, as expected, villages – instead of the states/municipalities – receive the right to transfer land-use rights to developers themselves, DOs are expected to gain relevancy.

Hong Kong

While HK's land management system basically resembles that of the British, the working of LVC mechanisms is different due to the land leasehold system that is operational in most of HK (except for the New Territories). Land premium incomes (collected on land sold in leasehold) are a substantial income source to the HK government, providing generous funding for urban infrastructure. This makes income from DOs less urgent. However, due to poor regulation, land-lease in HK often only allows collection of the initial premium, so that land value capture cannot take place during lease renewal. DOs do sometimes function here as a 'backup'; both in the urban areas and the rural areas (New Territories), since 1991, NDOs can be used by the government when there is a change of land use or via planning permits.

Taiwan

Taiwan operates an extensive system of LVC mechanisms that include, besides a classic direct tool (a land value increment tax – *tu di zeng zhi shui* – levied upon land transaction that provides for 20–40% of total tax revenue for the six major cities between 2003 and 2013), also several DOs based on direct and indirect rationales. In urban areas and in the conversion of farmland into non-agricultural uses, DOs are a percentage of the future land value, which matches with direct rationales. In non-urbanized areas, DOs are based on the costs of required investments in public infrastructure, which follows a clearer indirect rationale. Although fear of lofty operation costs and exceeding room for negotiations have led to adopting pre-specified formula, DOs do in practice offer much room for negotiations.

Republic of Korea

Since the 1960s, DOs in Korea have been part of land readjustment mechanisms which used to be the dominant land management strategy in the country. Both in the original land readjustment schemes (1966–1984) and the subsequent adjusted joint (hapdong) redevelopment schemes (1983–1998), LVC was based on N-NDOs. Developers must contribute in two different ways: by the provision of public facility land for streets, parks and other public infrastructure; and, in the joint schemes, by an additional land contribution for low-income housing. To countermeasure land speculation, skyrocketing land prices and privatization of development gains, the Development Gain Recapturing Act emerged in 1992, again involving a non-negotiable, direct DO. With this N-NDO declared ineffective, the government more recently initiated in 2009 as an experiment the pre-negotiation system. The pre-negotiation system (*sajeonhyeobsangjedo*) is a direct, negotiable DO, which argues that part of the development gain belongs to the community and should therefore be redistributed to the community. The extent, however, of negotiations is still limited; this DO is mandatory and there is hardly any negotiation possible about the size of it, although the scope of the contribution is negotiable.

Indonesia

Local governments in Indonesia compulsorily charge the developer to contribute to public facilities and infrastructure through N-NDOs that do not, however, provide much revenue. Additionally, municipalities sometimes require in exchange for the development permit (IMB) the free cession of fixed percentages of land for public infrastructure that are regulated in local bylaws but do in practice leave room for negotiating the form of infrastructure, thus a form of 'not-pure' NDO. Interestingly, a special corporate social responsibility (CSR) law offers one more possibility for the government to generate income for public infrastructure provision: it is obligatory for any corporation to implement a CSR policy. Often, this occurs after development has taken place, and is not related to land-use regulation decisions. However, some municipalities use this law as an NDO, i.e. to negotiate, as part of the process of granting development permits, contributions from private companies to public facilities and to improve the social and physical conditions in the surroundings of the development area. There are also, however, concerns about the lack of transparency in these negotiations.

2.2 Conclusions

Generally speaking, the trend in most countries seems to be a shift towards practices in which N-NDOs are combined with NDOs. Sometimes, NDOs gain importance, while sometimes, N-NDOs become predominant. This is often due to one or more of the following causes. First, N-NDOs experience legislative problems in their implementation and do often not bring in sufficient revenues for municipalities (this is more the case when N-NDOs are embedded in 'weak' property rights regimes and immature development control systems; see Section 3.4). Second, more market-friendly policies might un-favor N-NDOs, while NDOs are seen as more flexible to adapt to changing market conditions and/or policy contexts than are N-NDOs. NDOs are also easier to introduce, because they require less regulation. As a consequence, a trend towards NDOs appears. Third, NDOs often show problems of transparency, so with time they often become institutionalized and regularized into N-NDOs. In short, in some countries' perceived disadvantages of N-NDOs stimulate transitions towards NDOs, while in other countries, the opposite happens.

We think that a combined use of both NDOs and N-NDOs offers the possibility of optimizing their advantages while minimizing their disadvantages. NDOs can definitively offer the opportunity of adapting rapidly to new conditions (e.g. changes in market conditions) without legislative changes. However, if NDOs are not regularized to clarify the scope of negotiations soon enough, NDOs might still lead to important setbacks. Ideally, NDOs should be used to quickly adapt to changes and N-NDOs should soon follow them to clarify and consolidate the scope of the contributions. This can happen in a continuous process of trial-and-error experiences. In some contexts, NDOs might be the best and only option; while in other contexts, negotiations should disappear and obligations be charged only through statutory and 'inflexible' N-NDOs. Sometimes both should be complementary; negotiations can initially lead to a voluntary agreement, but in case the public sector and private landowners cannot achieve this, the public sector can then compulsorily charge N-NDOs. And sometimes both should coexist negotiations can lead to a voluntary agreement about additional contributions above the basic package of N-NDOs.

From a pragmatic point of view, the benefits of using NDOs and/or N-NDOs must be clear for all parties. For both the public sector and private landowners, these benefits usually relate to 1) the speed of development processes (negotiations sometimes delay processes, sometimes fasten them); 2) the flexibility of NDOs, in terms of 'market-oriented' size of the developer contribution (when market conditions allow, a higher developer contribution can be agreed upon, while poor market conditions lead to lower developer contributions); 3) the possibility to negotiate not only the developer contribution, but the content of land-use regulations as well; and 4) the public interest (negotiations have consequences for the transparency in the public decision-making, the public participation and the environmental quality of the resulting urban development). The choice for NDOs and/or N-NDOs always requires a careful evaluation of the context.

3. Embedment of developer obligations into governance forms for urban development

Another set of debates addresses how PVC in general, and DOs in particular, are embedded in different governance forms in urban development. The question is how this combination of DOs and forms of governance influences the effectiveness and efficiency of DOs.

3.1 Active and passive governance approaches to urban development

Public and private bodies play different roles in the different steps of land development (land purchase and assembly; financing, land preparation and provision of the necessary infrastructure; land disposition). This leads to two different forms of governance in land development (i.e. to different land policies). In the first, public bodies deploy themselves many or even all of these steps. In a second form of governance, private bodies are the ones in charge of all or almost all these steps (Alexander, 2001: 758–759, 2014: 538). A similar categorization distinguishes among 'active' and 'passive' forms of governance in urban land development (Van der Krabben & Jacobs, 2013: 775–776; Hartmann & Spit, 2015). Active forms of governance imply public bodies purchasing and assembling the land (Step 1), financing its preparation and development and providing the infrastructure (Step 2) and finally selling it (Step 3) to real estate developers or end users. In countries where land (or part of the land) is state owned (e.g. China, Hong Kong, Vietnam), Step 1 can be ignored. If governments sell the land (free- or leasehold) without developing it first (they sell 'raw' land), Step 2 can be ignored too. Passive forms of governance imply public bodies regulating the use of land and letting (a collective of) private bodies to do the rest of the work. While active forms of governance do not necessarily require the use of DOs (the net income from buying and selling the land should pay for the infrastructure costs), the passive forms obviously do. Of course, these are extreme models and practice shows a wide variety of mixed formulas. Forms of governance can be subcategorized (ordered from more active to more passive) as: a) nationalization of all land and public land development, b) public land banking and development, c) public-private land development, d) land readjustment and e) private land development. a) and b) include also those scenarios in which public bodies sell the 'raw' land without developing it first.

3.2 Collaborative planning and the increased relevance of negotiations

In many countries – but perhaps more in Europe than elsewhere – in recent decades, collaborative planning approaches were introduced, much in line with the turn into a *communicative* rationality in planning. Those collaborative strategies come in all kinds of forms, but have in common that responsibilities for the implementation of urban planning are shared by public and private stakeholders or even move from the public sector to private actors, in which case a transition from active to passive forms of governance takes place. The willingness of private and public stakeholders to collaborate is important for the effectiveness of value capture, and negotiation processes play a crucial role. Different variables might influence the effectiveness of this public-private cooperation and the possible negotiations. First, there are studies that show that cultural conditions can play an important role in the potential success of negotiations (Samsura et al., 2010). Second, institutional and legal conditions are important, as well. Among these institutional and legal conditions, we focus in this section first on the embedment of DOs into the broader governance approach to land development, i.e. their interaction with other land policy instruments. Later, in Section 4, we focus on another set of institutional and legal conditions that regulate the embedment of DOs into negotiation processes.

3.3 Embedment of developer obligations into governance approaches to land development

Whether DOs are negotiable or not, the fact is that in most countries their achievement depends on any sort of agreement between the public body that tries to charge obligations and the landowners/developers who must pay them. Most N-NDOs are compulsory in the sense that landowners cannot build if they do not contribute, but if they are not willing to build, public bodies cannot force them to contribute (except in some sorts of land readjustment; see ahead). This is partly why passive/collaborative approaches are criticized as being ineffective (see, for example, the discussion in Spain since the 1970s [Muñoz Gielen, 2010: 30–34] and in the US in the 1960s and 1970s [Van der Krabben & Jacobs, 2013: 775], or the discussions in Chapter 8 on Switzerland and Chapter 11 on Portugal about the lack of tools to control private-led urban development). In a genuine active governance approach, the dependence on agreement is theoretically lower, and thus, the effectiveness of value capture can be higher.[3] DOs play here no or a less prominent role, because contributions from developers here are most of the time obtained in exchange for the selling of land or land-use rights, not in exchange for land-use regulation decisions. However, DOs might still play a relevant role because using land-use regulation decisions as leverage, despite the public ownership of land, is often necessary; for example, when poorly regulated land leases only provide one-time initial premium payment, but subsequent rebuilding and densification cannot be subject anymore of rent payment. This is the case in Hong Kong, where DOs serve as a sort of 'backup' in those cases in which the land-lease does not allow charging redevelopment. China is another example of how land-use regulation decisions are used as leverage, even if land is public. Here, DOs are negotiated when developers already own land-lease rights but ask for additional development possibilities. In China, land-use planning is a top-down public responsibility, so these NDOs offer the possibility to developers to have a say in land-use regulation decisions. The expected reform in the allocation of development rights between local governments and rural villages will probably make land-use regulations more relevant, and hence give DOs a more prominent role.

In land readjustment (LR) regulations, landowners must jointly pay the contributions and provide the land needed for the public infrastructure (sometimes through DOs, sometimes through any other sort of PVC tool), while they share the finally serviced building plots. In some countries, public bodies have the statutory powers, under certain circumstances, to force

---

3 Along with the financial risks for the public body in charge, however, in case this body needs first to acquire the land. This is because an active approach without land previously in public hands requires public bodies making investments in buying land, without certainty about the return on the investments. When land is already in public hands, the risks are much lower.

reluctant landowners to work along the development. This is the case in Germany (*Umlegung*), Spain (*Reparcelación*), Korea (*Tojiguhoegjeonglisa-eob*) and Turkey, where the possibility of applying 'compulsory' LR does not require the support of any number of landowners (Germany and Spain) or at least not of all landowners (Korea[4] and Turkey). In this compulsory procedure, all landowners must give free access to their land to allow the readjustment of properties and the infrastructure provision, deliver some land needed for public infrastructure for free to the public body in charge and pay a corresponding share of the readjustment and infrastructure costs (or alternatively deliver some serviced building plots as payment in lieu, the 'cost-equivalent land').[5] Here LR can diminish dependency on agreement between public bodies and landowners, and offers thus the potential of increasing the effectiveness of PVC instruments (along with a limitation of individual property rights).

The mere presence of an LR regulation does not in itself reduce the dependency on agreement between public bodies and landowners. There are many countries with ineffective LR regulations, in the sense that they do not support PVC. For example, in Israel, properties can be compulsorily readjusted and municipalities often proceed with it. However, there is no legal provision (neither within the LR regulation nor outside it) that obliges landowners to provide the infrastructure or pay for it. As a consequence, after the readjustment of properties and the delivery of the property title of part of the land to the municipality, often the infrastructure is not provided so the development does not take place. Therefore, municipalities seek agreement with landowners or developers representing them in order to finance the public infrastructure (Muñoz Gielen & Mualam, 2017). Turkey also disposes of an LR regulation, which until the 1980s was used frequently, but it allowed only contributions for on-site, 'hard' infrastructure not exceeding 40% of the development area and excluding the costs of infrastructure provision. Consequently, in large-scale developments, municipalities since the 1990s have preferred to follow a straight private sector-led approach (model e), while LR is still applied mostly in smaller developments. Korea

---

4 In Korea, at least two-thirds of the landowners, owning at least two-thirds of the land, must agree with land readjustment.

5 Note that LR includes mainly indirect PVC instruments, because its main motivating rationale is the internalization of the costs of mitigation of the development impacts. This is the case, for example, with all the costs that can be charged to landowners in the German, Korean and Turkish LR regulations, and with almost all the costs in the Spanish LR regulations. However, LR can also include direct PVC instruments in case they also oblige landowners to share part of the economic value increase with the public, with the argument that this increase belongs partially or totally to the community (e.g. the previously mentioned Spanish N-NDO *cesiones*). LR always includes a package of minimum contributions (sometimes N-NDOs, sometimes other sorts of non-negotiable PVC tools), which sometimes coexist and are complementary with additional NDOs (e.g. Spain).

had since 1962–1983 a well-functioning LR in the reconstruction period after the Korean War, but it was abandoned because it allowed only to cover the costs of direct necessary public infrastructure and did not allow additional value capture (e.g. no social/affordable housing). Since then, municipalities prefer, as in Turkey, a straight private sector-led approach (model e). Poland and Switzerland have a totally voluntary LR regulation in place that does not support PVC (except, for Switzerland, in the canton Vaud; Lambelet & Viallon, 2018). Portugal has disposed of an LR regulation since 1999 (*Perequação*) that includes the statutory possibility of compulsory application, but in practice consent of all landowners is needed, which very much hampers its implementation (Morais de Sá & Dias Correia, 2018). Colombia has disposed of an LR regulation since 1997, but it is almost not applied in practice, despite the fact that it includes the possibility of compulsory readjustment in case the owners of at least 51% of the land supports it.

In passive or collaborative forms of governance (c, d and e), there is thus often a strong dependency on agreement with landowners and developers, although this dependency is lower when LR gives public bodies the statutory powers to force landowners to allow the development of their land and to pay their share of DOs.

Finally, other land policy instruments can influence the degree of dependency and hence the results of DOs as well: expropriation (called 'compulsory purchase' in the UK) and pre-emption rights (they give municipalities a first-buyer right). These coercive instruments may support public bodies' strategies to acquire land, influencing the degree of dependency among public and private stakeholders (if landowners do not agree to the contributions public bodies can threaten to acquire their land). Highly relevant for the outcomes of the use of expropriation and pre-emption powers is the compensation to be paid to the landowners, based on the value of the land either in its previous or in its future use. Many countries regulate that it is the future use that must serve as basis for compensation, for example the Netherlands, Poland (Zaborowski, 2018) and Portugal (Morais de Sá & Dias Correia, 2018). Some countries tried to regulate the previous uses as basis for compensation, but were not always successful in actually lowering compensation sums. In Italy, until the 1980s, compensation in case of expropriation was based on its previous use, but since then, judicial scrutiny has brought compensation paid closer to the future use value. In 2007, the Spanish central government, pursuing an effective (i.e. cheap) expropriation, prescribed that compensation sums must be based on the former uses, but it is not clear yet whether this provision endures judicial scrutiny (Muñoz Gielen & Lora-Tamayo Vallvé, 2018). Valtonen et al. (2017), comparing active municipal land policies in Finland and the Netherlands, note that these active land policies in Finland are 'supported' by expropriation law taking the 'previous use' value for compensation, while Dutch cities must pay full compensation based on 'future use' value.

But even when public bodies dispose of coercive instruments as compulsory LR or 'cheap' expropriation, negotiations do often still play a role.

First because even in case coercive instruments do actually give large powers to public bodies to impose N-NDOs on landowners, public bodies often pursue additional NDOs from landowners, so they need to negotiate. For example, in Germany, public bodies prefer to negotiate with landowners, because N-NDOs provide only basic infrastructure, and public bodies pursue larger contributions through negotiations, most notably in the city of Munich (Muñoz Gielen, 2016; Helbrecht & Weber-Newth, 2018: 124). A second reason that negotiations might still play a role is related to the property rights regime.

3.4 Embedment of developer obligations into the property rights regime

Problems in some countries with regard to ambiguity in property rights regimes and the immaturity of the development control system may put the use of developer obligations in a somehow different perspective. Particularly in developing countries, ambiguous property rights may result in the unequal treatment of landowners, but it may also put pressure on negotiations about developer obligations (Nguyen et al., 2017). The absence of a long-established planning culture that offers an 'institutionalized' (but not necessarily 'formalized') system of DOs sometimes puts local governments in a weak position to impose obligations, despite the fact that the regulation is there, and may even result in corruption. Instruments that were supposed to be coercive are not so much in practice, which can lead to more negotiations. I.e. DOs might formally be compulsory, but in practice they are 'evitable'. Nguyen et al. (2017) show for Vietnam how the local government, despite DO regulations, lacks the powers to actually impose sufficient obligations on private developers. Until the 1980s, LR in Spain, Korea and Turkey gave in theory much statutory power to municipalities, but landowners effectively opposed an enlargement of the minimum package of N-NDOs. In Spain, several modifications of the LR regulation were necessary to reduce since then the dependency on landowners. This led to the successful achievement of larger packages of N-NDOs. Interestingly, the diminished dependency reinforced the negotiation position of public bodies, which sometimes used this to increase also NDOs. In Korea and Turkey, municipalities diminished the use of LR because they were difficult to implement, and instead pursue private land development, accompanied with DOs, to increase the contributions (Turk, 2017). Nowadays, transitional countries like Poland and Vietnam, and developing countries like Indonesia, suffer the problem of ineffective DOs, because they cannot rely yet on long-standing experiences of dealing with private land development. Another sort of transitional country is the Netherlands, where the transition from active governance approaches to more private ones since the 1990s has not yet resulted in effective DOs. Here, as in Poland and Vietnam, local public bodies cannot rely on long-standing experiences with private land development.

3.5 Conclusions

In active governance approaches to land development, the public stakeholder's dependency on an agreement with a private developer is lower than in passive approaches; the public landowner can, in principle, choose from different private developers, and thus the effectiveness of public value capture tools can be higher. However, when the public stakeholder doesn't already own the land and must acquire it, this higher effectiveness comes with a financial risk, because of the uncertainty over the returns on the required public investments in land purchase.

In passive governance approaches to land development that use an LR regulation that gives public bodies the statutory powers to force landowners to work along the development, the public sector's dependency on agreement with private landowners is lower than in passive approaches without this sort of LR regulation, and thus the effectiveness of DOs can be higher (at the expense, one can argue, of unwilling private landowners).

When passive governance approaches to land development dispose of effective coercive instruments like expropriation or pre-emption rights, the dependency for public bodies on agreement is lower than in passive approaches without such instruments (again, at the expense of private landowners). Hence, with effective coercive instruments the effectiveness of DOs can be higher. Compensation regulation seems to play a crucial role here.

However, even passive governance approaches to land development that use an LR regulation that gives public bodies the statutory powers to force development, and that disposes of effective coercive instruments, do often experience a certain degree of dependency on agreement. Dependency is greater when ambiguity in property rights regimes and the immaturity of the development control weakens the performance of public bodies. This leads us to the following argument: that in passive governance approaches, the embedment of DOs into the negotiation process is relevant for their effectiveness.

4. Embedment of developer obligations into negotiation processes

Passive and collaborative forms of urban governance – as opposed to active urban governance – are common in many countries. As we just saw, in these forms of governance, there is always some degree of dependency among public and private bodies, and therefore bargaining often plays a crucial role. This section discusses several aspects of the embedment of DOs into the planning and negotiation process that are likely to be relevant for the results of this bargaining.

4.1 Conditioning development to agreement

In a first group of countries (that we know of: England, Spain, Portugal, Italy, Brazil, Colombia, Canada, Switzerland, Indonesia, Korea, NSW Australia), legislation gives public bodies the statutory powers to condition land-use regulation decisions[6] to the developer committing in an agreement to deploy and/or pay obligations. This is different from conditioning the building permit to the payment or implementation of N-NDOs, without any agreement (contract) backing it, thus a sort of administrative conditioning. N-NDOs can be formally an obligation that follows from those building permits, without any agreement securing their effective implementation. Many countries show that such an agreement is relevant for the effectiveness of DOs. First, because without a contract not compliance can only be enforced through administrative law (often withdrawal of the building permit alone), while in case there is an agreement, municipalities can also enforce through civil law. Second, because once the first land-use regulation decision is made that prescribes in a legally binding way the land use (most of the time the land-use plan), landowners are already secure about the use and building possibilities of their land. As a result of this certainty, higher expectation values are already capitalized in the market and serve as collateral, developers can rely on land price expectations and municipalities have no more leverage with which to negotiate, i.e. the ulterior issuing of permits is less relevant in the power relations between municipalities and developers.

Based on these statutory powers in the mentioned first group of countries, public bodies can thus rightfully deny the land-use regulation if the developer refuses to commit in a contract the effective implementation of his contributions. In a second group of countries (that we know of: the Netherlands, Canada in the 1960s), national legislation allows public bodies to engage in voluntary negotiations with developers, but if they refuse to reach an agreement, public bodies cannot, formally speaking, refuse the approval of the land-use regulation, i.e. public bodies cannot threaten to not approve the land-use regulation if the developer doesn't sign the agreement. Signing the agreement must be voluntary, i.e. not under the threat of not approving the land-use regulation.

In Poland, public bodies are not only not allowed to condition land-use regulations to an agreement, but actually they are even not allowed to link these regulations to agreements. Any agreement, even voluntarily agreed, that could be linked to a land-use regulation decision often fails to pass judicial scrutiny.[7] In addition, in Poland administrative conditioning is not possible, i.e. municipalities cannot even condition the building permit to the payment or implementation of N-NDOs.

---

6 For example, rezoning, additional development rights, relaxation of existing land-use regulations, issuing of building permits, property subdivision or readjustment decisions leading to new use and/or building possibilities, etc.
7 In Poland, there is one exception to this: the possibility of conditioning the building permit to an agreement with the traffic road authority regarding contributions needed for a basic package of access roads. It is, however, not legal to include other contributions in this agreement, and in any case decisions about land-use plans (the documents that create for the first time legally binding development possibilities) cannot be linked (let alone be conditioned) to any agreement.

This being said, in many countries (that we know of the Netherlands nowadays and Ontario in Canada in the 1960s, to a lesser extend Poland nowadays) public bodies nevertheless often condition land-use regulations even if there is no legal basis for this. However, the uncertainties about the legality of such practice hampers the effectiveness of DOs.

4.2 *Moment prescription obligations in relation to moment prescription future use and building possibilities: the economic 'incidence' of developer obligations*

When obligations are prescribed, in legislation or in policy, a very relevant question is what their economic 'incidence' is. This is who will really end up paying the obligations: the developer who buys the land and asks for a modification of the land-use regulations? Or will the obligations be passed on towards the previous landowner, by paying a reduced land price? (Misczynski, 1978: 112). Or, alternatively, will the future user/owner of the property end up paying them, by paying a higher price for the building (or by accepting a lower quality of the building or the public space)?

We argue here, in line with basic premises of the neo-classical theory of economic rent (also known as land rent theory, see Section 5.1 in the Introduction of this book), that the economic incidence of DOs depends on whether there is certainty about DOs before or after expectations appear about the future use and building possibilities, i.e. before or after any non-legally binding policy document (development or strategic plan) or legally binding zoning regulation creates expectations (the first sort of document) or certainties (the second sort) about future use and building possibilities. These expectations and certainties can have a substantial effect on land prices, and may create *hope values*. Certainty about DOs means that developers know beforehand which contributions they have to pay. Certainty requires two conditions: first, that the DOs are formally prescribed, in laws and/or policies; and second, that developers know that they will have to provide them. It is not enough that DOs are formally prescribed; it is also relevant that these contributions are not 'evitable', in the sense that developers know that municipalities will not easily cease to require them. Countries in which it is common practice for municipalities to 'forget' previously prescribed contributions do not provide certainty to developers, no matter how clear these contributions were prescribed beforehand in laws or policy (see Section 3.4).

When there is certainty about obligations before or at the time expectations/certainties appear about the future use and building possibilities, land prices tend to internalize the obligations, i.e. developers will tend to capitalize the costs of obligations into the land value and thus lower the price to pay for the land. Here the costs of DOs are passed to the landowner, so DOs act as genuine land value capture (LVC) tools, capturing windfall from the original landowners. As a consequence, one might expect that developers will be more willing to agree with the obligations. When certainty about obligations appears after hope values rise, there is a chance that land prices capitalize already the full value increase. Here land prices will not internalize the obligations, i.e. developers will pay a high price for the land and may enter into situations that they can no longer afford anymore to pay obligations. As a consequence, developers will not agree soon and negotiations will fail or end up with developers being given additional, more profitable use and building possibilities to compensate them (Misczynski, 1978; Muñoz Gielen & Tasan-Kok, 2010; Monk & Crook, 2016).

The experience in *Faria Lima* in São Paulo, and in Curitiba (both cities in Brazil), suggest that an a priori prescription of obligations (in both cities developers must buy development rights from the local government: the N-NDOs *Outorga Onerosa do Direito de Construir* and CEPACs) might have indeed a moderating effect on land prices. In Curitiba, these N-NDOs captured, between 2011 and 2016, as an average, an equivalent between 5.5% and 20% of the land value increments in the previous 20 years. If properly designed and implemented, they captured an equivalent up to above 50% (Marcelino, 2017).

It can also be argued that developers might end up passing on the costs of the obligations to buyers of the real estate by higher selling prices or providing lower-quality buildings and public space. There is much – but non-conclusive – writing about whether and how costs are passed on to homebuyers, i.e. whether housing markets behave as typical stock markets. We tend to conclude that, for sure if there is certainty about obligations beforehand, obligations will affect land prices and/or development profits, but not the final selling prices, since private developers selling new homes operate in a stock market, where the prices of new homes adjust to prices in the stock and not to the development costs.

The economic incidence of DOs is fundamental for their ethical meaning because it addresses the debates about who is the legitimate owner of the land value increase ('see sections 3.1 and 3.2 in chapter Introduction'). This variable is also fundamental for the organization of effective bargaining processes because it influences the chances of developers agreeing to pay contributions. Apart from the legitimacy issue, section 5.1 of the introductory chapter also referred to the economic argument raised by Henry George, Adam Smith and William Vickrey that a land value tax – a 'single tax' on land – is the most logical source of public revenue (compared to other public levies): while most taxes may have a negative impact on economic activity, a land value tax does not. Although some of the country chapters do discuss DOs as an alternative to increasing land value and property taxes (US, Canada), the 'historical' single tax discussion (land value tax to be preferred above other taxes) falls outside this book.

4.3 Transparency

A common topic in planning literature addresses the risks of developer obligations as a way of 'selling' of development permit against the public interest (see

234 Demetrio Muñoz Gielen and Erwin van der Krabben

e.g. Crow, 1998; Fox-Rogers & Murphy, 2015; Helbrecht & Weber-Newth, 2018). Do public bodies safeguard the public interest, or are they defenseless for the power of developer's interests? Many question this intense public-private participation in land and property development, arguing that it leads to dangerous collusion, limited competitiveness and even corruption (see e.g. Coiacetto, 2009; Hu & Zhang, 2015; Wong, 2015). The lack of transparency is often addressed as one important risk. Transparency in the application of DOs is seen as an important pre-condition, though not the only one, for their effectiveness and legitimacy. In collaborative planning approaches, two variables usually are the subject of negotiations: the development possibilities (what and how much is the landowner allowed to build?), and the contributions (what, of which quality and how much must the developer construct/pay?). Transparency about these variables most likely reduces the chance of collusion (and corruption). The relevant question in this book is whether transparency about these variables has any influence for the effectiveness of DOs.

Transparency before negotiations

A study on England, Spain and the Netherlands offers insight in this topic (Muñoz Gielen & Tasan-Kok, 2010). In all three countries, local public bodies usually create transparency in the early stages of the planning process, to different degrees, about future development possibilities. Local public bodies tend to increase certainty about the future development possibilities in order to improve transparency and accountability in their planning decisions. The findings in all three countries suggest that more transparency beforehand may result – from a local government's point of view – in less effective DOs. When municipalities publicly prescribe future, more profitable development possibilities early in the development process, this might inflate land prices (which tend to capitalize the hope value) and might also lead to the loss of a valuable negotiation tool.

However, it was not always possible to measure the actual effect of transparency about future building possibilities, mainly because the transparency was similar in all three countries. In addition, it turned out that transparency about future development possibilities is not always the only determinant variable, as another variable may play a more relevant role: the transparency about future contributions. We mean by 'transparency about contributions' that there is certainty beforehand about them. In other words, transparency about future building possibilities, if accompanied by transparency about future contributions, does not necessarily negatively influence the effectiveness of DOs. The experiences in Spain, England and the Netherlands support this conclusion because differences in these countries in transparency about contributions correlate with differences in the effectiveness of DOs, and both are apparently causally connected. In Spain since the 1970s, and in England since the 1990s, there has been an increasing transparency about future contributions, which led there to increased contributions. In the

Netherlands, there is little transparency, i.e. often Dutch developers don't know before buying the land and starting negotiations which obligations they have to construct and/or pay. For example, nowadays only around one-fourth of Dutch municipalities prescribe in policy which contributions should developers pay for large, off-site infrastructure, leaving most of the contributions to be defined during the negotiations. This uncertainty has a negative influence on contributions. Some of the other countries presented in this book seem to support this speculation. In Switzerland, due to the strong decentralization of planning competences, cantons and communes (municipalities) have in practice the room to delude federal attempts to create certainty beforehand about developer contributions. They rather tend to leave it to the negotiations, the same as in the Netherlands, which often creates uncertainty beforehand about the contributions. This uncertainty has a negative influence on contributions (Lambelet & Viallon, 2018). Poland, where contributions can in practice be eluded, also shows the pernicious effect of uncertainty about contributions.

There are two explanations for the positive effect of transparency beforehand about future contributions. First, transparency may have a deflating impact on the price of land, as developers do indeed take account of future contributions when calculating the price to be paid to the landowner, and lower land prices augment the financial leeway for contributions (see Section 4.2). Second, transparency strengthens the moral legitimacy and technical argumentation of public officers when they require contributions from developers.

Transparency after negotiations

In all three countries – England, Spain and the Netherlands – there is transparency afterwards about the development possibilities: these are formally prescribed in legally binding, statutory land-use regulations. This is also the case in most of the studied countries in this book. There are, however, large differences regarding the transparency about the finally obtained contributions: while in England and Spain development agreements are public,[8] in the Netherlands only a brief summary of those agreements, excluding much of the details about what exactly did the developer implement and/or pay, are made public.[9] Because transparency is the lowest in the Netherlands and so are the contributions of landowners there (compared with England and Spain), in a first thought one could conclude that low transparency afterwards influences the effectiveness of DOs. The argument could be that

---

8 Other countries in this book in which developer agreements are public, that we know of, are Poland (the only formal NDO, i.e. the contract with the traffic authority including only basic road infrastructure), Australia (New South Wales), Chile, Canada (Ontario) and Italy.
9 The other country in this book, that we know of, in which agreements are not public is Turkey.

low transparency afterwards diminishes the public acceptance of DOs in general, and this somehow harms the effectiveness of DOs.

Nuances about the influence of formal transparency

Other evidence brings important nuances to the speculation that formal transparency afterwards alone (publication of the results of negotiations) is relevant for public acceptance and effectiveness of DO. In Spain, development agreements are public, thus creating transparency about the finally agreed contributions. Contrary to the speculation that transparency about negotiated contributions leads to public acceptance, in Spain public acceptance of DOs is low, as they are often seen as the result of corruption. Contrary, too, to the speculation in Spain that public acceptance leads to effective DOs, despite the lack of public acceptance, DOs are quite effective. So, there seems not to be a clear causal link between formal transparency afterwards, public acceptance and effectiveness of DOs.

Some country chapters bring more light to this, and seem to support also the speculation that transparency beforehand about future contributions has a positive effect. The cases introduced in Chapter 8 on Switzerland suggest that there might be a relation between politicization, community involvement, public acceptance and effective DOs, but not with transparency afterwards – at least transparency in the formal sense. Development agreements there are not public afterwards, and it is the degree of previous politicization and community involvement (through political will, local referenda and the attention of media) that increases the public knowledge about the obligations and makes them more certain beforehand and less 'avoidable' (but still, to a large extent, 'flexible') in the negotiations. This increases the obtained obligations. The causal relation here seems to be that politicization and community involvement increase the political will to obtain contributions, and this seems a fundamental ingredient for effective DOs. In the cities of Toronto (Canada), Sesto San Giovani, Milano (Italy), Istanbul (Turkey), Santa Monica and San Francisco (US), public and political involvement in the negotiations, independently from the formal transparency about de results of negotiations, has increased the amount of contributions as well (see Amborski, 2017 for Toronto).

We thus tend to conclude that it is certainty about future contributions and community and political involvement in early stages of the development process (before contributions are agreed) that provides effective DOs, and – to a minor extent – formal transparency afterwards (i.e. legal obligation to fully publish the results of negotiations).

4.4 Economic appraisal feasibility obligations

In many countries, DOs are criticized because they are said to jeopardize the economic feasibility of the development. Contributions can be high, for example in the City of Toronto, in Ontario, Canada, the combined local and regional DOs may be as high as $88,391 (CDN, about 59,000 Euro) for a single family and semi-detached home. Landowners and developers consistently pose this argument, and in less buoyant real estate markets, public bodies are often reluctant to prescribe high obligations. This discussion has often led to the use of economic appraisals to determine a 'reasonable' level of obligations: for example, the economic feasibility studies of N-NDOs in the Spanish general land-use plans (*Plan General de Ordenación Urbana*), the calculation of maximum N-NDOs that landowners can bear in the Dutch development contribution plan (*Exploitatieplan*), the system of appraisals to measure the 'reasonable' amount of NDOs (*planning obligations*) in England and both N-NDOs (Section 7.11 contribution plans) and NDOs (voluntary planning agreements) in NSW Australia.

Our hypothesis is that the maturity of real estate appraisal professionals and methods, together with clear regulations, can contribute to the appropriateness and feasibility of such economic appraisals and thus to more effective DOs. The country chapters did not, however, provide clear evidence on this topic. In this regard, the only relevant finding can be found in the Brazillian CEPACs, introduced in the 1990s in the city of São Paulo. Here, development rights are sold in the stock market through public electronic auctions that have absolute transparency. The prices of development rights are here thus determined by the free play between offer and demand, avoiding any discussion about the accuracy of appraisal methods (Sandroni, 2010; Smolka, 2013: 53–57).

4.5 Conclusions about the embedment of developer obligations in the negotiation process

If public bodies condition land-use regulations based on a clear legal authorization to refuse them in case the developer doesn't agree to commit in a contract to the implementation of the contributions, this not only reduces the chances of collusion, but also increases their bargaining advantages and hence the effectiveness of DOs.

When certainty about DOs appears before expectations appear about the future development possibilities of the land (thus, when there is certainty and transparency beforehand about DOs), land transactions tend to internalize these obligations, i.e. the costs of obligations are passed on to the landowner (or at least limit the developer's profit). Hence, developers are more inclined to agree paying the contributions.

Transparency about future developer obligations and about the results of negotiations, achieved through formal transparency but mostly through community involvement in the decision-making, increases the chance of effective DOs.

Clear regulation and maturity of real estate appraisal methods can contribute to a non-controversial application of economic appraisals. This can improve the acceptability of DOs – and thus, their effectiveness.

5. Limits to the scope of developer obligations

When reviewing the experiences in different countries, we can conclude that the scope of DOs is increasingly large. Initially, in many countries, DOs based on indirect rationales (i.e. internalization of development impacts) required only investments in 'hard' infrastructure directly related to the development, particularly traffic measures: access roads, parking areas, etc. The link between this infrastructure and the development is evident, and does not arise much discussion. With time, many countries 'stretched' this link to include also 'hard' infrastructure not directly related to the development, possibly located outside the development area, and also 'soft' or 'social' infrastructure, of which the link with the development is not always clear, or at least arouses more discussion. This includes not only public facilities (schools, kindergartens, green spaces, etc) and sustainable measures (energy efficiency of buildings, etc.), but also social/affordable housing. Also, in many countries, this enlargement of the scope of contributions went effectively along with an enlargement of the quality of public infrastructure constructed or paid by landowners and developers.

Some examples illustrate how far contributions can go. In Ontario, Canada, from the few hundreds of dollars for a single family detached house charged in the 1960s, the most recent data shows that all DOs combined (local and regional) in most municipalities in the Greater Toronto Area surpass the amount of $40,000 (CDN, about 26,000 Euro) for a single family detached house, with the highest charges being in the City of Brampton at $84,044 (CDN, about 54,000 Euro) and recently in the City of Toronto at $88,391 (CDN, about 59,000 Euro) (Amborski, 2017). Another example of extreme high contributions is the City of Vitoria, in Spanish Basque Country, were the municipality asked and obtained more than 70% of social and affordable housing units in all urban extension areas of that city. Most Spanish cities serve also as an example of large contributions towards public infrastructure: landowners used to cede for free to the public 60–80% of the development area in urban redevelopment and 45–60% in peri-urban sites. In NSW Australia, the estate government charges an N-NDO in greenfield developments to finance regional infrastructure (among others, the special infrastructure contribution).

Does this imply that there are no limits to the scope (i.e. sort, quality and amount) of DOs, based on indirect rationales? Apart from an obvious one (the economic feasibility: DOs cannot jeopardize development profit), there are other limitations that actually demarcate how far public bodies can go when they ask contributions from developers based on indirect rationales. In many countries, public debate and political discussion deal with the limits to the scope of DOs.[10] As a consequence, legislation and/or jurisprudence rules

---

10 For example, during the parliamentarian discussion previous to the approval in 2016 of the Chilean *Ley de Aportes al Espacio Público* (LEAP), a decisive discussion was that DOs are not supposed to charge for the 'historical' deficit of urban infrastructure. Similar discussions are held in many other countries.

on some basis requirements and limits, so there is no absolute freedom to prescribe or agree all sorts of contributions. If there is policy detailing the scope of contributions, this policy must also fit within these requirements and limits. If there is no policy base, and obligations are purely negotiated, they still must comply, too. Here follow some examples of such requirements:

- Public purpose: the obligation should have a public purpose or interest, a catchall term that includes, for example, social and environmental goals or, e.g. in Spain and many Latin-American countries, the equal distribution of betterment and costs among all landowners;
- Connection: there must be a connection between the obligation and the development that contributes. For example, in the US, this is referred to as 'rational nexus', in Canada as the 'nexus test' (Amborski, 2017), in England as 'reasonable relationship', in NSW Australia as 'demonstrable nexus' (for its local N-NDO), in the Netherlands (for its N-NDO) as 'profit' and 'causality' (*profijt* and *toerekenbaarheid*) and in Chile as 'proportionality' (*proporcionalidad*). This requirement uses to apply more for N-NDOs, while for some N-NDOs and especially for NDOs, the connection requirement applies not so much, or not at all. For example, N-NDOs in NSW Australia meant for financing regional infrastructure do not need to fulfill the 'demonstrable nexus' that rule local N-NDOs;
- Obligations are earmarked: obligations (in case of monetary contribution) cannot be spent for other goals than those for which they have been prescribed (in case of N-NDOs) or agreed (in case of NDOs); in some jurisdictions (e.g. England and Ontario and Alberta in Canada), municipalities must regularly report the actual spending of these funds. In England, obligations must be given back to developers if they are not spent on the agreed goals within a certain period of time (often five years);
- Proportionality: all developments should be charged following any form of proportionality to avoid an unequal and arbitrary treatment of one developer in relation to others.

These requirements are present in many countries – but we should not conclude that in all of them, these criteria are homogeneously and coherently applied all through the jurisdiction. While in the US, for example, federal jurisprudence and state legislation developed common requirements for all developments, in Alberta, Canada, jurisprudence applies these requirements differently, depending on the specifics of the case. But also in the US, with its quite homogeneous requirements for the whole country, the interpretation given in the different states might vary considerably.[11] In Portugal, despite

---

11 See the example in Chapter 2 on the US of how differently state legislators apply the US Supreme Court's *exactions* doctrine – for example, California does not consider inclusionary housing zoning as an exaction, avoiding thus the 'rational nexus' test – or how differently this test is applied in California, Illinois and Rhode Island to justify charging affordable housing on commercial (non-residential) developments.

the fact that fiscal and planning law require a rational nexus in order to charge obligations, constitutional law does not allow earmarking the revenues, leaving considerable room for municipalities to spend them on other policy goals.

In theory, these requirements apply only to DOs based on indirect rationales. DOs based on direct rationales (the economic value increase belongs to the community, and not to the landowner) have – in theory – only the limitation of economic feasibility. Here public bodies do not need, theoretically speaking, to comply with any of the previously mentioned requirements. We found some evidence, however, that nuances this conclusion. For example, the revenues generated with the CEPACs in São Paulo (a sort of N-NDO), despite being based on direct rationales, can only be spent for public urban infrastructure located in the area. Another example is Spain, where landowners must cede for free to the municipality enough serviced building plots to host the public development rights (*cesiones*, a sort of N-NDO). These serviced building plots must, however, formally speaking, be used to build affordable housing[12] This suggests that despite the fact that 'direct' DOs are in theory not bound to the same requirements and limits as 'indirect' DOs, the strength of indirect rationales do actually limit their scope. This is to say that these mentioned requirements and limits might thus be also relevant, to a certain extend, for 'direct' DOs.

Conclusions

DOs based on indirect rationales were often initially limited to 'hard' infrastructure directly related to the development, specially traffic measures, but with time extended towards off-site infrastructure without a direct link, and towards 'soft' and 'social' infrastructure. In most countries, DOs – indirect DOs especially, but also DOs based on direct rationales – follow some basic criteria: they serve a public purpose, are somehow connected to the development that contribute, are earmarked and cannot be spent for other goals, and are somehow proportionally allocated among all developments. These criteria reinforce the legitimacy of DOs and hence their effectiveness. Depending on the specific context, they are interpreted more or less strictly.

6. Final reflections about the role of developer obligations in municipal financial health

Cities around the world often struggle to generate sufficient revenue for funding of urban growth, and to do this in a sustainable and socially acceptable way. This is particularly the case for megacities facing rapid

---

12 There is, however, evidence that municipalities often do not do such, but rather sell these plots and use the revenue for other policy goals.

urbanization and population growth. In most countries, cities rely, to a certain extent, on the national government's financial contributions. However, in many jurisdictions, cities plea for greater financial and fiscal autonomy to support urban growth, urban renewal, climate adaptation measures and energy transition. So, increasing fiscal autonomy, to be obtained among others through public value capture (PVC) tools, is on the (political) urban agenda in many jurisdictions. Along this line, modern public finance theory advocates both a decentralized and localized revenue structure, with a clear division of expenditure responsibilities (Bahl et al., 2013) and a more diversified revenue structure for cities (Chernick et al., 2010). Decentralized revenue structures add to accountability, in terms of democratic accountability to the local population, and to authority, in terms of the ability to manage expenditures and to determine revenues (Bahl et al., 2013: 151). A more diversified revenue structure supports a more stable income for cities. PVC tools charged by local governments obviously fit well in such a localized and diversified finance approach.

Another body of literature takes a more critical approach to localized revenue structures (including PVC tools), claiming that they are part of neoliberal governance (see e.g. Peck, 2012; Lin & Zhang, 2014) and the financialization of urban development policies (see e.g. Weber, 2015; Qun et al., 2015; Aalbers et al., 2017). Weber, for instance, argues that the focus of American cities on the use of tax increment financing as an income source may lead to poor planning decisions and extracts potential revenue for other goals than real estate development.

This book offers insight into the potentials of one specific sort of PVC tool: developer obligations (DOs). DOs are charged only on those who profit from land-use regulations decisions right at the moment when they dispose of liquidity (and not on the old widow living in a city center apartment inherited from her working-class husband), which increases their social and political acceptability. Also, they don't always require extensive legislative preparation, so municipalities can easily introduce them.

We will first further reflect on the role that DOs can have in the financing of municipalities, and will then end with some conclusions about those aspects that deserve further investigation.

6.1 The role of developer obligations in municipal financial health

DOs are contributions made in exchange for land-use regulation decisions, and they require somebody wanting to develop land (either greenfield or urban transformation). If there is no need of major rezoning or urban redevelopment, and if this does not increase the economic value of land and properties on it, DOs do not offer many possibilities. Because of this dependence on urban development, oscillations in real estate markets lead to oscillations in collected DOs. Therefore, there is no guarantee for local authorities that DOs will provide a stable source of income. So, a first conclusion could be that DOs are potentially an effective instrument to finance capital investments in new urban infrastructure, and to a lesser extent to pay current expenditures.[13] Other PVC instruments, notably property taxes and land taxes, offer, because of their regular collection, a more stable source of income (but may be more difficult to implement in some jurisdictions). And of course, other local taxes and central governmental financial transfers towards municipalities are essential for sustainable municipal finances.

Nevertheless, the literature and previous chapters offer many examples of cities where DOs produce a fundamental share of all revenues, which suggests that, especially in areas of active real estate markets, DOs have the potential to become a fundamental source in municipal finances, if maximized. For example, in São Paulo and Curitiba (Brazil), the N-NDOs *Outorga Onerosa do Direito de Construir* and CEPACs can provide 10% or more of the total new capital investments (new construction and improvements of urban infrastructure) (Smolka, 2013: 42, 53–57). In some counties of the US state of Florida, DOs provide between 10% and more than 20% of the local budget (Burge, 2010: 189). In Seoul (Korea), during the 1960s and 1970s, property taxes did not provide much, leaving the N-NDOs as the only significant public value capture instrument (Kresse et al., 2017: 20). In Spain, since the 1980s, N-NDOs and NDOs, besides providing cash funding for municipal budgets, provide also almost all new public infrastructure in the country except strategic large regional and national infrastructure like airports, seaports, highways, railways and improvements of existing infrastructure in consolidated urban areas. This leads in newly developed areas to landowners and developers ceding for free between 45% (in low density, peri-urban developments) and 80% (in dense urban developments) of the development area, and constructing all public spaces and roads there (Muñoz Gielen, 2010: 156–161, 2016: 84). In England, NDOs also provide large contributions in infrastructure and affordable housing (Muñoz Gielen, 2010: 205–210), and in NSW Australia, DOs are a primary source of local government funding. In many cities in Ontario, Canada, DOs can be substantial. One important reason of the increase of DOs in Canada is that they represent an alternative to increasing the property tax. In Qatar, a country with a zero-tax regime, a very incipient planning system and no history of PVC, NDOs are actually the only PVC tool ever deployed (Ibrahim & Saleh, 2016).

---

13 Public expenditures in public infrastructure can be categorized into capital and current expenditures. The latter refers to operation and maintenance costs in the provision of urban services. Those are regular and recurring costs, and are usually financed by current operating revenues, like user fees and taxes. Capital expenditures, on the other hand, refer to usually one-time investments in long-lived assets used to provide public services (roads, schools, parks, health care centers and other 'hard' infrastructures like sewage, power plants and public transportation systems, social and affordable housing, etc.) (Marcelino, 2017: 10–11).

The scope of DOs might also include some large infrastructure, but we did not find many examples of DOs financing a country's main infrastructure, like motorways or railways interconnecting different cities and the like. DOs seem thus so far to have mostly a local character, which makes sense because land-use regulation decisions largely remain, in most countries, within the realm of local public bodies' competences. DOs also have, however, the potentiality of funding regional and national infrastructure, as NSW Australia and Ontario in Canada show. Here, state and provincial governments use DOs to finance regional infrastructure and services.

6.2 *Final reflections*

We advocate a generalization of the use of DOs, together with other PVC tools, in line with the strengthening of public development control and a clarification of the property rights regime with respect to DOs. We believe that proper value capture mechanisms can contribute, together with solid and sustainable public land-use planning, to achieve the social function of property in urban development, i.e. to balance private profits and public costs, and increase the accountability of public actions in urban development. NDOs, if not jeopardizing N-NDOs and if properly regulated, are definitely worth considering: they offer more flexibility to adjust to the local situation and may thus offer at least the potential to 'cream off' a larger part of the development gain. The use of NDOs also seems to fit well with the communicative rationality in spatial planning (Healey, 1992), emphasizing interactions and negotiations between public and private stakeholders taking part in complex decision-making processes. It assumes there is 'room to maneuver' in these processes, and that the effective use of this may add to more successful planning.

Many side effects of DOs, however, may occur. DOs are said by many to have contributed to a (neoliberal) financialization of urban planning, to an unequal treatment of different landowners, to an undermining of plan-led planning systems (urban development guided by public planning) in favor of development-led (the market guides urban development), to corruption in urban governance, to an uneven play between developers and local public bodies, to the 'selling' of development rights and to many other undesired outcomes. For sure, many public bodies give in to the temptation to use DOs only for generating revenue. We are aware of many ill-designed, poorly regulated DOs, and as well of well-designed and properly regulated DOs that are, however, poorly embedded in the broader land policy regime. The risks are obvious and operate within the tension between public urban planning goals and financial considerations (which are important for public urban planning goals, as well). Placed for the accomplished fact, however, that DOs have become central in urban planning and development, we believe that ignoring their potentiality – especially those of negotiated DOs – does not help to avoid their undesired effects. We hope that this book contributes to a better understanding and use of them.

References

Aalbers, M. B., Van Loon, J. & Fernandez, R. (2017), 'The Financialization of a Social Housing Provider', *International Journal of Urban and Regional Research*, Vol. 41, No. 4, pp. 572–587.

Alexander, E. R. (2001), 'Governance and Transaction Costs in Planning Systems: A Conceptual Framework for Institutional Analysis of Land-Use Planning and Development Control – The Case of Israel', in *Environment and Planning B: Planning and Design*, Vol. 28, pp. 755–76.

——— (2014), 'Land-Property Markets and Planning: A Special Case', *Land Use Policy*, Vol. 41, pp. 533–540.

Amborski, D. (2017), *Tensions Regarding Developer Obligations in the Province of Ontario*. Paper in 11th Annual Conference International Academic Association Planning, Law and Property Rights, Hong Kong, China, February, p. 27.

Bahl, R. W., Linn, J. F. & Wetzel, D. L. (eds.). (2013), *Financing Metropolitan Governments in Developing Countries*. Boston: Lincoln Institute of Land Policy.

Bailey, S. J. (1990), 'Charges for Local Infrastructure', *The Town Planning Review*, Vol. 61, No. (4), pp. 427–453.

Barker, K. (2004), *Review of Housing Supply. Delivering Stability: Securing our Future Housing Needs*. London: Barker Review, March, p. 149.

Burge, G. (2010), 'The Effects of Development Impact Fees on Local Fiscal Conditions', in Ingram & Hong (eds.). (2010), pp. 182–212.

Calavita, N. (2015), 'Practive Value Capture', *Zoning Practice*, American Planning Association No. 6.

Calavita, N. & Wolfe, M. (2014), *White Paper on the Theory, Economics and Practice of Public Benefit Zoning*. Sponsored by the East Bay Housing Organizations under a HUD-funded Sustainable Communities Grant provided to ABAG/ Metropolitan Transportation Commission.

Callies, D. L. & Grant, M. (1991), 'Paying for Growth and Planning Gain: An Anglo-American Comparsion of Development Conditions, Impact Fees and Development Agreements', *The Urban Lawyer*, Vol. 23, No. 2, pp. 221–248.

Campbell, H. & Henneberry, J. (2005), 'Planning Obligations, the Market Orientation of Planning and Planning Professionalism', *Journal of Property Research*, Vol. 22, No. 1, pp. 37–59.

Chernick, H., Langley, A. & Reschovsky, A. (2010), *Revenue Diversification and the Financing of Large American Central Cities*. Working paper prepared for the 32nd Annual Research Conference for Public Policy Analysis and Management, Boston. www.lincolninst.edu/pubs/.

Coiacetto, E. (2009), 'Industry Structure in Real Estate Development: Is City Building Competitive?' *Urban Policy and Research*, Vol. 27, No. 2, pp. 117–135.

Corkindale, J. (2004), *The Land Use Planning System: Evaluating Options for Reform*, Hobart Paper 148, London: Institute of Economic Affairs, p. 113.

Crook, T. (2016), 'Planning Obligations Policy in England: *de facto* Taxation of Development Value', in Crook et al. (eds. 2016), pp. 63–114.

Crook, T., Henneberry, J. & Whitehead, C. (eds.). (2016a), *Planning Gain. Providing Infrastructure & Affordable Housing*, RICS Research, Wiley Blackwell.

——— (2016b), 'Summary and Conclusions', in Crook et al. (eds.). (2016a), pp. 269–289.Crow, S. (1998), 'Planning Gain: There Must be a Better Way', *Planning Perspectives*, Vol. 13, pp. 357–372.

Delafons, J. (1990), *Development Impact Fees and Other Devices*, Monograph 40, Berkeley: Institute of Urban and Regional Development. http://escholarship.org/uc/item/5mt8q2rh.

Department for Communities and Local Government. (2006), *Valuing Planning Obligations in England*. London: DCLG Publications, May.

Fox-Rogers, L. & Murphy, E. (2015), 'From Brown Envelopes to Community Benefits: The Co-Option of Planning Gain Agreements Under Deepening Neoliberalism', *Geoforum*, Vol. 67, pp. 41–50.

Gozalvo Zamorano, M. J. & Muñoz Gielen, D. (2017), 'Non-Negotiable Developer Obligations in the Spanish Land Readjustment: An Effective Passive Governance Approach That "de facto" Taxes Development Value?' *Planning Practice & Research*, Vol. 32, No. 3, pp. 274–296, DOI:10.1080/02697459.2017.1374669.

Hartmann, T. & Spit, T. (2015), 'Dilemmas of Involvement in Land Management – Comparing an Active (Dutch) and Passive (German) Approach', *Land Use Policy*, Vol. 42, pp. 729–737.

Healey, P. (1992), 'An Institutional Model of the Development Process', in *Journal of Property Research*, Vol. 9(1), pp. 33–44.

Healey, P., Purdue, M. & Ennis, F. (1996), 'Negotiating Development: Planning Gain and Mitigating Impacts', *Journal of Property Research*, Vol. 13, No. 2, pp. 143–160.

Helbrecht, I. & Weber-Newth, F. (2018), 'Recovering the Politics of Planning: Developer Contributions and the Contemporary Housing Question', *City*, Vol. 22, No. 1, pp. 116–129.

Hu, Z. & Zhang, K. (2015), 'Game Playing Analysis of Planning and Supervision Collusion in Real Estate Land', *The Open Cybernetics & Systemics Journal*, Vol. 9, pp. 2086–2091.

Ibrahim, H. & Saleh, A. F. M. (2016), *Promoting Sustainable Housing and Urban Development for Qatar Through PPP Model*. Proceeding in ICUP International Conference on Urban Planning, Nix, Serbia, November, pp. 201–206.

Ingram, G. K. & Hong, Y.-H. (eds.). (2010), *Municipal Revenues and Land Policies*. Cambridge, MA: Lincoln Institute of Land Policy, p. 536.

Jacobsen, F. & McHenry, C. (1978), 'Exactions on Development Permission', in Hagman, D. & Misczynski, D. J. (eds.), *Windfalls for Wipeouts: Land Value Capture and Compensation*. Washington, DC, Chicago, IL: Planners Press American Planning Association, pp. 342–366.

Kresse, K., Kang, M. & Kim, S. (2017), *Value Capture from Development Gains to Public Utility: Case of Seoul, Republic of Korea*. Paper in 11th Annual Conference International Academic Association Planning, Law and Property Rights, Hong Kong, China, February, p. 52.

Lambelet, S. & Viallon, F. X. (2018), *Written Questionnaire and Appendix About Transparency*, February.

Lawhon, L. (2003), 'Development Impact Fee Use by Local Governments', in *Municipal Year Book*. Washington, DC: International City Management Association, pp. 27–31.

Lin, G. C. S. & Zhang, A. Y. (2014), 'Emerging Spaces of Neoliberal Urbanism in China: Land Commodification, Municipal Finance and Local Economic Growth in Prefecture-Level Cities', *Urban Studies*, Vol. 52, No. 15, pp. 2774–2798.

Loughlin, M. (1981), 'Planning Gain: Law, Policy and Practice', *Oxford Journal of Legal Studies*, Vol. 1, No. 1, pp. 61–97.

Marcelino, M. A. (2017), *How Investments in Urban Services Can Be Financed by the Land Value Capture Instrument "Sale of Development Rights"* – *The Case of Curitiba*. Master thesis, MSc Programme in Urban Management and Development, IHS Rotterdam, p. 113.

Misczynski, D. J. (1978), 'The Question of Incidence', in Hagman, D. & Misczynski, D. J. (eds.), *Windfalls for Wipeouts: Land Value Capture and Compensation*. Washington, DC, Chicago, IL: Planners Press American Planning Association, pp. 112–141.

Monk, S. & Crook, T. (2016), 'International Experience', in Crook et al. (eds.). (2016), pp. 227–268.

Morais de Sá, A. & Dias Correia, P. V. (2018), *Written-questionaire*.

Muñoz Gielen, D. (2010), *Capturing Value Increase in Urban Redevelopment*. Leiden, The Netherlands: Sidestone Press, p. 478.

—— (2016), 'Proposal of Land Readjustment for the Netherlands: Analysing Its Effectiveness from an International Perspective', *Cities*, Vol. 53, pp. 78–86.

Muñoz Gielen, D. & Lenferink, S. (2018), 'The Role of Developer Obligations in Financing Large Public Infrastructure After the Economic Crisis in the Netherlands', *European Planning Studies*, Vol. 26, No. 4, pp. 768–791. DOI:10.108 0/09654313.2018.1425376.

Muñoz Gielen, D. & Lora-Tamayo Vallvé, M. (2018), *The use of compulsory property acquisition and land readjustment in urban densification in Spain*, in Searle (ed.), *Compulsory Property Acquisition for Urban Densification*. Routledge Complex Real Property Rights Series. Routledge, Oxon, New York, pp. 81–93.

Muñoz Gielen, D. & Mualam, N. (2017), *Comparison of German, Spanish and Israeli Land Readjustment Regulations from the Point of View of Their Effectiveness in Capturing Land Value Increase*. Presentation in 11th Annual Conference International Academic Association Planning, Law and Property Rights, Hong Kong, China, February.

Muñoz Gielen, D. & Tasan-Kok, T. (2010, article, first author), 'Flexibility in Planning and the Consequences for Public Value Capturing in UK, Spain and the Netherlands', *European Planning Studies*, Vol. 18, No. 7, pp. 1097–1131.

Nguyen, T. B., Van der Krabben, E., Spencer, J. H. & Truong, K. (2017), 'Collaborative Development: Capturing the Public Value in Private Real Estate Development Projects in Ho Chi Minh City, Vietnam', *Cities*, Vol. 68, pp. 104–118.

Qun, W., Yongle, L. & Siqi, Y. (2015), 'The Incentives of China's Urban Land Finance', *Land Use Policy*, Vol. 42, pp. 432–442.

Peck, J. (2012), 'Austerity Urbanism: American Cities Under Extreme Economy', *City*, Vol. 16, No. 6, pp. 626–655.

Peddle, M. T. & Lewis, J. L. (1996), 'Development Exactions as Growth Management and Local Infrastructure Finance Tools', *Public Works Management & Policy*, Vol. 1, No. 2, pp. 129–144.

Pinilla, J. F. (2017a), *Developers Obligations as a Land Value Capture Tool. Practice and Lessons from Colombia*. Paper in 11th Annual Conference International Academic Association Planning, Law and Property Rights, Hong Kong, China, February, p. 19.

—— (2017b), *Written Questionaire*, March.

—— (2017c), *Written Questionaire*, December.

—— (2018), *Written Questionaire*, February.

Pogliani, L. (2017), *Infrastructure and Value Capture in Italy and the Challenge of Milano Railways Agreement*. Paper in 11th Annual Conference International Academic Association Planning, Law and Property Rights, Hong Kong, China, February.

——— (2018), *Written Questionaire*, February.

Samsura, D. A., van der Krabben, E. & van Deemen, A. (2010), 'A Game Theory Approach to the Analysis of Land and Property Development Processes', *Land Use Policy*, Vol. 27, No. 2, pp. 564–578.

Sandroni, P. (2010), 'A New Financial Instrument of Value Capture in São Paulo: Certificates of Additional Construction Potential', in Ingram, G. K. & Hong, Y-H. (eds.), *Municipal Revenues and Land Policies*. Cambridge, MA: Lincoln Institute of Land Policy, pp. 218–236.

Searle, G., Gurran, N. & Gilbert, C. (2017), *Do Negotiated Government-Developer Agreements Bring Adequate Public Benefit? Sydney's Voluntary Planning Agreements*. Paper in 11th Annual Conference International Academic Association Planning, Law and Property Rights, Hong Kong, China, February.

Smolka, M. O. (2013), *Implementing Value Capture in Latin America: Policies and Tools for Urban Development*. Cambridge, MA: Lincoln Institute of Land Policy, p. 72.

Turk, S. S. (2017), *Changing from Use of Voluntary Method Towards Use of Negotiated Developer Obligations in Turkey*. Paper in 11th Annual Conference International Academic Association Planning, Law and Property Rights, Hong Kong, China, February, p. 21.

Valtonen, E., Falkenbach, H. & Van der Krabben, E. (2017), 'Risk Management in Public Land Development Projects: Comparative Case Study in Finland and the Netherlands', *Land Use Policy*, Vol. 62, pp. 246–257.

Van der Krabben, E. & Jacobs, H. M. (2013), 'Public Land Development as a Strategic Tool for Redevelopment: Reflections on the Dutch Experience', *Land Use Policy*, Vol. 30, pp. 774–783.

Viallon, F-X. (2017a), *Economic Value Capture in Swiss Land Policy: How Much Is Enough?* Paper in 11th Annual Conference International Academic Association Planning, Law and Property Rights, Hong Kong, China, February, p. 9.

——— (2017b), *Written Questionaire*, March.

Weber, R. (2015), 'Selling City Futures: The Financialization of Urban Redevelopment Policy', *Economic Geography*, Vol. 86, No. 3, pp. 251–274.

Wong, S. (2015), 'Real Estate Elite, Economic Development, and Political Conflicts in Postcolonial Hong Kong', *The China Review*, Vol. 15, No. 1, pp. 1–38.

Zaborowski, T. (2017), *Polityka przestrzenna kształtowania koncentracji osadnictwa Anglii i Niemiec. Cele i instrumentarium planistyczne*. Warszawa: Wydawnictwa Uniwersytetu Warszawskiego.

——— (2018), 'Land Acquisition and Land Value Capture Instruments as Determinants of Public Urban Infrastructure Provision: A Comparison of the Polish Legal Framework with Its German Counterpart', *Geographia Polonica*, Vol. 91, No. 3.

Index

Institutions

Cases